ON LONGING

ON LONGING

Narratives of the Miniature, the Gigantic, the Souvenir, the Collection

Susan Stewart

Duke University Press Durham and London 1993

Tenth printing in paperback, 2007
© 1993 Duke University Press
All rights reserved
Printed in the United States of America on acid-free paper ∞
Typeset in Palatino
Originally published by Johns Hopkins University Press in 1984.
Library of Congress Cataloging-in-Publication Data appear
on the last printed page of this book.

For my mother and grandmothers—
Delores Stewart, Alice Stewart, and Nellie Brown

TABLE OF CONTENTS

PREFACE/HYPERBOLE

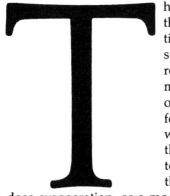

his essay centers on certain metaphors that arise whenever we talk about the relation of language to experience or, more specifically, whenever we talk about the relation of narrative to its objects. These metaphors—history and stasis, inside and outside, partiality and transcendence—form the focus of the discussion in this work as I ask: How can we describe something? What relation does description bear to ideology and the very invention of that 'something'? and, analogously, What does exaggeration, as a mode of signification, exaggerate? Narrative is seen in this essay as a structure of desire, a structure that both invents and distances its object and thereby inscribes again and again the gap between signifier and signified that is the place of generation for the symbolic. Therefore my reader will discover that I am particularly interested in the social disease of nostalgia as I examine the relations of narrative to origin and object, and that herein lies the reason I have chosen a kind of ache as my title. For the word *longing* has a number of meanings which, taken together, in fact encompass this study of narrative, exaggeration, scale, and significance: yearning desire, the fanciful cravings incident to women during pregnancy, belongings or appurtenances.

If we look to the first meaning of *longing*, "yearning desire," we see that, according to the list of examples in the *OED*, it experiences a split in the eighteenth century. In 1713 (Addison) we find: "Whence this pleasing hope, this fond desire, this longing after immortality?"

And in 1748 (*Anson's Voyage*): "Our native country, for which many of us by this time began to have great longings." My point is not to note the death of immortality, but rather to note that the location of desire, or, more particularly, the direction of force in the desiring narrative, is always a future-past, a deferment of experience in the direction of origin and thus eschaton, the point where narrative begins/ends, both engendering and transcending the relation between materiality and meaning. Yet the particular content of this desire is subject to historical formation. A hundred and twenty-seven years before *Anson's Voyage*, Burton wrote: " 'Tis a childish humour to hone after home, to be discontent at that which others seek; to prefer, as base Icelanders and Norwegians do, their own ragged island before Italy or Greece, the gardens of the world. . . . All places are distant from heaven alike, the sun shines haply as warm in one city as in another, and to a wise man there is no difference of climes; friends are everywhere to him that behaves himself well, and a prophet is not esteemed in his own country" (*Anatomy of Melancholy*, pt. 2, sec. 3, mem. 4, p. 175). Who is the homesick partner in this dialogue? By the mid eighteenth century he has a name and his own category of insanity, his own refusal of the present.

The second meaning of *longing*, "the fanciful cravings incident to women during pregnancy," takes us closer to an imagined location of origin, be it the transcendent with its seeming proximity to the immortal or the rural/agrarian with its seeming proximity to the earth; for it is in pregnancy that we see the articulation of the threshold between nature and culture, the place of margin between the biological "reality" of splitting cells and the cultural "reality" of the beginning of the symbolic. Out of this dividing—this process of differentiation and relation—the subject is generated, both created and separated from what it is not; and that initial separation/joining has a reproductive capacity that is the basis for the reproductive capacity of all signifiers. Following Kristeva ("Motherhood According to Giovanni Bellini"), we might focus here on the "elsewhere" of pregnancy as such a threshold: in French, *enceinte*, "walled in," the enclosure by which maternity is both valorized and made marginal; in English one might say "my confinement." As a place apart, the threshold of pregnancy is characterized by an overabundance of the natural/instinctual at the same time that it is the precondition of the cultural/symbolic. Kristeva writes that "[in pregnancy] this tendency toward equalization, which is seen as a regressive extinction of symbolic capabilities does not, however, reduce differences; it resides within the smallest, most archaic, and most uncertain of differences. It is powerful sublimation and indwelling of the symbolic within instinctual drives. It affects this series of 'little differences–resemblances'. . . . Before founding society in the same stroke as signs and communications, they are the precondition of the latter's existence . . ." (p. 240).

The instinctual "cravings" of maternity are "fanciful" (cravings/carvings), for as symptoms of ingestion they represent both the generalized and the internalized longing that the very adjective *fanciful* seeks to naturalize as a longing for biological perpetuation. Maternity's generation of the series—that is, the generation of the object *and* object relations—is an incorporative gesture; and it is in the interdependence of the elements of the series that their regenerative power resides. Hence the derivation of the second meaning of *longing*—"the longing mark," or impression, left by the mother's desire. Trace or scar, this impression finds its synonym in the generative metaphor of writing, which here is an unconscious inscription upon the developing consciousness of the child and the eruption of the mark that before had no name.

The third meaning of *longing*, "belongings or appurtenances," continues this story of the generation of the subject. I am particularly interested here in the capacity of narrative to generate significant objects and hence to both generate and engender a significant other. Simultaneously, I focus upon the place of that other in the formation of a notion of the interior. Here we might remember the meaning of appurtenance as appendage, the part that is a whole, the addition to the body which forms an attachment, transforming the very boundary, or outline, of the self. The function of belongings within the economy of the bourgeois subject is one of supplementarity, a supplementarity that in consumer culture replaces its generating subject as the interior milieu substitutes for, and takes the place of, an interior self. Thus in the beginning of this essay I focus upon certain conventions of description as they developed in postindustrial genres, particularly conventions of point of view, "exactness," distance, and temporality. The reader who arose from the mechanical reproduction of literature is a reader acutely aware of the disjunction between book as object and book as idea. And the solitude of his or her reading takes place within the milieu of the bourgeois domestic, a milieu of interior space miming the creation of both an interior text and an interior subject.

These conventions of description are intimately bound up with the conception of time as it is both portrayed in the work and partaken of by the work. By means of its conventions of depiction, temporality, and, ultimately, closure, narrative here seeks to "realize" a certain formulation of the world. Hence we can see the many narratives that dream of the inanimate-made-animate as symptomatic of all narrative's desire to invent a realizable world, a world which "works." In this sense, every narrative is a miniature and every book a microcosm, for such forms always seek to finalize, bring closure to, a totality or model.

The miniature is considered in this essay as a metaphor for the interior space and time of the bourgeois subject. Analogously, the gigantic is considered as a metaphor for the abstract authority of the state and the collective, public, life. In examining narratives of the miniature and the gigantic, I attempt to outline the ways in which these discourses of the self and the world mutually define and delimit one another. The problems uncovered in such narratives—problems of inside and outside, visible and invisible, transcendence and partiality of perspective—point to the primary position the body must take in my argument. The body is our mode of perceiving scale and, as the body of the other, becomes our antithetical mode of stating conventions of symmetry and balance on the one hand, and the grotesque and the disproportionate on the other. We can see the body as taking the place of origin for exaggeration and, more significantly, as taking the place of origin for our understanding of metonymy (the incorporated bodies of self and lover) and metaphor (the body of the other). It is this very desire of part for whole which both animates narrative and, in fact, creates the illusion of the real.

At the conclusion to the essay I look at two devices for the objectification of desire: the souvenir and the collection. The souvenir may be seen as emblematic of the nostalgia that all narrative reveals—the longing for its place of origin. Particularly important here are the functions of the narrative of the self: that story's lost point of identity with the mother and its perpetual desire for reunion and incorporation, for the repetition that is not a repetition. The souvenir seeks distance (the exotic in time and space), but it does so in order to transform and collapse distance into proximity to, or approximation with, the self. The souvenir therefore contracts the world in order to expand the personal. I go on to examine the ways in which the collection furthers the process of commodification by which this narrative of the personal operates within contemporary consumer society. A final transformation of labor into exchange, nature into marketplace, is shown by the collection. Significantly, the collection marks the space of nexus for all narratives, the place where history is transformed into space, into property. Whereas the first part of this essay examines narratives that are generated by objects, the second part examines the ways in which the souvenir and the collection are objects generated by means of narrative. The creation of such narrated objects depends upon the fictions and abstractions of the bourgeois self on the one hand and the exchange economy on the other. In the final phases of late capitalism, history itself appears as a commodity.

Thus this essay is an exploration of the meaning of exaggeration, but in saying so I do not mean to privilege any given notion of the normal. Under a use-value economy, exaggeration takes place in relation to the scale of proportion offered by the body. Although this body is culturally delimited, it functions nevertheless as the instrument of lived experience, a place of mediation that remains irreducible beyond the already-structured reductions of the sensory, the direct relation between the body and the world it acts upon. Yet once the abstractions of exchange are evident, exaggeration must be seen in relation to the scale of measurement, and thereby the scale of values, offered by a more abstract domain of social convention—and that social convention achieves its ideological force by virtue of the powers of authority. Although we must acknowledge, as Marx did, that the senses and the very notion of "lived experience" are the products of social history, it seems worthwhile to distinguish between levels of abstraction within this given formulation of the direct and the mediated. Furthermore, to distinguish between such levels begins to give us an account of the process by which the body itself can become a commodity. This process of alienation further emphasizes the legitimacy of a social notion of an "authentic body"; in other words, we must take into account the fact that the possibility of an unalienated subject and an unmediated relation to nature can find expression only within an equally ideological, even utopian, sphere.

If authority is invested in domains such as the marketplace, the university, or the state, it is necessary that exaggeration, fantasy, and fictiveness in general be socially placed within the domains of anti- and nonauthority: the feminine, the childish, the mad, and the senile, for example. In formulating the loci of authority and exaggeration in this way, we necessarily and nostalgically must partake in the lost paradise of the body and the myths of the margin, the outside. Exaggeration always reveals the cheap romance that is reality, but then it must move on.

This essay focuses upon a Western tradition because I wanted to limit what is already an interdisciplinary scope and because the modes of exaggeration discussed relate to a particular set of historical developments. Yet the essay itself is a collection and not a chronicle: I am more concerned with presenting a display of heterogeneity than with accounting for a model of causality. Except for some remarks on tourist art, I have left out any discussion of the rich non-Western tradition of experiments with scale and the fantastic. Forms such as the Japanese netsuke, the Persian and Indian miniatures, the Indonesian and Chinese giants, and the miniature genres of Somali poetry could not be discussed without doing extraordinary violence to their meaning in context.

The notes and bibliography that follow this essay are meant to be an acknowledgment of intellectual and, at times, pragmatic debts, but I would like to note that in particular the works of Bakhtin, Bachelard, and Baudrillard have broken ground for a semiotic analysis and critique of the relations between narrative and "the system of objects."

Parts of this essay were read at the international semiotics conference "Il linguaggio del gioco" held in Montecatini Terme in October 1979; at meetings of the Modern Language Association, the American Folklore Society, and the Temple University English Department's Journal Club in 1981 and 1982; and at the Tudor and Stuart Club of the Johns Hopkins University in 1982. The comments of the participants on those occasions were inestimably useful. Funds from two Temple University Summer Research grants and participation in a National Endowment for the Humanities Summer Seminar in the sociolinguistics of literature, led by John F. Szwed at the University of Pennsylvania, provided valuable resources. I would like to thank the following colleagues in particular for various kinds of help, from preliminary encouragement to final revision: Tim Corrigan, Amanda Dargan, Stanley Fish, Edward Hirsch, Philip Holland, Debora Kodish, Gary Saul Morson, Craig Schafer, Amy Shuman, Alan Singer, Barbara Herrnstein Smith, John Szwed, Jane Tompkins, and Ana Cara Walker. Nadia Kravchenko typed the manuscript with a sense of grace and precision, and my editor at The Johns Hopkins University Press, William P. Sisler, once again served as diplomat and ally. Nora Pomerantz gave the proof her careful attention. Finally, I want to thank Daniel Halevy and Jacob Stewart-Halevy, who were happy to help me see this book to its conclusion.

ON LONGING

PROLOGUE

Our language can be seen as an ancient city: a maze of little streets and squares, of old and new houses with additions from various periods; and this surrounded by a multitude of new boroughs with straight regular streets and uniform houses.

—Wittgenstein

Back toward town we glided, past the straight and thread-like pines, past a dark tree-dotted pond where the air was heavy with a dead sweet perfume. White slender-legged curlews flitted by us, and the garnet blooms of the cotton looked gay against the green and purple stalks. A peasant girl was hoeing in the field, white-turbaned and black-limbed. All this we saw, but the spell still lay upon us.

—W. E. B. DuBois

 *et me begin with the invisibility and blindness of the suburbs. Between classes, a fundamental slippage— the absence of the landscape of voyage. The suburbs present us with a negation of the present; a landscape consumed by its past and its future. Hence the two foci of the suburbs: the nostalgic and the technological. A butterchurn fashioned into an electric light, a refrigerator covered by children's drawings, the industrial "park," the insurance company's "campus." The celibacy of the suburbs articulates its inversion of nature: the woman becomes a sun, the man a revolving moon. Here is a landscape of apprehension: close to nature, and not consumed by her; close to culture, close enough to consume her. In the topography of the suburbs is revealed the topography of the family, the development, a network of social relations and their articulated absences. To walk in the suburbs is to announce a crippling, a renunciation of speed. In the suburbs only outsiders walk, while the houses are illuminated as stages, scenes of an uncertain action. In these overapparent arrangements of interior space, confusion and distance mark the light.*

The countryside: space ideal, space of childhood and death. The forest remote, water mirroring not ourselves but the infinite distance of sky. Within patterns of nature, we search for traces of the human: a tiny rowboat pulled up to shore, the oars folded and asleep. Perhaps a figure, but microscopic, and on the edge of some oblivion—a cliff, or the other side of the painting. Everywhere signs of cultivation and wilderness: the plowed field of poetic lines, the ax left leaning against a colossal tree. The countryside unfolds, maplike before

us, simultaneous and immediate. And yet always the problems of horizon and distance, the problems of depth and breadth. As we begin to traverse the field of vision, the tragedy of our partial knowledge lies behind us. The distance becomes infinite, each step an illusion of progress and movement. Our delight in flying comes from the revelation of countryside as sky and sea, from the transcendence we experience over vast spaces. Yet to see the thin and disappearing signature of the jet is to see the poverty of this flight to omniscience; in each photo appears the grim machinery of the wing. In the notion of return, of cycle, of the reclamation of landscape, lies the futility and productive possibility of human making.

To walk in the city is to experience the disjuncture of partial vision/partial consciousness. The narrativity of this walking is belied by a simultaneity we know and yet cannot experience. As we turn a corner, our object disappears around the next corner. The sides of the street conspire against us; each attention suppresses a field of possibilities. The discourse of the city is a syncretic discourse, political in its untranslatability. Hence the language of the state elides it. Unable to speak all the city's languages, unable to speak all at once, the state's language becomes monumental, the silence of headquarters, the silence of the bank. In this transcendent and anonymous silence is the miming of corporate relations. Between the night workers and the day workers lies the interface of light; in the rotating shift, the disembodiment of lived time. The walkers of the city travel at different speeds, their steps the handwriting of a personal mobility. In the milling of the crowd is the choking of class relations, the interruption of speed, and the machine. Hence the barbarism of police on horses, the sudden terror of the risen animal.

Here are three landscapes, landscapes "complete" and broken from one another as a paragraph is. And at the edge of town, the camp of the gypsies.

1. ON DESCRIPTION AND THE BOOK

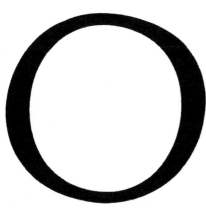ut of these landscapes, the distinction of point of view. In a world where access to speed is access to transcendence, point of view is particularly a narrative gesture. The point of view of landscape is no longer still, is instead a matter of practice and transformation. Modernism's suspicion of point of view can be seen as a critique of omniscience, but a critique rooted in a self-consciousness that proclaims an omniscience of its own ontology, its own history. Point of view offers two possibilities: partial and complete. What remains silent is the third and anonymous possibility—blindness, the end of writing.

In allegory the vision of the reader is larger than the vision of the text; the reader dreams to an excess, to an overabundance. To read an allegorical narration is to see beyond the relations of narration, character, desire. To read allegory is to live in the future, the anticipation of closure beyond the closure of narrative. This vision is eschatological: its obsessions are not with origins. For Bunyan at the end of *The Pilgrim's Progress*, for example, the reader's failure at closure will result in repetition, a further inscription of the narrative upon the world. For Bunyan, repetition proclaims the cyclical and identical patterns of history. Each turn through the text will result in the same reading. The locus of action is not in the text but in the transformation of the reader.[1] Once this transformation is effected, point of view is complete, filled out to the edges. And wherever we look, we see the work of this closure—the image is indelibly stamped upon the world.

This confidence in the circularity of history and the complete vision of closure is broken with the advent of the industrial revolution, the advent of a new kind of realism and a novel kind of "psychological" literature. As Ian Watt has told us,[2] two shifts in the concept of realism took place at the beginning of the eighteenth century. First, from the Renaissance onward, a tendency to replace collective experience with individual experience had evolved. And second, the particularity of everyday life and the individual's experience in *this* world became the locus of the real.[3] Thus the realism of allegory has been displaced, has moved from the reader's "quickening," an internal recognition of signs through reading, to the reader's apprehension of an immediate environment that is nevertheless external and continually changing. The reader is in an observer's position, yet his or her vision remains partial because of this externality of time and space. The eschatological vision of allegory makes the reader the producer of the text in the sense that closure can be achieved only through conversion. But the production of the eighteenth-century novel is divided between the author and his reader, and the reader's production is subsidiary to, and imitative of, the author's work. We may see the picaresque on the interface between these two forms, the picaro an outsider, a "reader" of a set of locations on the one hand, yet, on the other hand, simply another character, whose partial vision as an outsider makes him or her ridiculous. In this generic progression, the convention of the "wandering viewpoint" has emerged,[4] a convention whereby the reader is situated *within* the text, moving alongside a diversely coordinated set of textual time systems. Thus a new process of reading evolves from this new form of realism, a reading which gives the reader the status of a character. The reader comes to "identify with" the position of Tom Jones, Pamela, Joseph Andrews, with the "proper name" and not with a lesson, a signified. The reader becomes a character, a figure who looks for signs or clues—not a reader of signs and clues that fit together into a moral puzzle solved through the eschatology of closure, but a reader of signs for their own sake, a reader of correspondences between the signs of the world, the immediate environment of everyday life, and the signs of the novel. Thus the sign in the realistic novel leads not to the revelation of a concealed meaning uncovered but to further signs, signs whose signified becomes their own interiority, and hence whose function is the production and reproduction of a particular form of subjectivity.

In this productive mapping of sign upon sign, world upon world, reality upon reality, the criterion of exactness emerges as a value. And exactness, always a matter of a concealed slippage between media, is moved from the abstract, the true-for-all-times-and-places of allegory, to the material, the looking-just-like, that sleight of hand which is the basis for this new realism. The allegorical figure who moves in a binary fashion within a world by means of correct and incorrect actions is replaced by a member looking for signs. Exactness is a mirror, not of the world, but of the ideology of the world. And what is described exactly in the realistic novel is "personal space," the space of property, and the social relations that take place within that space. We must remember that Crusoe sees the social as a mark upon, a tainting of, his private space, and greets the trace of the human with "terror of mind": "Then terrible Thoughts rack'd my Imagination about their having found my Boat, and that there were People here; and that if so, I should certainly have them come again in greater Numbers, and devour me; that if it should happen so that they should not find me, yet they would find my Enclosure, destroy all my Corn, carry away all my Flock of tame Goats, and I should perish at last for meer Want."[5] Yet the illusion of the emperor surrounded by his riches, the illusion of Crusoe, lord of the island, is the most inimically social of all illusions.

The movement from realism to modernism and postmodernism is a movement from the sign as material to the signifying process itself. The reflexivity of the modernist use of language calls attention not to the material existence of a world lying beyond and outside language but to the world-making capacity of language, a capacity which points to the arbitrariness of the sign at the same time that it points to the world as a transient creation of language. Like the first juncture between pre- and post-eighteenth-century fiction, this shift toward the sign itself can be linked to the development of the political economy. The exchange value of language, a value we see at work in oral genres even in modern society (e.g., the reciprocity of puns, the joke-swapping session), is replaced by a form of what we might, in analogy, call surplus value. Literary discourse is performed not within the ongoingness of conversation but in the largely private production and apprehension of the text, and the relationship between literary production and consumption becomes one of increasing distance in time and space. The forms of alienation arising from preferences for difficulty and the exotic as qualities of the modernist text reflect an increasing distance between the forces of literary production and those of literature's general consumption. At the same time, they reveal the concentration of those productive forces resulting in and from the hegemony of mass culture.

In his essay *The Tourist: A New Theory of the Leisure Class*, Dean MacCannell suggests that we see the relation between commodities as a "semiotic" one: "In Marx's treatment of it, the system of commodity production under capitalism resembles nothing so much as a language. A language is entirely social, entirely arbitrary and fully capable of generating meanings in itself."[6] Yet to say that the system of commodity production "resembles" language is not enough; it is necessary to outline the nature of that resemblance, to note the symbolic nature of the commodity once it is transformed from use value to exchange value and defined within a system of signs and their oppositions. "It is possible to consider the exchange of commodities as a semiotic phenomenon not because the exchange of goods implies a physical exchange, but because in the exchange the *use value* of the goods is transformed into their *exchange value*—and therefore a process of signification or *symbolization* takes place, this later being perfected by the appearance of money, which *stands for something else*," writes Umberto Eco.[7] Hence the notion of a "pure semiotic" realm of exchange; a realm analogous to the most reductive accounts of a pure "poetic language" (Hugo Ball, for example) would find its locus in the gift shop and in the deliberate superfluousness of "tokens of affection."

If we consider the relation between commodity production and the organization of fictive forms as part of an entire semiotic system, we can posit an isomorphism between changes in genre and changes in other modes of production. Not the least important implication of this relation is the influence of generic changes upon the prevailing notion of history as narrative. In other words, the distances between audience and performer in a culture's genre repertoire outline the place of the self as agent, actor, and subject of history.

Just as genre may be defined as a set of textual expectations emergent in time and determined by (and divergent from) tradition, so history may be seen as a convention for the organization of experience in time. Yet historical and generic conventions cannot be mapped upon the real; rather, these conventions are emergent in the prevailing ideological formations that are the basis for the social construction of the real. Here we might take our position from Vološinov:

> Genres are definable in terms of specific combinations of features
> stemming from the double orientation in life, in reality, which each
> type of artistic "form of the whole" commands—an orientation at once
> from outside in and from inside out. What is at stake in the first
> instance is the actual status of the work as social fact: its definition in
> real time and space; its means and mode of performance; the kind of
> audience presupposed and the relationship between author and

audience established; its association with social institutions, social mores and other ideological spheres; in short—its full "situational" definition.[8]

Rooted in the ideological, the literary genre determines the shape and progress of its material; but, at the same time, the genre itself is determined by the social formations from which it arises. The relation between literary producer and consumer will be reflected in the form of the genre. Consider, for example, the rule of turn-taking, which plays such an important part in our concept of "conversation" and in the various "conversational genres": repartee, verbal dueling, riddling, punning, telling proverbs, telling jokes and joking, and constructing narratives of personal experience. The reciprocity of the utterance underlies both fictive and nonfictive forms in these conversational contexts. But with the creation of fictive worlds that are removed in time and space from the context of situation, an increasing distance is placed between producer and consumer and the symmetry of conversational reciprocity is replaced by the specialized values of performer and spectator. The spectacle, the stage play, the novel, exemplify this increasing distance between performer and audience.

In his careful exploration of these distances in relation to folkloric forms, Roger Abrahams has suggested that

> at some arbitrary point in the unarticulated—but obviously unconsciously sensed—spectrum of performer-audience relationships, folklorists decide that there is too great a distance between the performer and his audience to call an enactment folklore. . . . A similar and equally arbitrary cut-off point is observable in the realm of material folklore. In this case, however, the relationship with which we are concerned is between *maker* and *user*, not performer and audience. At some point of the maker-user relationship spectrum, the removal between the two becomes so pronounced that we call it a product of technology, not material folklore.[9]

We might go on to address the historical and ideological formations underlying these shifts in genre. For example, in a reciprocal-exchange economy, performer and audience are functions of situation, functions into which (if only theoretically) any social member can step. But in a society in which these roles are specialized, the role becomes larger than the member who assumes it; the role is determinate. The mysterious power of our metaphor of "the person behind the mask, the person underneath all this 'role playing'," arises from the stratification brought about by the latter phenomenon. Rather than being in time, in history, these latter and increasingly fictive genres are viewed as being outside time and unmodified by the contingencies and responsibilities of historical time. The product of technology is not a function of a mutual context of making and use. It works to make invisible the labor that produced it, to appear as its own object, and thus to be self-perpetuating. Both the electric toaster and *Finnegans Wake* turn their makers into absent and invisible fictions.

An important dimension of these relationships between audience and performer, subject and agent, the collective and the individual, is the difference between speeds of performance. Conversational genres, and even, more generally, the genres of face-to-face interaction, are marked by the simultaneous and reciprocal experience of time and space undergone by both performers and audience. It is only with the advent of mechanical reproduction that this original temporal and spatial context has become physically manipulated. In his classic essay "The Work of Art in the Age of Mechanical Reproduction," Walter Benjamin outlined some possible consequences of this technological revolution. The authority of the object, the authority of the "original," is jeopardized, the object is detached from the domain of tradition, the work of art is emancipated from its dependence upon ritual, and, consequently, exhibition value begins to displace cult value, the increased mass of participants in the arts results in a new mode of participation: "A man who concentrates before a work of art is absorbed by it. . . .In contrast, the distracted mass absorbs the work of art."[10] Although Benjamin was concerned primarily with the impact of technological innovation in the visual arts, the impact of printing on the verbal arts also must be considered. Except for such children's genres as tongue twisters, visual puns, and feats of memorization, the verbal arts do not concern themselves with the manipulation of speed or with the manipulation of the physical space surrounding the utterance. With the invention of print, however, the material aspects of the discourse emerged as an aesthetic factor. While oral verbal art unfolds in time, written verbal art unfolds in time and space; the book offers a concrete physical textuality, an "all-at-onceness" of boundaries which the oral performance allows to elide into the surrounding context of situation. Yet, in the way it is bound, the book denies us a transcendent simultaneity; we must unfold the pages in time, and this unfolding bears little relation to the actual speed of the text. With print, the time of the performance becomes remote and the text's potential for the fictive is increased. We might consider that the fantastic possibilities the book presents have their antecedents in those oral genres—like the Irish *märchen* tradition—that take as their context the night lit only by fire. In Ireland, *Fiannaíocht sa ló* (storytelling in the daytime) was said to be

unlucky. While some learned tales while haymaking or digging pota-
toes during the daytime, the most prevalent context was the night:
fishermen at sea at night as they waited to draw in their nets, or men
and women passing the night, making fish nets and telling tales to
one another.[11] The blank spaces of night, the blinding whiteness of the
page before print, offer themselves to the fantastic, to a reading of fire
or the tracks of animals. Although the technology of artificial light destroyed the context of the oral fantastic, the technology of the artificial
word created a space for its eruption. In each case these storytelling
contexts metaphorically and physically remove themselves from the
immediate and historical context of everyday life.

The printed text is cinematic before the invention of cinema. The
adjustable speed of narration, the manipulatability of the visual,
turns the reader into a spectator enveloped by, yet clearly separated
from, the time and space of the text. Michel Butor has offered an
illuminating discussion of the reader's position:

> As soon as we can speak of a literary "work," and hence as soon as we
> approach the province of the novel, we must superimpose at least three
> time sequences: that of the adventure, that of writing it, that of reading
> it. The time sequence of the writing will often be reflected in the
> adventure by the intermediary of a narrator. We generally assume a
> progression of speeds between these different "flows": thus, the author
> gives us a summary, which we read in two minutes (he might have
> spent two hours writing it), of a narrative which a certain character
> might have told in two days, of events extending over two years. Thus
> we have organizations of narrative of different speeds.[12]

Butor goes on to say that in reading dialogue and in reading letters
embedded in the text, we are aware of "going the same speed as" the
characters of the novel. Hence we have the problem of speaking/
reading plays—a reading which borders on enactment and performance. In the simultaneity of print, with its rather remarkable capacity for storing information, we find an increasingly complex set of time
systems. The project of the realistic novelist is to move a complex set
of characters through a complex set of interrelated actions; in other
words, to acquire a rather fantastic omnipotence with regard to a
rather mundane world. In *Tom Jones,* for example, Books IV through
XVIII are titled by the amount of time they depict, a time which is the
time of the text's representation: "Containing the Time of a Year,"
"Containing a Portion of Time Somewhat Longer Than Half a Year,"
"Containing About Three Weeks," "Containing Three Days," and so
on. Thus we can further distinguish between authorial time (time of
writing) and the reader's time (time of reading the text) as extratextual

temporalities, and the narrator's time (time of the storytelling act) and the time that is portrayed through the text's representation (time of depicted events) as intratextual temporalities.[13] Because this particular novel is a history of a central character, told by an omniscient narrator, we have a further disjuncture between Tom's experience of events (the time of the representation), the reader's experience of events (vacillating between the point of view of the narrator and the point of view of Tom), and the narrator's "experience" of events, the last being the experience of the storytelling act. Hence the narrator must resort to "meanwhile" strategies if the work is to have a continuity miming the continuity of our experience in everyday life. Chapter 8 of Book X ("In Which the History Goes Forward About Twelve Hours"), "In Which the History Goes Backward," therefore begins: "Before we proceed any farther in our history, it may be proper to look a little back in order to account for the extraordinary appearance of Sophia and her father at the inn at Upton. The reader may be pleased to remember that in the ninth chapter of the seventh book of our history we left Sophia, after a long debate between love and duty, deciding the course as it usually, I believe, happens in favour of the former." With these complex disjunctions between different experiences of temporality, the narrative voice and, consequently, the time of the narration reach for transcendence through the use of metanarrative comments like this one. The omniscient narrator works to disguise the temporality of his or her own voice, to assume an all-at-onceness and all-knowingness that is seductive to the reader, for that position of omniscience presumably will be available to the reader once he or she reaches the novel's closure. At closure we have "graduated," we have finished the book; we have not simply taken one more turn through a forest of signs as we do in allegory. The ideological aspects of the narrative voice also must be considered here, for rather than splitting into binary allegorical camps (we have only to think of bumper stickers that say "I've got it"), the realistic novel presents a set of conflicting ideologies, conflicting points of view, in part through the device of conflicting extratextual and intratextual time systems. The triumph of the omniscient narrator is worked in pulling the reader out of sympathy with any particular time system other than his or her own. Sophia's debate between love and duty is seen through the ironic distancing of "deciding the course as it usually, I believe, happens."

This absent location of origin and authority in the novel might be compared to other postliterate modes of aesthetic production. Just as the reader impossibly aspires to take the position of the narrator, standing above and outside the narrative, so, Benjamin explains, does the audience take the position of the camera in watching a film.

> The camera that presents the performance of the film actor to the public need not respect the performance as an integral whole. Guided by the cameraman, the camera continually changes its position with respect to the performance. The sequence of positional views which the editor composes from the material supplied him constitute the completed film. It comprises certain factors of movement which are in reality those of the camera, not to mention special camera angles, close-ups, etc. . . . This permits the audience to take the position of a critic, without experiencing any personal contact with the actor. The audience's identification with the actor is really an identification with the camera.[14]

In his projections regarding the popular apprehension of film, Benjamin was not able to anticipate the ways in which the technology would discipline the audience into particular modes of seeing or the ways in which that technology itself would develop. Nevertheless, with the advent of film, interpretation has been replaced by watching, by an eye that suffers under an illusion of nakedness, an illusion shared with the camera's "naked" eye. Here we see the increasing historical tendency toward the self-sufficient machine, the sign that generates all consequent signs, the Frankenstein and the thinking computer that have the capacity to erase their authors and, even more significantly, to erase the labor of their authors. The current bifurcation of popular film in America into the horror movie and the special-effects movie displays this phenomenon of reflexive signification. The popularity of *Star Wars* and *E.T.* would seem to derive at least in part from the ways in which these two modes are combined and then suffused with a generalized nostalgia for the generic history of film itself. Indeed, it is the very productivity and self-referentiality of these cinematic signs, their absolute erasure of a physical referent, that renders their excessiveness tolerable for an audience. The true horror movie would be the one envisioned by the audience of Lumière's *Arrival of a Train at a Station* on the night of December 28, 1895. As the train "approached" them at a 45° angle on the screen, they stampeded from the basement room on the Boulevard Capucine which Lumière had rented for the screening.[15]

In a suggestive article on the relation between the development of film and the development of late capitalism, Stanley Aronowitz has stated that "film is the synchronous art form of late capitalism. The film-machine is the enemy of time no less than mass production; it reproduces desire as its product, removes the referent, the signified, and leaves only the act of signifying."[16] Here the mode of production has as its principal obligation the reproduction of itself. Similarly, the growth of the mechanical reproduction of American folk music effected the movement from "country music," played at the speed of the audience, the speed of dance and the body, to "bluegrass," a music which is often evaluated for the way it pits the limits of skill against the limits of aural speed. Bluegrass does not mime the movements of the body; it mimes the movements of the machine that reproduces it: "The Orange Blossom Special" is a testament to technology; its referent is the history of mechanical innovation and not simply the history of musical innovation. In another parallel, the complex technology of "holographic art" erases its author and its referent; what matters is that it works, not that it points to something outside itself. Its contents seem strangely unmotivated, strangely out of key with the technical sophistication of its mechanisms: a woman's face, a parrot in a cage, scenes that resemble those of romantic greeting cards. Content is emptied of interpretability. While modernist art delighted in "making strange" the everyday, this technological art delights in turning the strange into the obvious, in mapping mystery onto cliché. Holographic art is an art like that of commercial television, a mystification of technology accomplished in a gesture which proclaims the innocuousness of all *content*. In fact, without this univocal and mimetic content, we would not be able to distinguish artistic from scientific uses of the holograph.

In these postliterate genres, the time system of the viewer is collapsed into the time system of a machine that has erased its author. No matter how many buttons there seem to be on the television set, there are only two: on and off. The buttons that would be absolutely forbidden to the television would be the buttons Vertov and Chaplin liked to push as authors: the one that speeds up the action and the one that reverses. Once the viewer can manipulate these dimensions, he or she becomes aware of the textuality, the boundaries of the work. Through such manipulations, the viewer can become both reader and authority, in control of the temporality and spatiality of the work, and hence able to reclaim it by the inscription of an interpretation that has the power of interruption and negation. In other words, the progressive movement from the body's reciprocality to technological abstraction in the mode of production of the art form effects a transformation of the subject. In the former mode of production, the subject is performer or agent of tradition; in the second mode of production, the subject is performed, constituted by the operation of the *device* or the differentiation of roles determined by the mode of production itself. For a simple example of this differentiation, we might look to the European circus, whose multiple rings are not so much a simultaneous play as they are the articulation of class difference. What happens in the center ring (its splendor and pyrotechnics, its invention of anthropology and history) is available only peripherally to those with second- and third-class tickets. Furthermore, we might note that recent revolutionary art movements—street theater and happenings, for example—have attempted a reduction of this differentiation, although of necessity this reduction has been self-conscious and nostalgic in its attempts to replace the mechanical and individual with "the homemade" and the communal.

Manipulation and reversibility mark their other: the conventional view of time in the everyday lifeworld. This convention holds time to be linear, narrative, and undifferentiated by hierarchy; it is a convention that defines "being" in everyday life as "one thing after another." But from another stance—that offered by the model of fiction—the time of everyday life is itself organized according to differing modes of temporality, modes articulated through measurements of context and intensification. Time in the everyday lifeworld is not undifferentiated and unhierarchical—it is textual, lending itself to the formation of boundaries and to a process of interpretation delimited by our experience with those boundaries. While consciousness may be described as a "stream," it is only through the reflective and anticipatory processes of understanding that we are able to articulate even that quality of "streamness." Here we might remember Kenneth Burke's assertion that "there are no forms of art which are not forms of experience outside of art." [17] The prevailing notion that everyday time is a matter of undifferentiated linearity may be linked to the prevailing forms of experience within the workplace. Such a notion presents us with an assembly line of temporality, an assembly line in which all experience is partial, piecemeal.

But this would be experience *without language,* for it is by language that we articulate the world "behind" and "beyond" the immediate context at hand. Language gives form to our experience, providing through narrative a sense of closure and providing through abstraction an illusion of transcendence. And it is at this point that the social nature of experience becomes apparent, for language is a social phenomenon; it is only by means of our inherited and lived relation to language that the temporality of our experience becomes organized and even organizable. If the form of experience is that of an "unmediated flow," it is only language which enables us to define this indefiniteness. And because of the social formation of language, because language cannot be abstracted from the ideological sphere that is both its creator and creation, we must question the function of this prevailing notion of experience.

Perhaps one of the strongest models of a presumed disjunction between everyday life and art, stream of consciousness and self-consciouness, is presented in the invisible social space of reading and writing, a space defined temporally and spatially as outside and above the quotidian. Although reading may give form to time, it does not count in time; it leaves no trace; its product is invisible. The marks in the margins of the page are the marks of writing, not the marks of reading. Since the moment of Augustine's reading silently to himself,[18] reading has inhabited the scenes of solitude: the attic, the beach, the commuter train, scenes whose profound loneliness arises only because of their proximity to a tumultuous life which remains outside their peripheries. The reader speaks only to the absent writer; the writer speaks only to the absent reader. We cannot "write along" with someone; aside from Colette and Willy in the novel factory, the writer is alone. And whereas reading may assume or even manipulate the speed of thought, writing obeys the speed of the body, the speed of the hand. If thought outdistances writing, the text must become flooded with signification; if writing outdistances thought, we find the convention of the computer poem and by extension, the "mindless" secretary. Because writing by hand assumes the speed of the body, it is linked to the personal. It is not quite polite to type condolence notes and heartfelt letters to friends or lovers. To sign your name, your mark, is to leave a track like any other track of the body; handwriting is to space what the voice is to time. The moral righteousness of burning one's own letters and diaries is the righteousness of the suicide, not of the avenging murderer. But the record that cannot be burned with the rest is the record that cannot be recorded: the time that cannot count in the diary is the time of writing the diary.

The Sadness Without an Object

The functions that the everyday and its concomitant languages, inhabitants, and temporalities serve are at least two. First, they quantitatively provide for history; second, they qualitatively provide for authenticity. The temporality of everyday life is marked by an irony which is its own creation, for this temporality is held to be ongoing and nonreversible and, at the same time, characterized by repetition and predictability. The pages falling off the calendar, the notches marked in a tree that no longer stands—these are the signs of the everyday, the effort to articulate difference through counting. Yet it is precisely this counting that reduces difference to similarities, that is designed to be "lost track of." Such "counting," such signifying, is drowned out by the silence of the ordinary.

Consider once more the example of Crusoe. Crusoe is surrounded by the social, but it is the social in the abstract—truly a *langue*, a Cartesian ideal, of the social—that we see here. Inversely, Crusoe's sense of time has only the sun as its model, a model which he loses sense of precisely because it cannot be organized abstractly. Missing the comforts of social time, Crusoe in his journal counts not days but objects and the labor that has accomplished their possession or creation:

> Thus I liv'd mighty comfortably, my Mind being entirely composed by resigning to the Will of God, and throwing my self wholly upon the Disposal of his Providence. This made my Life better than sociable, for when I began to regret the want of Conversation, I would ask my self whether thus conversing mutually with my own Thoughts, and, as I hope I may say, with even God himself by Ejaculations, was not better than the utmost Enjoyment of humane Society in the World.
>
> I cannot say that after this, for five Years, any extraordinary thing happened to me, but I liv'd on in the same Course, in the same Posture and Place, just as before; the chief things I was employed in, besides my yearly Labour of planting my Barley and Rice, and curing my Raisins, of both which I always kept up just enough to have sufficient Stock of one Year's Provisions before hand. I say, besides this yearly Labour, and my daily Labour of going out with my Gun, I had one Labour to make me a Canoe, which at last I finished.[19]

The absolute tedium of Crusoe's days is the tedium of this antiutopia of objects, an island of objects existing solely as their use value. Marx similarly described Crusoe's world:

> Let us now picture to ourselves, by way of change, a community of free individuals, carrying on their work with the means of production in common, in which the labour-power of all the different individuals is consciously applied as the combined labour-power of the community. All the characteristics of Robinson's labour are here repeated, but with this difference, that they are social, instead of individual. Everything produced by him was exclusively the result of his own personal labour, and therefore simply an object of use for himself.[20]

If *Robinson Crusoe* is an eschatological work, its eschaton is the moment when the ship (and not the naked footprint) appears on the horizon and use value is transformed into exchange value. The crucial moment in which Crusoe decides to take the money from the ship marks the onset of this anticipation. In this is the "capitalist" tone of the work, and not simply in Crusoe's desire to possess things.

Robinson Crusoe presents us with the saturation point of "ordinary language," language as pure use value, language as inventory over utterance. If there was ever a character who spoke in ordinary language, it is Friday. Yet Friday must be disciplined into speaking ordinary language. He begins his dialogue with Crusoe on the level of *"if God much strong, much might as the Devil, why God no kill the Devil, no make him no more do wicked?"* Crusoe's response is, "And at first I could not tell what to say, so I pretended not to hear him, and ask'd him what he said." After more frustration with the question, Crusoe says: "I therefore diverted the present Discourse between me and my Man, rising up hastily, as upon some sudden Occasion of going out; then sending him for something a good way off."[21] Eventually Crusoe teaches Friday to simply say "yes" and "no," reducing his language to a pure function of immediate context and perpetuating a much larger imperialist tradition of leveling the vox populi.

For Crusoe, time is space to be uncovered, parts of the island left unexplored. The measurement of time is distance; time is a matter of the discovery and acquisition of nature. And because this sense of time stands only in relation to the material world, it has no capacity for reciprocity or for reversal. Time and material goods are stockpiled in Crusoe's world; there is no space for play and exchange until the moment of closure. Similarly, the conventions of everyday life assume an absolute referentiality between ordinary language and the material world. Hence, within this mythology, the primitive, the folk, the peasant, and the working class speak without self-consciousness, without criticism, and without affectation. Yet what is hidden within (or beneath) this flat surface of "ordinary language" is the range of genres that still characterize a face-to-face mode of social interaction: gossiping, flirting, promising, joking, making conversation, doing introductions, and so on.

The function of these "invisible" genres is not to serve as purely utilitarian modes, to serve as "pointers" toward the material world. Rather, it is to maintain, manipulate, and transform the ongoing social reality from which such individual genres have arisen. Furthermore, we may include within this function not only face-to-face genres but all genres. In the place of "ordinary" and "poetic" ones we might substitute "face to face" versus "literary" genres as distinctions useful for articulating differing methods of engagement with the text, differing modes of production and consumption. Or we might replace the standard/poetic distinction with a distinction between nonfictive and fictive genres—a distinction which would allow us to examine ideological formations as they alternately create "the real" and "the imaginary" of social life. In any case, to take as a first step a division between standard and poetic language is to engage in a wholesale and simultaneous trivialization of the word and the work of art.

The crisis that this distinction between standard and deviation attempts to erase, or perhaps simply to avert, is the crisis of the sign—the gap between signifier and signified, which Derrida and others have termed the myth of presence in Western metaphysics. To have an ordinary language which proceeds as if it were part of the material world and a poetic language made of deviations from ordinary language is to ignore the slippage between language and referent which makes all language, from the outset, a deviation from "standardness" or "quality," a deviation which in fact is the productive possibility of language's existence as a social phenomenon. The utilitarian vision of an ordinary language perfectly mapped upon the material needs of the everyday is a vision of language before the Fall: speaking from the heart or from nature as the vox populi is mythically able to do. Thus the folk are seen to rise in one voice because of their lack of consciousness of difference.[22] Such theories of language can be placed amid other Western cults of the primitive: the celebration of madness in romanticism and modernism, the cult of the child, the cult of the pastoral—cults that have never been held by the mad, the child, or the folk themselves.

But if we view this crisis of the sign from an emphasis upon language, what becomes problematic is the gap between language and speech, between the abstraction that is language and the practice that is speech. Hence the structuralist focus on the sentence and its transformations rather than upon the utterance and its situations. And if we view this problem as one of transformations of context, we can begin to approach language as utterance, language used within speech situations, and to see the arbitrariness of the sign dissolve into an ontological crux. The arbitrary nature of the sign may hold within the relation of word and thing, but it is transformed into a nonarbitrary relation by social praxis. Here we might compare the arbitrariness of the sign to the "arbitrariness" of exchange value. Although exchange value bears no intrinsic relation to either the material nature of the commodity or the amount of labor that has gone into the formation of the commodity, in the sense that it is socially determined it is not arbitrary. "Hence," wrote Marx, "exchange value appears to be something accidental and purely relative, and consequently an intrinsic value, i.e. an exchange value that is inseparably connected with, inherent in commodities, seems a contradiction in terms. . . . Therefore, first: the valid exchange values of a given commodity express something equal; secondly, exchange value, generally, is only the mode of expression, the phenomenal form, of something contained in it, yet distinguishable from it."[23] Such an appearance of arbitrariness serves the social function of creating the illusion of a "free market." My point is that we find the conventions for using language emerging in the material social praxis of utterance and not through the abstract measurement of an imperfect *parole* against a perfect *langue*. By framing our use of language in this way, we witness a shift in idealization, a shift which moves the ideal from the *langue* to the situation. Context, the situation of the utterance in face-to-face communication, becomes privileged. In these two positions, the abstract and singular vocality of *langue* and the concrete and multivocal situation of the utterance, we can see voiced two conflicting ideological positions. To privilege either view is to stop the vital movement of the sign. Bakhtin, writing under the name of Vološinov, has characterized this movement, which he calls the social "multiaccentuality" of the sign, as follows:

> Class does not coincide with the sign community, i.e. with the community, which is the totality of users of the same set of signs for ideological communication. Thus various different classes will use one and the same language. As a result, differently oriented accents intersect in every ideological sign. Sign becomes an arena of class struggle.
>   This social multiaccentuality of the ideological sign is a very crucial aspect. By and large, it is thanks to this intersecting of accents that a sign maintains its vitality and dynamism and the capacity for further development. . . .
>   The very same thing that makes the ideological sign vital and mutable is also, however, that which makes it a refracting and distorting medium. The ruling class strives to impart a supraclass, external character to the ideological sign, to distinguish or drive inward the struggle between social value judgments which occurs in it, to make the sign uniaccentual.

Bakhtin goes on to say that the inner dialectical quality of the sign comes out fully in times of revolutionary change and social crisis, but that because of the social tendency toward conservatism this contradiction does not fully emerge in everyday life.[24] Thus not only is an ideological function at work in the separation of ordinary and poetic (semiotic and symbolic) language and its hierarchization of access to meaning, but such an ideological function is at work as well in the always-political imposition of univocality. The gap between signifier and signified, the irreconcilable state of difference (which, accepted, tends toward the schizoid), is taken up by social life and dispersed into the "free play" of art and the grounded "base" of the everyday, a base which, with difficulty, must suppress its own access to heterogeneity.

The conservatism of everyday life arises from its emphasis upon convention, repetition, and the necessity of maintaining a predictable social reality.[25] The function of "making conversation," for example, is mainly the exercise of statements of membership, statements which will allow for the continuance and proper closure of the conversation itself. Hence the reflexive nature of everyday reality, its capacity for mirroring itself through the creation of the rule-governed and rule-creating behavior we know as the traditional, behavior which appears to be outside and beyond the situation and which is at the same time the very creation of the situation. We can see in the structuralist's assumption of an ideal of language a romanticism of apprehension, a romanticism to be fulfilled at the moment when *langue* is realized on earth. And in the contextualist's privileging of context of situation we see a romanticism directed toward a lost point of origin, a point where being-in-context supposedly allowed for a complete and total-ized understanding. In order to examine our relations to this point of origin, the point before the splitting of signifier and signified, the point of union between utterance and context, let us turn to a set of formations—the quotation, the fiction, and the book—and the varieties of nostalgia in which they are engaged.

This privileging of origin, of "original" context, is particularly manifested in the ambivalent status of the quotation, for the quotation lends both integrity and limit to the utterance by means of its "marks." In detaching the utterance from its context of origin, the quotation marks textualize the utterance, giving it both integrity and boundary and opening it to interpretation. The quotation appears as a severed head, a voice whose authority is grounded in itself, and therein lies its power and its limit. For although the quotation now speaks with the voice of history and tradition, a voice "for all times and places," it has been severed from its context of origin and of original interpretation, a context which gave it authenticity. Once quoted, the utterance enters the arena of social conflict: it is manip-ulatable, examinable within its now-fixed borders; it now plays with-in the ambivalent shades of varying contexts. It is no longer the possession of its author; it has only the authority of use. At the same time, the quotation serves to lend the original an authenticity it itself has lost to a surrounding context. The quotation mark points not only inward but outward as well. What stands outside the quotation mark is seen as spontaneous and original; hence our generic conventions of speaking from the heart, from the body, from nature.

In the quotation, we see at work the two primary functions of language—to make present what can only be experienced abstractly, and to textualize our experience and thereby make it available for interpretation and closure. The act of quoting intensifies these processes, which are at work in all language use, much as the framing of carnival marks the intensification and display of all other textual scenes of social life. In quotation and in carnival we see a process of restoration and a process of disillusionment, for the boundary of the text is both fixed and made suspect, and, because of the ongoingness of time and space, this placing is never complete. Henri Lefebvre has suggested that "la fête ne se distinguait de la vie quotidienne que par l'explosion des forces lentement accumulées dans et par cette view quotidienne elle-même."[26] The carnival presents a reply to everyday life which is at the same time an inversion, an intensification, and a manipulation of that life, for it exposes and transforms both pattern and contradiction, presenting the argument and the antithesis of everyday life in an explosion that bears the capacity to destroy that life.

Quotation thereby leads us to a set of terms bound up in this double process of restoration and disillusion: the image, the reflection, and, above all, the repetition. To posit a repetition is to enter the abstract and perfect world of art, a world where the text can appear and reappear despite the ongoingness of the "real world." And yet, without this repetition, without this two-in-the-place-of-one, the one cannot come to be, for it is only by means of difference that identity can be articulated.[27] In quotation we find the context of production transformed and the utterance detached from the authority of that context. In fiction, reframing the utterance transforms both the context of production and the mode of production. As Bateson has explained in his studies of the message "This is play," the play message signifies a transformation of interpretive procedures, a transformation partaken of by members of the situation and which they understand as a device for entering into an abstract and metaphorical play world.

Play, and fiction as a form of play, exaggerate the capacity that all reported speech bears—the capacity to re-create contexts other than the context at hand, the capacity to create an abstract world through language. And the crisis of the sign, the gap between signifier and signified, is reproduced at the level of context: the gap between the reported speech and the speech of origin. The repetition the fiction presents is an imaginary repetition, for it need not have the authority of the "happened before." What is fictive is the "original context"; the pure fiction has no material referent. Hence fiction subverts the myth of presence, of authorial context, of origin, and at the same time asserts the ideological by insisting upon the reality-generating capacity of language.

Fiction allows us to see that repetition is a matter of reframing, that in the repetition difference is displayed in both directions, just as "identity" is created. We thus cannot see the repetition as secondary, or auxiliary, to the original, for instead of supplementing or supplanting the original, it serves to create the original. Analogously, the fiction, whether conventionally labeled "realistic," "absurd," "fantastic," or "exact," does not reflect its subject so much as it creates its subject; each fiction contaminates the imaginary purity of everyday life by denying the privileged authority of immediate, lived context and that context's subsequent "authenticity" of experience.

Because fiction "occurs" in a world simultaneous to and "outside" everyday life, it interrupts the narrativity, the linearity of that life. The weaving of fictive genres throughout this linearity lends to everyday life a lyric quality, a quality of recurrence and variation upon theme. Even the personal-experience story, the narrative genre that perhaps most mimes the conventional linearity attributed to our everyday experience of temporality, serves to structure that narrative within larger conventions, indeed generic conventions, for interpreting experience. And such structuring echoes others' engagement with both everyday temporality and the temporality of "personal narrative." The personal-experience story is most impersonal in its generic conventions and may be compared to the novel in its continuing involvement with and transformation of previous performances of its genre. Here the progress of the individual life history, whose repetition is seen as a cumulative one, is in fact the progress of the genre, the refinement of notions of character, incident, action, and scene in relation to changing cultural values.

All fictions, both oral and written, lend lyric structure to our experience, but the convergence of fictiveness and print is particularly conducive to an experience of simultaneity and a metaphorical existence that is both substitutive and predicative. Whereas speech unfolds in time, writing unfolds in space, and print's formation by a process of mechanical reproduction gives the book both material existence through time and an abstract existence across a community of readers. Furthermore, the community, like the author's ideal and gentle reader, is a largely imaginary construction, an abstraction unavailable to any given author or reader at any given moment, and yet which must of necessity be assumed at such moments. Hence the reproduction of the text is simultaneously quite literal and autonomous of authorial intention: each reader creates not a new interpretation but a new text and an author whose "authority" is determined by the ideology of literary convention, including the social formation known as "the literary life," as much as by conventions of intentionality. The tension we see at work between tradition and situation in the face-to-face communities that engage in oral genres is displaced in written forms by their turning of the reader into performed/performer. The author's experience of this tension is that of a reader creating a new text, a new temporality, out of those experiences, both real and imagined, which he or she had apprehended and given structure to.

The simultaneity of the printed word lends the book its material aura; as an object it has a life of its own, a life outside human time, the time of the body and its voice. Hence the transcendent authority of the classic and the classicism of all printed works. The book stands in tension with history, a tension reproduced in the microcosm of the book itself, where reading takes place in time across marks which have been made in space. Moreover, because of this tension, all events recounted within the text have an effect of distancing, an effect which serves to make the text both transcendent and trivial and to collapse the distinction between the real and the imagined. The ideological nature of the work becomes apparent here as the ideal supplants the "merely real." The printed word always tends toward abstraction, for it escapes both the necessity of a material referent and the constraints of an immediate context of origin; it is always quotation.

Similarly, in its absolute closure, its clarity of beginnings and endings, the printed work finds an analogous practice in narrative. While "lived" history is perceived as open work, work without established beginning or established ending, it is the accomplishment of narrative to provide both origin and eschaton, a set of provisions that are profoundly ideological in the closure they present. Narrative is "about" closure; the boundaries of events form the ideological basis for the interpretation of their significance. Indeed, without narrative, without the organization of experience, the event cannot come to be. This organization is an organization of temporality and an establishing of the causality implicit in temporality, but narrative closure is offered outside the temporality of our everyday lives. It is not caught up within that temporality, but rather is performed with self-consciousness, with a manipulation of point of view within its own story time, the context of its performance.

Although narrative offers transcendence, it lacks authenticity, for its experience is *other*. The printed word suffers doubly from this lack, for not only has it lost the authenticity of lived experience—it has lost the authenticity of authorial voice as well. Who is speaking? It is the voice of abstraction, a voice which proclaims its absence with each word. In this outline of experience we can see a simultaneous and contradictory set of assumptions. First, the assumption that immediate lived experience is more "real," bearing within itself an authenticity which cannot be transferred to mediated experience; yet second, the assumption that the mediated experience known through language and the temporality of narrative can offer pattern and insight by virtue of its capacity for transcendence. It is in the meeting of these two assumptions, in the conjunction of their *symptoms*, that the social disease of nostalgia arises. By the narrative process of nostalgic reconstruction the present is denied and the past takes on an authenticity of being, an authenticity which, ironically, it can achieve only through narrative.[28]

Nostalgia is a sadness without an object, a sadness which creates a longing that of necessity is inauthentic because it does not take part in lived experience. Rather, it remains behind and before that experience. Nostalgia, like any form of narrative, is always ideological: the past it seeks has never existed except as narrative, and hence, always absent, that past continually threatens to reproduce itself as a felt lack.[29] Hostile to history and its invisible origins, and yet longing for an impossibly pure context of lived experience at a place of origin, nostalgia wears a distinctly utopian face, a face that turns toward a future-past, a past which has only ideological reality. This point of desire which the nostalgic seeks is in fact the absence that is the very generating mechanism of desire. As we shall see in our discussion of the souvenir, the realization of re-union imagined by the nostalgic is a narrative utopia that works only by virtue of its partiality, its lack of fixity and closure: nostalgia is the desire for desire.

The prevailing motif of nostalgia is the erasure of the gap between nature and culture, and hence a return to the utopia of biology and symbol united within the walled city of the maternal. The nostalgic's utopia is prelapsarian, a genesis where lived and mediated experience are one, where authenticity and transcendence are both present and everywhere. The crisis of the sign, emerging between signifier and signified, between the material nature of the former and the abstract and historical nature of the latter, as well as within the mediated reality between written and spoken language, is denied by the nostalgic's utopia, a utopia where authenticity suffuses both word and world. The nostalgic dreams of a moment before knowledge and self-consciousness that itself lives on only in the self-consciousness of the nostalgic narrative. Nostalgia is the repetition that mourns the inauthenticity of all repetition and denies the repetition's capacity to form identity.[30] Thus we find that the disjunctions of temporality traced here create the space for nostalgia's eruption. The inability of the sign to "capture" its signified, of narrative to be one with its object, and of the genres of mechanical reproduction to approximate the time of face-to-face communication leads to a generalized desire for origin, for nature, and for unmediated experience that is at work in nostalgic longing. Memory, at once impoverished and enriched, presents itself as a device for measurement, the "ruler" of narrative. Thus near-sightedness and far-sightedness emerge as metaphors for understanding, and they will be of increasing importance as this essay proceeds.

Interior Decorations

Nostalgia's longing for absolute presence in the face of a gap between signifier and signified reminds us that narrative is a signifying phenomenon made up of another signifying phenomenon: language "means" before narrative takes it up. Here is another face of the problem of ordinary/poetic language: language detached from its history, from the contradictions arising from its experience in real speech situations, would be empty, would be barren not only of exchange value but of use value as well. Because it is manufactured from this stock of utterances, the literary is neither new nor deviant, but rather is what Soviet semioticians have called a "secondary modelling system":

> It is possible to conclude that if from one perspective the assertion that poetic language is a particular case of natural language is well-founded, then from another perspective the view that natural language is to be considered a particular case of poetic language is just as convincing. "Poetic language" and "natural language" are particular manifestations of more general systems that are in a state of continual tension and mutual translation, and at the same time are not wholly mutually translatable; therefore the question of the primacy of one or the other communication-modelling system is determined by the functional direction of a specific act of translation, that is, by what is translated into what.[31]

Because, as a result of its particular mixing of the complex of languages available at the moment of its performance and of its detachment from a context of origin, the literary work cannot admit of synonymity, it displays within its physical closure the impossibility of closure on the level of interpretation. It displays the oxymoron of the sign: while the signifier may be material, the signified cannot be.

So long as a literary genre allows for a distinction in point of view(s),[32] a set of conflicting languages will be in tension both within the text and in relation to the interpreter's language. These conflicting languages arise not just from the relations between various stances regarding what is said but also from the relations between what is said and what is not said. It is in patterns of signification that we derive the ideological, for what is not said bears the burden of cultural assumptions; the what-everyone-knows does not need to be articulated. Yet these unarticulated assumptions are in fact the most profoundly ideological of all assumptions, for they suffuse every aspect of consciousness. In this tension between identity and difference, the unarticulated and the defined, lies the work of the speech situation. But literary genres present not only the tension of the speech situation; they also present a tension between tradition and performance, between past instances of the genre and the instance at hand. Literature does not represent speech acts in the sense that a tape recording might represent them. Literature comes with the weight, the burden, of literary history, with conventions shaping the form of representation, conventions that both arise from and effect the conventions for oral discourse. In a footnote to her *Toward a Speech Act Theory of Literary Discourse*, Mary Louise Pratt writes: "It will be argued that literature is often or always didactic, that is, intended to have some world-changing or action-inducing force. I think it can be shown, however, that this aim has to be viewed as indirect in an analysis of literary speech acts, since its achievement depends on first achieving the representative aim. All exempla work this way and differ in this respect from direct persuasion."[33] But in saying this, Pratt herself is both ignoring and, through the unsaid, articulating the literary convention that lyric structure argues and narrative structure (to which she limits her study) "describes"; hence lyric structure seeks to "persuade," while narrative structure seeks to "inform." "Directness" is a feature of generic style. My point is that it is the very closure of narrative, its "unmotivatedness," which places it within the realm of the ideological. Whereas the univocality of the traditional lyric may clearly define an *other*, an alternative, or opposing, voice, it is narrative's illusion of multivocality which conceals the shaping force of intentionality, of the authorial voice in history. Narrative is ideological both in its "unsaid" quality and in the fact that its descriptive power lies in its ability to make visible, to shape the way we perceive the landscape of action, and hence to shape the way we perceive our relation to that landscape. We cannot assume the existence of a "representative" aim independent of an ideological aim, for representation always strives, through manipulation and the forced emergence of detail, to create an ideal that is the "real." The continual use of an "ethnographic present" in anthropological writing is a good example of this denial of the ongoingness of experience and the multivocality of points of view. It is not lived experience which literature describes, but the conventions for organizing and interpreting that experience, conventions which are modified and informed by each instance of the genre.

What does it mean to describe something? Descriptions must rely upon an economy of significance which is present in all of culture's representational forms, an economy which is shaped by generic conventions and not by aspects of the material world itself. While our awe of nature may be born in the face of her infinite and perfect detail, our awe of culture relies upon a hierarchical organization of information, an organization which is shared by social members and which differs cross-culturally and historically. Not our choice of subject, but our choice of aspect and the hierarchical organization of detail, will be emergent in and will reciprocally effect the prevailing social construction of reality. As genres approach "realism," their organization of information must clearly resemble the organization of information in everyday life. Realistic genres do not mirror everyday life; they mirror its hierarchization of information. They are mimetic in the stance they take toward this organization and hence are mimetic of values, not of the material world.[34] Literature cannot mime the world; it must mime the social. It cannot escape history, the burden of signification borne by language before literature takes it up.

Here we must go beyond the conventions of description, which mask its independent life and functions. The unsaid assumption underlying all descriptions is experience beyond lived experience, the experience of the other and of the fiction. In description we articulate the time and space that are absent from the context at hand, the lived experience of the body. Our interest in description may be stated most often as an interest in style, but in fact it is equally an interest in closure. All description is a matter of mapping the unknown onto the known. To have an "indescribable" experience is simply to confirm the ideology of individual subjective consciousness. Each time we present a description, each time a description is "taken up" as the real, the social utopia of language, the belief in the signifying capacity of language and uniform membership in that capacity on the part of speakers, is confirmed. And where writing is concomitant with authority, the validity of written description will be held to transcend any contradictions everyday experience may present. In this otherness from the everyday, every text bears the potential of a sacred text.

Thus an adequate description is always a socially adequate description. It has articulated no more and no less than is necessary to the membership of the sign. Independent of this social organization of detail, description must threaten infinity, an infinity which stretches beyond the time of speech in a gesture which points to speech's helplessness when bereft of hierarchy. To describe more than is socially adequate or to describe in a way which interrupts the everyday hierarchical organization of detail is to increase not realism but *the unreal effect of the real*. If such writing as that of the *nouveau roman* seems inhuman, unmotivated, it is because the surface of detail has been leveled to significance without hierarchy; it does not tell us enough and yet it tells us too much. The tension that novelists like Puig or Robbe-Grillet present combines an objective surface of detail with a hidden and necessarily subjective subject, a subject formed from the pattern of its absences. Butor has characterized this mode of writing as a "structural inversion": "We might emphasize the importance of a given moment by its absence, by the study of its surroundings, thus making the reader feel that there is a lacuna in the fabric of what is being narrated, or something that is being hidden."[35] This "objective" style takes the stance, the point of view, of an observer who looks from a distance that is "realistic." Yet it is the even-handedness, the amoralistic (because unhierarchical) nature, of this stance which undermines its realism, much as the unconscious undermines the superficial realism of everyday life. Such objectivity may be seen as well in the work of contemporary "superrealists" such as Richard Estes. In Estes's work we are overwhelmed by a detail that in everyday life has become taken for granted; thus this detail is presented so realistically it becomes illusory. The cityscapes Estes chooses to paint are cultural scenes; their detail is human, made within the signifying practices of man, and yet inhuman in that such paintings resist the imposition of "humanism" upon them. We are overwhelmed by surface in these works, by the reflections of these scenes in the very glass they depict. Everything points to the surface of the paint, a surface made glaring by its lack of texture, by the absence of its mark. This is why a photographic reproduction of an Estes work is boring; there is nothing to distinguish it from a photograph of the material landscape itself. The painting has sprung into being like the magical commodities that contextualize it. In Estes's work or in the sculptures of Duane Hanson we search for clues of the subjective in the midst of an objective surface; hence our delight when we uncover the artist's signature (the "Estes" which Estes invariably conceals somewhere in each work) or, amid the Hansons, when the tourist turns out to be a real tourist after all.

As the form of realism shifts to individual experience in its temporal and spatial context, the context of the interior of bourgeois space, it is the details of that context which become described, and such details must be described according to the conventions of bourgeois life. Laurence Sterne concluded that the "nonsensical minutiae" of everyday life, the "little occurrences of life" are what exhibit the truth of character. And if detail lends hierarchy and direction to our everyday lives, so does it lend hierarchy and detail to the novels of realism. It is the mark of a successful realistic novel that it be frittered away by detail. We can see in eighteenth- and nineteenth-century realistic novels echoes of two major themes of bourgeois life: individuation and refinement. If reality resides in the progress of the individual, it is that individual's context which should be used to define him or her. The description of the material world, the world of things, is necessary for a description of the hero's or heroine's progress through that world, and the "finer" the description, the "finer" the writing. Such description provides a categorization of value; its catalog links the abstractness of language to the materiality of things. In his *Semiotics of Poetry* Riffaterre concludes: "As reality, the details are indeed minor. As words, however, minor details are worth noticing merely because they have been recorded: their insignificance is but the other face of their importance as signs. . . . This semantic given is the model for all the other details, which function not just as picturesque notations or constituents of reality, but as embodiments of the semiotic constant."[36] Within this semiotic universe, the material object is transformed completely to the realm of exchange value. There is no *point* to the detail in bourgeois realism aside from its function within the world of signs, its message that it is the trace of the real. The ornament does not dress the object; it defines the object. We find an analogy to our position in Guy Debord's critique of the spectacle forms of what might be termed the semiotics of late capitalism. "It [spectacle] is not a supplement to the real world, its added decoration. It is the heart of the realism of the real society."[37] His point—that the semiotic system works independent of, and even absorbs, intrinsicality—is well displayed in a recent *New Yorker* advertisement for Rolex watches, which compares the precision of its promoted commodity with the "precision" of the late John Cheever's fiction:

Rolex. For those who set the measure of the times.
John Cheever. Best selling novelist and master of the short story.
An award winning author who savors the bittersweet taste of American life in timeless narration.
Detail illuminates John Cheever's writing. Just as detail inspires every Rolex craftsman. Created like no other timepiece in the world. With an unrelenting, meticulous attention to excellence in a world fraught with compromise. The Rolex Oyster Perpetual Day-Date Superlative Chronometer.
A great work designed to stand the test of time.

The substitutability of Cheever's signs for the sign of the watch signals not only the commodification of the artwork but also the mutuality of exchange within the system of objects. The recent film *Diva*, with its emphasis upon the articulation of the brand name (again the substitution of the Rolex in a gesture of "trading up" as one "trades in"), makes an analogous point: the ideology of trading up always promises an imaginary social mobility for the subject, an improvement in "style of life" that is here a virtual transformation of time.

Refinement has to do with not only the articulation of detail but also the articulation of difference, an articulation which has increasingly served the interests of class. Baudrillard, in his study of the bourgeois system of objects, noticed this class-related phenomenon of refinement; for example, he described the bourgeois interior as dependent upon the discretion of "tints and nuances." Colors such as gray, mauve, and beige mark a moral refusal of color in the bourgeois world. "De la coleur surtout: trop spectaculaire, elle est une menace pour l'intériorité."[38] The sign itself is dissolved into its differences from other signs within a system of signs: the material world is made symbolic according to the signifying practices of class. Hence the naïveté of semiotics in assuming signs that are not symbols; particularly in the era of late capitalism we can see all aspects of the material world become symbolic of class relations, all signs referring with careful discrimination to their place in the system of signs.

Thus far we have been addressing the detail in relation to the description of the material world: the world as still life. And just as the still life is a configuration of consumable objects, so the book's minute description of the material world is a device which tends to draw attention to the book as object. The configurations of print and the configurations of context-as-décor bear an intimate relation which oral genres, pointing to the time and space of the body, do not partake of. Description of the material world seems self-motivated, seems to be directed toward a presentation without direction. Thus, whereas the still life speaks to the cultural organization of the material world, it does so by concealing history and temporality; it engages in an illusion of timelessness. The message of the still life is that nothing changes; the instant described will remain as it is in the eye of the beholder, the individual perceiving subject. As Louis Marin has suggested, "Et cependant, avant d'être peinture de vie silencieuse, la nature morte a eu pour fonction et objectif, de parler, de murmurer à l'oreille du contemplateur, un certain discours qui ne pouvait être compris là encore que de ceux qui possédaient consciemment ou inconsciemment les codes hautement élaborés d'une culture."[39] The still life stands in a metonymic relation to everyday life; its configuration of objects does not frame another world so much as it enters the frame of this world, the world of individual and immediate experience in a paradise of consumable objects. Here we can see that all description is depiction, an effort to enclose a seemingly infinite amount of detail within an absolute frame. That frame is the social convention of adequacy, which functions to provide closure. Description allows us to "see" remote experience, to "picture it in our minds," and we do so by a process of intertextual allusion and comparison. If the notion of depiction implies a relativity and authorship which a more "scientific" notion of description does not, it is because we simultaneously have need for an ideology of individual creativity in the first case and an ideology of replicability and transcendent viewpoint in the second.

Narrative closure articulates boundary in such a way as to separate one temporality from another, to point to the disjunction between context of narration and the context of the narrated event. When narrative moves into the "detailed" description of action rather than material life, it calls attention to itself as a manipulation of temporality. A detail of movement is a skewing of narrative time, a manipulation of the reader's access to knowledge. In the detail of movement we see the possibility of using detail to digress, to inscribe a circle around an object in order not to divulge it, and at the same time the possibility of using detail to tantalize. The digression stands in tension with narrative closure. It is narrative closure opened from the inside out. It holds the reader in suspension, or annoyance, for it presents the possibility of never getting back, of remaining forever within the detour. Fantasy literature in particular exploits this device of narrative looping, for the fantasy presents what is framed as an absolute other world, and so the detour does not have the hierarchical constraints that a realistic narrative must internalize. Digression in narrative might be seen as the equivalent, on the discourse level, of syntactical embedding. Just as syntactical embedding is a matter not just of additional information but of a restructuring of information in such a way as to throw light upon and help define the position of the speaker in relation to the material and the listener in context, so narrative digression articulates the narrative voice, its control over the material, and consequently its control over the reader's passage toward closure. Instead of offering the reader transcendence, the digression blocks the reader's view, toying with the hierarchy of narrative events. What counts and what doesn't count must be sorted. The digression recaptures the tedium of the journey, the incessant and self-multiplying detail of landscape, a detail which nearly erases the landmark by distracting the reader's attention.

In the detail of the scene we see nature transformed into culture: the material world is arranged and transformed with regard to the exigencies of plot or in order to allow the reader to enter the signifying practices of the work. In the detail of action we see narrative triumph over everyday temporality, forcing the reader to participate in the speed of the narrative. In either case the reader must acknowledge with a statement of membership the community of readers. The text will draw upon and transform the ideological practices brought to it by the reader in this dialogue between inside and outside: the book as both idea and object, finalizable as meaning and materiality at once; the interpenetration of milieu and inference, sign and symbol, that marks the function of details for the bourgeois subject.

Space of Language

Speech leaves no mark in space; like gesture, it exists in its immediate context and can reappear only in another's voice, another's body, even if that other is the same speaker transformed by history. But writing contaminates; writing leaves its trace, a trace beyond the life of the body. Thus, while speech gains authenticity, writing promises immortality, or at least the immortality of the material world in contrast to the mortality of the body. Our terror of the unmarked grave is a terror of the insignificance of a world without writing. The metaphor of the unmarked grave is one which joins the mute and the ambivalent; without the mark there is no boundary, no point at which to begin the repetition. Writing gives us a device for inscribing space, for inscribing nature: the lovers' names carved in bark, the slogans on the bridge, and the strangely uniform and idiosyncratic hand that has tattooed the subways. Writing serves to caption the world, defining and commenting upon the configurations we choose to textualize. If writing is an imitation of speech, it is so as a "script," as a marking of speech in space which can be taken up through time in varying contexts. The space between letters, the space between words, bears no relation to the stutters and pauses of speech. Writing has none of the hesitations of the body; it has only the hesitations of knowing, the hesitations which arise from its place outside history—transcendent yet lacking the substantiating power of context.

The abstract and material nature of language, apparent in speech as sound and significance, is all the more apparent in writing. This oxymoron of the sign, the material nature of the signifier in contrast to the abstract nature of the signified, has posed a particular problem for Marxist aesthetics. Raymond Williams tries to resolve the matter by drawing a distinction between inner sign—inner language—and the material sign, one located within consciousness and the other located in social life.[40] But in what way can we say that inner language is different from social language? Certainly not in its degree of sociability, for the language we use to formulate, experiment, fantasize, and reason "internally," that is, without speech, is the same language, with the same history, be it "personal" or "cultural," that we use in our relations with others throughout our everyday lives. The social cannot be abstracted from language; to perform such an abstraction would be to posit a personal beyond history, a gesture which quite obviously serves certain class interests. In *A Theory of Semiotics*, Umberto Eco provides a gloss on this point as part of a larger argument regarding semiotic *content:*

> We can say that *cultural units are physically within our grasp.* They are the signs that social life has put at our disposal: images interpreting books, appropriate responses interpreting ambiguous questions, words interpreting definitions and vice-versa. The ritual behavior of a rank of soldiers interpreting the trumpet signal "at-tention!" gives us information about the cultural unit (at-tention) conveyed by the musical sign-vehicle. Soldiers, sounds, pages of books, colors on a wall, all these *etic* entities are physically, materially, *materialistically testable.* Cultural units stand out against society's ability to equate these signs with each other, cultural units are the semiotic *postulate* required in order to justify the very fact that society does equate codes with codes, sign-vehicles with meanings, expressions with contents.[41]

It is not through any intrinsic quality of the sign but rather through the interpretive acts of members of a sign community that the sign comes to have meaning. Hence the transmutability of all signs, their capacity to serve as signified or signifier, independent of their physical properties. The semiotic universe is an abstract and interpretive universe constructed by means of concrete social practices.

The aesthetic, as a dimension of the semiotic, celebrates the transformation of the material by the abstract. The capacity of all play and fictions to reframe context is a transformation performed by means of signifying practices, the transformation of use value into exchange value by means of signification. It is not surprising that the age of late capitalism is marked by the aestheticization of commodities and the commercial exploitation of sexuality. It is not the materiality of signs which makes them subject to ideological formations here; it is their immateriality, their capacity to serve the interests of those formations regardless of their physical form. Although the cult of the artist has celebrated such an immateriality as a form of transcendence, this immateriality can as well be seen as what links aesthetic forms to specific historical and social content. Art exaggerates the double capacity of the sign, the transformative power of all signs. The signs of art signify within an immaterial context, but the signs of other contexts display an equally immaterial signified, are equally capable of becoming significant.[42]

The oxymoron of the sign is particularly foregrounded in the book: book as meaning versus book as object; book as idea versus book as material. And because the social shape of reading has become inner speech, the book as meaning and idea is all the more distanced from the book as object and material. In this deliberate and artificial split lies the gap between the leisurely bourgeois reader and the "intellectual worker," between the cardboard front for books and the thumbed edition. The two faces of paperback publishing, the mass-market and the academic paperback, further complicate this focus of the book, for in the mass-market paperback, the book is consumable, destroyed by reading, and in the academic paperback the "value" of academic discourse is displayed within the pulp of cheap materials. In his essay on the book as object, Butor criticizes the consumerism of commercial publishing for bringing about this state of affairs:

> When the book was a single copy, whose production required a considerable number of work hours, the book naturally seemed to be a "monument" (*exegi monumentum aere perennius*), something even more durable than a structure of bronze. What did it matter if a first reading was long and difficult; it was understood that one owned a book for life. But the moment that quantities of identical copies were put on the market, there was a tendency to act as if reading a book "consumed" it, consequently obliging the purchaser to buy another for the next "meal" or spare moment, the next train ride.[43]

Butor is gratified to see that the *Discourse on Method* is available in every train station, but he mourns the loss of the monumental book here, a mourning which may be translated into a nostalgic mourning for the classic, for the book as a transcendent cultural artifact. In the realm of market competition, speed is the auxiliary to consumption, and the rapid production and consumption of books, their capacity for obsolescence in material form, necessarily seems to transform their content. If the book can be consumed, so can the idea; if the book is destroyed, the idea is destroyed. The consumer approaches memory not simply with nostalgia but with an abundance of bad faith. This bourgeois conjunction of sign and signified is apparent in the dramatic rescue of the classics offered in advertisements for gilt-and-leather volumes of "The World's Greatest Literature."

So long as the production of books remained within the artisanal sector, a wide range of the population was denied access to them. It was only the mass production of books that created a crisis in value. Before mass production, form and content presented an illusion of wholeness. Thus the book collector is caught up in the maniacal desire of the museologist; his or her nostalgia is for an absolute presence between signifier and signified, between object and context. Like other collectors, he or she must substitute seriality and external form for the moment of production and its firsthand knowledge. In his *Curiosities of Literature*, D'Israeli writes:

> The passion for forming vast collections of books has necessarily existed in all periods of human curiosity; but long it required regal munificence to found a national library. It is only since the art of multiplying the productions of the mind . . . that men of letters have been enabled to rival this imperial and patriotic honour. The taste for books, so rare before the fifteenth century, has gradually become general only within these four hundred years: in that small space of time the public mind of Europe has been created.[44]

The royal predilection for giving libraries the names of their benefactors ("The emperors were ambitious at length to give their names to the libraries they founded")[45] has in more modern times been transferred to the identification of the reader with the books he or she possesses, to the notion of self as the sum of its reading. Consider the juxtaposition of D'Israeli's criticism of the bibliomania of those who collect books for their own sake with his approval of the "tasteful ornamentation of books":

> This passion for the acquisition and enjoyment of *books* has been the occasion of their lovers embellishing their outsides with costly ornaments, a rage which ostentation may have abused: but when these volumes belong to the real man of letters, the most fanciful bindings are often emblems of his taste and feelings. The great Thuanus procured the finest copies for his library, and his volumes are still eagerly purchased, bearing his autograph on the last page. A celebrated amateur was Grollier; the Muses themselves could not more ingeniously have ornamented their favorite works. I have seen several in the libraries of curious collectors. He embellished their exterior with taste and ingenuity. They are gilded and stamped with peculiar neatness; the compartments on the binding are drawn and painted, with different inventions of subjects, analogous to the works themselves; and they are further adorned by that amiable inscription, *Jo. Grollierii et amicorum!*— purporting that these literary treasures were collected for himself and for his friends![46]

Only "taste," the code word for class varieties of consumption, articulates the difference here.

The book as pure object abandons the realm of use value and enters an ornamental realm of exchange value. Valéry describes with distaste the example of Edmond de Goncourt:

> And now for another and very different example, showing the absurd lengths to which even the most distinguished collector may go when the desire for variety leads him to forget the basic function of a book and the binding fitted to it. After having the first editions of his friends' works bound in parchment, Edmond de Goncourt had their portraits painted on the covers by the artists he considered most appropriate to the sitters: for Daudet, Carrière, for Zola, Raffaelli, etc. Since the books could not bear the slightest handling without damage, they were condemned to sit eternally in a glass case. . . . Is that what a real book is meant for?[47]

Writing can be displayed as both object and knowledge. The possibilities for its objective display are restricted to its physical properties, to the limits of its mode of production. At the outer limits of these possibilities are transformations in the mode of its production and transformation of its physical properties. Valéry records: "I remember seeing and—with a certain horror—daring to handle a ritual of black magic, or perhaps it was the text of a black mass, bound in human skin; a frightful object—there was still a tuft of hair on the back of it. All aesthetic questions apart, there was a very evident kinship between the grisly exterior and the diabolical content of this abominable book."[48] In this remarkable example, a series of correspondences are collapsed: binding and content, body and soul. This object inverts the value which holds that the cultural always triumphs over the natural, over labor, and over death. The volume is horrible in much the same way that the pyramids are horrible: it is a monument to death, to the total transformation of labor into exchange value. The taboo here is the transformation of the living body into the merely material, the doubling of human labor moving spirit into matter. The book has murdered its content. We may compare this volume to the Dadaist book/objects. One in particular was covered by a forbidding configuration of needles. The book stands self-contained, inviolable in this case, testing the boundaries of our notion of "book." As the skin-bound book tests the limits of the book's physical properties, other volumes speak of an infinity of production that then becomes their history—not the history of their writing, or what we call literary history, but the history of their making as objects. Describing "the most curious book in the world," Bombaugh writes:

The most singular bibliographic curiosity is that which belonged to the family of the Prince de Ligne, and is now in France. It is entitled *Liber Passionis Domini Nostri Jesu Christi, cum Characteribus Nulla Materia Compositis*. This book is neither written nor printed! The whole letters of the text are cut out of each folio upon the finest vellum; and, being interleaved with blue paper, it is read as easily as the best print. The labor and patience bestowed in its completion must have been excessive, especially when the precision and minuteness of the letters are considered. The general execution, in every respect, is indeed admirable; and the vellum is of the most delicate and costly kind.[49]

Like the *molas* of the San Blas Cuna, this volume reverses the usual pattern by which writing, as a craft, inscribes the world. It is through the absence of inscription (perhaps better described as the inscription of absence) that this text speaks. The text does not supplement nature here, it takes from it, marking significance by means of a pattern of nonmarks; it is the difference between the tattoo and the brand.

This patterning of significance returns us to the problem of quotation and the display of writing as knowledge. Allusion to the abstract world, the world created through speech and perpetuated through time in writing, is a dominant aspect of discourse in the literate world. The quotation as allusion points to the abstract exchange value of printed works, their value as statements of membership and class. And literature enters the field of exchange, a field articulated by writing, the exchange of letters, IOU's, "deeds," all acts of reciprocity that reveal the conflicting realms of the material and the abstract, the real and the ideal, praxis and ideology.

2. THE MINIATURE

Micrographia

The book sits before me, closed and unread; it is an object, a set of surfaces. But opened, it seems revealed; its physical aspects give way to abstraction and a nexus of new temporalities. This is the distinction between book and text which Derrida has described in *Of Grammatology:*

> The idea of the book is the idea of a totality, finite or infinite, of the signifier; this totality of the signifier cannot be a totality, unless a totality constituted by the signified preexists it, supervises its inscriptions and its signs, and is independent of it in its ideality. The idea of the book, which always refers to a natural totality, is profoundly alien to the sense of writing. It is the encyclopedic protection of theology and of logocentrism against the disruption of writing, against its aphoristic energy, and, as I shall specify later, against differences in general. If I distinguish the text from the book, I shall say that the destruction of the book, as it is now under way in all domains, denudes the surface of the text. That necessary violence responds to a violence that was no less necessary.[1]

The metaphors of the book are metaphors of containment, of exteriority and interiority, of surface and depth, of covering and exposure, of taking apart and putting together. To be "between covers"—the titillation of intellectual or sexual reproduction. To be outside the cover, to be godlike in one's transcendence, a transcendence of beginning collapsed into closure, and, at the same time, to be "closed out."

37

The closure of the book is an illusion largely created by its materiality, its cover. Once the book is considered on the plane of its significance, it threatens infinity. This contrast is particularly apparent in the transformations worked by means of the miniature book and minute writing, or micrographia. Minute writing experiments with the limits of bodily skill in writing: the remarkableness of minute writing depends upon the contrast between the physical and abstract features of the mark. Nearly invisible, the mark continues to signify; it is a signification which is increased rather than diminished by its minuteness. In those examples of micrographia which form a picture we see an emphasis upon healing the skewed relation between meaning and materiality. The miniature book delights in tormenting the wound of this relation, but the micrographic drawing says that, in fact, there is not an *arbitrary* relation between sign and signified but a *necessary* one. In a set of prints published recently in *The Georgia Review*, for example, the minute configurations of an author's words "spelled out" or depicted the author's portrait.[2] Such works transform the map into the globe; they say that writing, if approached from a sufficiently transcendent viewpoint, can become multidimensional.

Reading the book of nature became a *topos* of the Renaissance, but placing the book in nature may antecede it. D'Israeli, in *Curiosities of Literature*, equivocally describes "the Iliad of Homer in a nutshell, which Pliny says that Cicero once saw, it is pretended might have been a fact, however to some it may appear impossible. Ælian notices an artist who wrote a distich in letters of gold, which he enclosed in the rind of a grain of corn." He also mentions the English Bible that Peter Bales, an Elizabethan writing master, enclosed "in an English walnut no bigger than a hen's egg. The nut holdeth the book; there are as many leaves in his little book as the great Bible, and he hath written as much in one of his little leaves as a great leaf of the Bible."[3] Minute writing is emblematic of craft and discipline; while the materiality of the product is diminished, the labor involved multiplies, and so does the significance of the total object. Curtius writes:

> Now to reading conceived as the form of reception and study, corresponds writing conceived as the form of production and creation. The two concepts belong together. In the intellectual world of the Middle Ages, they represent as it were the two halves of a sphere. The unity of this world was shattered by the invention of printing. The immense and revolutionary change which it brought about can be summarized in one statement: Until that time, every book was a manuscript. Merely materially then, as well as artistically, the written book had a value which we can no longer feel. Every book produced by

copying represented diligence and skilled craftsmanship, long hours of intellectual concentration, loving and sedulous work.[4]

The labor was the labor of the hand, of the body, and the product, in its uniqueness, was a stay against repetition and inauthenticity. The appearance of minute writing at the end of the manuscript era characterizes the transformation of writing to print: the end of writing's particular discursive movement; its errors made by the body; its mimesis of memory, fading and, thus, in micrographia, diminishing through time as well as in space.

On the interface between the manuscript and printing, the miniature book is a celebration of a new technology, yet a nostalgic creation endowed with the significance the manuscript formerly possessed. McMurtie gives an account of the rise of miniature-book printing during the fifteenth century:

> In the nature of things, books of small size will be found rarely among the incunabula of the earliest days of printing—say from 1450 [to] 1470. Type at first was cast in relatively large sizes, and the books printed with them, if not folios, were almost always quartos of fairly generous dimensions. But by the last decade of the century, books in smaller sizes, though still relatively few, made their appearance more frequently. Refinements in the art of punch cutting and type casting made it possible to produce with remarkable ease types in the smaller sizes which were prerequisite to the printing of books of really small format.[5]

While convenience of handling was the first reason given for printing small books, printers gradually came to vie with each other to print the smallest book as a demonstration of craftsmanship for its own sake. And the small book required greater skill on the part of the binder as well as on the part of the printer. The leather had to be skived very thinly, the corners sharply defined, and the tooling done with minute care.[6]

The earliest small book was the *Diurnale Moguntinum*, printed by Peter Schoeffer in Mainz in 1468. From the beginning, the miniature book speaks of infinite time, of the time of labor, lost in its multiplicity, and of the time of the world, collapsed within a minimum of physical space. In the fifteenth century, small books of hours (measuring two square inches, set in gold, and worn suspended from the belt by a charm or rings) were made for the merchant princes of Florence and Venice.[7] Calendars and almanacs were and are favorite subjects for the printer of miniature books. The microcosmic aspects of the almanac make it particularly suited for miniaturization. For example, *A Miniature Almanack*, printed in Boston in the early nineteenth century, has a frontispiece which reads "Multum in parvo"; it includes the days of the month, days of the week, a calendar, the sun's rising and setting times, the moon's rising and setting times, the full sea at Boston, advice on "Right Marriage," "Qualities of a Friend," and "Popularity," a "List of Courts in the New England States," the "Rates of Postage," "The times of holding the Yearly Meetings of Friends in the Continent of America," a "Money Table," "A Table Shewing the number of days from any day of one month to the same day in any other month," a "Table of interest, per day, at 6% on any number of dollars from one to Twelve Thousand," and "A List of the Post Towns, on the main road from Brewster, Maine to St. Mary's, Georgia."[8] Thus the book encapsulates the details of everyday life, fitting life inside the body rather than the body inside the expansive temporality of life. Similarly, the Bible as the book of greatest significance, the book holding the world both past and future, is a volume often chosen for miniaturization.

It is the hand that has produced these volumes and the hand that has consumed them—they are an affront to reason and its principal sense: the eye. The miniature book speaks from the convention of print, but, just as importantly, from the invention of the microscope, the mechanical eye that can detect significance in a world the human eye is blind to. In Robert Hooke's journal, *Micrographia; or, Some Physiological Descriptions of Minute Bodies Made by Magnifying Glasses, with Observations and Inquiries There Upon* (1665), we sense this discovery:

> April 22 1663, Leeches in Vinegar. Bluish Mold on Leather; April 29th. A Mine of Diamonds in Flint. Spider with Six Eyes; May 6th, Female and Male Gnats; May 20th, Head of Ant. Fly like a Gnat. Point of a Needle; May 27th, Pores in petrified wood. Male Gnat; June 10th, Sage-Leaves appearing not to have cavities; July 8th, Edge of a Razor. Five Taffeta Ribbons. Millepede; July 16th, Fine Lawn. Gilt edge of Venice Paper; August 5th, Honeycomb Sea-weed. Teeth of a Snail. Plant growing on Rose-Leaves.

In the conclusion to his preface Hooke wrote: "And it is my hope, as well as belief, that these my Labours will be no more comparable to the productions of many other Natural Philosophers, who are now everywhere busie about greater things; then my little Objects are to be compar'd to the greater and more beautiful Works of Nature, a Flea, A Mite, a Gnat, to an Horse, an Elephant, or a Lyon."[9] The modesty of Hooke's remark can hardly help but strike us as ironic: the almost playful subject of his new instrument and its scope; the toy had not yet been put to work. It is significant that Hooke called his journal *Micrographia*, that somehow it was the *writing* of the natural, the previously unreadable, which now stood revealed. While the miniature book reduces the world to the microcosm within its covers, the microscope opens up significance to the point at which all the material world shelters a microcosm. For a modern corollary, picture the project undertaken by W. E. Rudge of Mt. Vernon, New York, in 1928: Rudge made a miniature New York phone book, the pages 4 3/4 by 6 1/4 inches and the entire book 3/4 of an inch thick. It could be read with the aid of a glass designed by a retired rear admiral. In that glass the eight million stories of the Naked City opened into an accordion of significance.[10]

The social space of the miniature book might be seen as the social space, in miniature, of all books: the book as talisman to the body and emblem of the self; the book as microcosm and macrocosm; the book as commodity and knowledge, fact and fiction. The early artisanal concern with the display of skill emphasizes the place of the miniature book as object, and more specifically as an object of person, a talisman or amulet. The fact that the miniature book could be easily held and worn attaches a specific function to it. Its gemlike properties were often reflected in its adornment by real gems. Occasionally miniature books were made with metal pages. James Dougald Henderson writes: "The most beautiful example of this type of book which has come to my notice is of silver gilt, three quarters of an inch high, with a narrow panel on the front cover in which is enameled in natural colors a pansy with stem and leaves. On the remaining portion of the front cover is an engraved cobweb from which hangs a spider. The body is a pearl and the head is a wee ruby."[11] Henderson doesn't bother to mention the title of the book—that is obviously not the point. However, we might find significance in the choice of flower and insect here. The pansy is the flower with a human face and thereby always a kind of portrait miniature. And the spider is perhaps the most domestic of insects, making her own home within a home. This book/jewel, carried by the body, multiplies significance by virtue of the tension it creates between inside and outside, container and contained, surface and depth. Similarly, Charles H. Meigs of Cleveland made a "Rubáiyát 7/16th of an inch by 5/16th of an inch at the turn of the last century. Three copies do not cover a postage stamp and one was set in a ring worn by the author for safe-keeping."[12] The first American miniature book, measuring 3 3/8 by 2 1/8 inches, could in fact, be worn metaphorically:

A Wedding Ring (Boston, 1695)

A WEDDING RING
Fit for the finger
Or, the Salve of Divinity
On the Sore of Humanity

. . . .

Laid open in a Sermon, at a
Wedding in Edmonton
By William Secker, preacher of the Gospel.[13]

Henderson writes that "in the period from 1830 [to] 1850 no stylishly gowned lady in England was complete unless her handbag carried one of the dainty little jeweled *Schloss Bijou* almanacs, about half the size of a postage stamp, enclosed in a small solander case and this in turn reposing in a tiny silk or plush lined and leather bound case in which was also a diminutive magnifying glass shaped like a hand mirror."[14]

Just as speech is structured by its context, so is there an effort here to join the content and form of writing. The mirror that is also a microscope, that both reflects and reveals, reappears in the other face of the miniature book, its pedagogic uses, for such books "serve not only as an adornment of some dusty trinket cabinet, but have served as the primary basis of education and interest for many a tot in centuries gone by."[15] Fourteenth- and fifteenth-century hornbooks, 3 to 4 inches long, with a handle, were shaped like hand mirrors and made of square pieces of wood. Paper was applied to the wood, and on this surface was inscribed a cross, followed by the alphabet, and concluding with the Lord's Prayer. Cow's horn was placed over the paper to protect it. To make the lesson even more appealing, hornbooks were sometimes made from gingerbread that had been shaped in molds.[16] If the lesson was well done, the child could eat the book, thus consuming the lesson both metaphorically and literally.

Early-seventeenth-century miniature Bibles, like John Taylor's rhyming "Thumb Bible," published in London by Hamman in 1614, were designed especially for use by children.[17] The preface to the Reverend Edmund S. Janes's miniature Bible, published in Philadelphia by W. N. Wiatt in the 1850's, explains:

> It therefore becomes a matter of immense importance, that their attention should be profitably directed, and their feelings morally and religiously influenced: that thus their minds may be properly occupied, and their hearts rightly exercised. And certainly nothing is more admirably calculated to accomplish this desirable object than those bible stories, or narratives, which are level to their capacities. . . . It was this conviction that induced the author to compile (at the request of the publisher) this little volume. He hopes it may take the place of foolish little picture books that afford no useful instruction, and exert no happy virtuous influence. This little volume has an excellence which similar publications have not had; the language is entirely scriptural.[18]

And the author of *Wisdom in Miniature; or, The Youth's Pleasing Instructor*, "a pocket companion for the youth of both sexes in America," printed in New York by Mahlon Day in 1822, had a similar goal: "It was my aim to crowd as many select sentences as I could into a small compass, to make this book a convenient portable pocket companion for the use of Young People."[19] This work concludes with "Short Miscellaneous Sentences: Alphabetically Digested; which may be easily retained in the memories of youth." We see an effort to connect the book to the body; indeed, to make a "digestible" book and at the same time a linking of the aphoristic thinking of religious didacticism with the miniature book's materially compressed mode of presentation.

The invention of printing coincided with the invention of childhood,[20] and the two faces of children's literature, the fantastic and the didactic, developed at the same time in the miniature book. The foolish little picture books that the Reverend Janes objected to were the chapbooks of fairy and folk tales, the inheritance of the Bibliothèque Bleu, the translation of the oral folk forms of the fantastic into the printed fantastic. Instead of offering nuggets of wisdom for the child to consume, these books presented an infinite and fabulous world which had the capacity to absorb the child's sense of reality. The miniature here became the realm not of fact but of reverie. After the advent of romanticism, the miniature book frequently served as a realm of the cultural other. The smallest printed book in the world, Eben Francis Thompson's edition of *The Rose Garden of Omar Khayyám* (3/16 by 5/16 of an inch), followed Meig's attempt to collapse the significance of the Orient into the exotica of a miniaturized volume. And in the twentieth century the miniature became the servant of advertising. Books with metal pages were put out to advertise hotels and local attractions for tourists in the 1920's, for example, and *Life* and *Saturday Evening Post* in 1916 and 1925, respectively, published miniature editions for advertising purposes.[21]

Such experiments with the scale of writing as we find in micrographia and the miniature book exaggerate the divergent relation between the abstract and the material nature of the sign. A reduction in dimensions does not produce a corresponding reduction in significance; indeed, the gemlike properties of the miniature book and the feats of micrographia make these forms especially suitable "containers" of aphoristic and didactic thought. Furthermore, on the interface between the manuscript and printing, as modes of production they are linked to the souvenir, the amulet, and the diminutive world of childhood. In describing these forms, my text has become embroidered with details, ornaments, and figurations. Thus these forms bring us to a further aspect of this divergent relation between meaning and materiality: the problem of describing the miniature. For the miniature, in its exaggeration of interiority and its relation to the space and time of the individual perceiving subject, threatens the infinity of description without hierarchization, a world whose anteriority is always absolute, and whose profound interiority is therefore always unrecoverable. Hence for us the miniature appears as a metaphor for all books and all bodies.

Tableau: The Miniature Described

We have looked at the ways in which the miniature book illustrates the conjunction of the material and abstract nature of the sign, emphasizing that the reduced physical dimensions of the book will have only peripheral bearing upon the meaning of the text. Thus the miniature book always calls attention to the book as total object. But we must also consider the *depiction*, or description, of miniatures within the text, the capacity for all writing, and especially fictive writing, to be like Hooke's *Micrographia*—that is, to be a display of a world not necessarily known through the senses, or lived experience. The child continually enters here as a metaphor, perhaps not simply because the child is in some physical sense a miniature of the adult, but also because the world of childhood, limited in physical scope yet fantastic in its content, presents in some ways a miniature and fictive chapter in each life history; it is a world that is part of history, at least the history of the individual subject, but remote from the presentness of adult life. We imagine childhood as if it were at the other end of a tunnel—distanced, diminutive, and clearly framed. From the fifteenth century on, miniature books were mainly books for children, and in the development of children's literature the depiction of the miniature is a recurring device.

In writing, description must serve the function of context. The locus of speech and action must be "filled in" for the reader, who suffers from the exteriority of print; the distance between the situation of reading and the situation of the depiction is bridged by description, the use of a field of familiar signs. What disappears in writing is the body and what the body knows—the visual, tactile, and aural knowledge of lived experience. Thus, whenever we speak of the context of reading, we see at work a doubling which undermines the authority of both the reading situation and the situation or locus of the depiction: the reader is not in either world, but rather moves between them, and thereby moves between varieties of partial and transcendent vision. Situation within situation, world within world—there is a vacillation between the text as microcosm and the situation of the reader as microcosm. Which contains which is unresolved until closure.

This mutual exteriority of "real" and textual worlds results in part from the problem that language can imitate only language: depiction and representation of the physical world in language are matters of concealed suture, matters of a mutuality of procedures by which the community maintains the fiction of linguistic representation. Thus, to speak of miniaturization in narrative is to engage in this fiction, for the ways in which the physical world can be miniaturized are not carried over into devices for the linguistic depiction of the miniature. The depiction of the miniature works by establishing a referential field, a field where signs are displayed in relation to one another and in relation to concrete objects in the sensual world.

Solomon Grildrig's introduction to *The Miniature: A Periodical Paper* might serve as an introduction to this literary method:

> I consider myself as one who takes a picture from real life, who
> attempts to catch the resemblance, or pourtray the feature of existing
> objects, so that the representation may impartially, and exactly describe
> the perfections or defects, beauties or deformities of the original. It is
> not for me to attempt the bolder strokes, and nervous outlines which
> the pencil of *Raphael* exhibit, nor can I expect that *my* portraits should
> glow with the vivid coloring which a *Titian* might express. My attempts
> will follow the style of a MINIATURE, and while the touches are less
> daring, while less force, and richness of imagination may be
> conspicuous in the following sketches, they may perhpas derive some
> merit in a humbler scale, from correctness of design, and accuracy of
> representation. This style indeed will be more appropriate, as it is in
> the lesser theatre of life that it will be employed, and as juvenile folly,
> or merit will often be the subjects of my lucubrations.[22]

The writing of miniaturization does not want to call attention to itself or to its author; rather, it continually refers to the physical world. It resists the interiority of reflexive language in order to interiorize an outside; it is the closest thing we have to a three-dimensional language, for it continually points outside itself, creating a shell-like, or enclosed, exteriority. "Correctness of design" and "accuracy of representation" are devices of distance, of "proper perspective," the perspective of the bourgeois subject. If they are especially appropriate to the "lesser theatre of life," it is because they allow the reader to disengage himself or herself from the field of representation as a transcendent subject.

The field of representation in the depiction of the miniature is set up by means of a method of using either implicit or explicit simile. Each fictive sign is aligned to a sign from the physical world in a gesture which makes the fictive sign both remarkable and realistic. The narrative of Tom Thumb, first mentioned in print in Scot's *Discoverie of Witchcraft* (1584), affords a good example of this technique.[23] Consider this passage from Charlotte Yonge's children's work, *The History of Sir Thomas Thumb* (1856):

> A son was born in the cottage by the wood side, but had ever man such a son? He was no larger than the green top of the twayblade blossom, and though perfect in all his limbs, it was not possible to feel that a thing so light and soft rested on the hand; and his mother, as she laid him gently on the thistle-down with which she had filled an acorn cup, knew not whether she were glad or grieved that she had the wish fulfilled which she had spoken. Owen gently sighed, and thereby almost blew his son away. . . .
>
> No mis-shapen limbs, no contorted features were there, but all was sweet and beautiful, the bright eyes like blue speed well buds, and the delicate little frame fresh and fair as the young blossom on the sweet-briar bough.
>
> Truly, for the first few days he grew so fast, he soon exchanged his acorn cup for a walnut shell, and outgrowing that again, had to sleep in the warm nest of the long-tailed tit mouse.[24]

The description here is not only directed toward the visual—it evokes the sensual as well, the hand being the measure of the miniature. The miniature has the capacity to make its context remarkable; its fantastic qualities are related to what lies outside it in such a way as to transform the total context. Thistledown becomes mattress; acorn cup becomes cradle; the father's breath becomes a cyclone. Amid such transformations of scale, the exaggeration of the miniature must continually assert a principle of balance and equivalence, or the narrative will become grotesque. Hence the "all was sweet and beautiful." The model here is nature and her harmony of detail. This space is managed by simile and by the principles of equivalence existing between the body and nature. Scale is established by means of a set of correspondences to the familiar. And time is managed by means of a miniaturization of its significance; the miniature is the notation of the moment and the moment's consequences. The delight and irony with which Yonge writes "Truly, for the first few days he grew so fast" establishes the pace of the miniature; it is not necessary to tell us that at some point Tom will stop growing; it is clear that that point is where description ends and action begins.

Because of the correspondences it must establish, writing about the miniature achieves a delirium of description. The arrested life of the miniature object places it within a still context of infinite detail. Gulliver's outline of "the inhabitants of Lilliput" might serve as an example:

> Although I intend to leave the Description of this Empire to a particular Treatise, yet in the mean time I am content to gratify the curious Reader with some general Ideas. As the common Size of the Natives is somewhat under six Inches, so there is an exact Proportion in all other Animals, as well as Plants and Trees: For Instance, the tallest Horses and Oxen are between four and five Inches in Height, the Sheep an Inch and a half, more or less; their Geese about the Bigness of a Sparrow; and so the several Gradations downwards, till you come to the smallest, which, to my Sight, were almost invisible; but Nature hath adapted the Eyes of the *Lilliputians* to all Objects proper for their View: They see with great Exactness, but at no great Distance. And to show the Sharpness of their Sight towards Objects that are near, I have been much pleased with observing a Cook pulling a Lark, which was not so large as a common Fly; and a young Girl threading an invisible Needle with invisible Silk. Their tallest trees are about seven Foot high; I mean some of those in the great Royal Park, the Tops whereof I could but just reach with my Fist clenched. The other Vegetables are in the same Proportion: But this I leave to the Reader's Imagination.[25]

Here we see not only a set of correspondences to the familiar but also the way in which that set of correspondences generates a metonymic extension of what has been described. Gulliver is able to leave the rest to the reader's imagination because he has established the proper principles of proportion. Indeed, he has left little to imagine! The progression of gestures in this passage marks a movement from the most visible to the least visible. At the point at which the invisible thread enters the invisible needle, we return to trees, and the sequence invites another round—from naked eye to microscope, from exterior to interior.

In *The Poetics of Space*, Bachelard writes that "because these descriptions tell things in tiny detail, they are automatically verbose."[26] We might add that this verboseness is also a matter of multiplying significance. The procedure by which description multiplies in detail is analogous to and mimetic of the process whereby space becomes significance, whereby everything is made to "count." The depiction of the miniature moves away from hierarchy and narrative in that it is caught in an infinity of descriptive gestures. It is difficult for much to *happen* in such depiction, since each scene of action multiplies in spatial significance in such a way as to fill the page with contextual information. Minute description reduces the object to its signifying properties, and this reduction of physical dimensions results in a multiplication of ideological properties. The minute depiction of the object in painting, as Lévi-Strauss has showed us in his analysis of the lace collar of François Clouet's *Portrait of Elizabeth of Austria*,[27] reduces the tactile and olfactory dimensions of the object and at the same time increases the significance of the object within the system of signs. When verbal description attempts to approximate visual depiction, we find a further reduction of sensory dimensions and, because of the history of the word as utterance in lived social practices, an even greater ideological significance.

This tendency of the description and depiction of the miniature to move toward contextual information and away from narrative also transforms our sense of narrative closure, for in the miniature we see spatial closure posited over temporal closure. The miniature offers a world clearly limited in space but frozen and thereby both particularized and generalized in time—particularized in that the miniature concentrates upon the single instance and not upon the abstract rule, but generalized in that that instance comes to transcend, to stand for, a spectrum of other instances. The miniature offers the closure of the tableau, a spatial closure which opens up the vocality of the signs it displays. In his classic article "Epic Laws of Folk Narrative," Axel Olrik discusses the tableau as follows:

> In these scenes, the actors draw near to each other: the hero and his horse; the hero and the monster: Thor pulls the World Serpent up to the edge of the boat; the valiant warriors die so near to their king that even in death they protect him; Siegmund carries his dead son himself. . . . One notices how the tableaux scenes frequently convey not a sense of the ephemeral but rather a certain quality of persistence through time: Samson among the columns in the hall of the Philistines; Thor with the World Serpent transfixed on a fishhook; Vidarr confronting the vengeance of the Fenris Wolf; Perseus holding out the head of Medusa. These lingering actions—which also play a large role in sculpture—possess the singular power of being able to etch themselves in one's memory.[28]

Thus there are two major features of the tableau: first, the drawing together of significant, even if contradictory, elements, and thereby the complete filling out of "point of view"; and second, the simultaneous particularization and generalization of the moment. The tableau offers a type of contextual closure which would be inappropriate to genres rooted in the context of their utterance; the tableau effectively speaks to the distance between the context at hand and the narrated context; it is possible only through representation, since it offers a complete closure of a text framed off from the ongoing reality that surrounds it. Here we might think not only of sculpture but also of the photograph, which has made possible the dramatization and classicization of the individual life history. Such "still shots," say, before the family car or the Christmas tree, are always profoundly ideological, for they eternalize a moment or instance of the typical in the same way that a proverb or emblem captions a moment as an illustration of the moral working of the universe. Thus, while these photographs articulate the individual, they do so according to a well-defined set of generic coventions. It is not simply that the family album records an individual's rites of passage; it does so in such a conventionalized way that all family albums are alike.

The French surrealist Raymond Roussel used the tableau as the basis for a lifelong experiment with problems of description. In his poems "La Vue" and "Le Concert" (1904), the narrator concentrates on the depiction of representation itself: a tiny picture set in a penholder in "La Vue," an engraving on the letterhead of a piece of hotel stationery in "Le Concert." In both cases Roussel has chosen an already defined space of representation—the picture and the engraving—and he has chosen to "rewrite" it in the necessarily incomplete medium of language. The exteriority of the interpretive field, the exteriority of the narrator's speech in relation to what he sees, is even more strongly realized in "La Source" (also in the 1904 volume), which begins with the narrator watching a young couple having lunch:

Tout est tranquille dans la salle où je dejeune
Occupant une place en angle, un couple jeune
Chuchote avec finesse et gaieté; l'entre tien
Plein de sous-entendus, de rires, marche bien.

The narrator then describes for fifty pages the spa pictured on the label of his bottle of mineral water before returning to the young couple, "chuchote toujours des choses qu'on n'entend pas."[29] The double removal of a representation of a representation is also present in the numerous tableaus of *Impressions of Africa*. In the following scene we see the device at work:

Standing upright behind the funeral slab was a hoarding covered in black material, which presented to the viewer a series of twelve water colours, arranged symmetrically, in four rows of three. The resemblance between the characters suggested that the pictures were concerned with some dramatic narrative. Above each image, by way of a title, one could read certain words, traced with a brush.

In the first painting a non-commissioned officer and a fair-haired woman in flashy clothes were lounging in the back of a luxurious victoria; the words *Flora and the Sergeant-Major Lécurou* summarily identified the couple.

> Next came *The Performance of Daedalus,* represented by a large stage
> on which a singer in Grecian draperies appeared to be singing at the
> top of his voice; in the front of a box the sergeant-major could be seen,
> sitting beside Flora, who was gazing through her opera glasses at the
> performer.[30]

The narrator goes on to describe the remaining ten watercolors. These
tableaus may be seen as illustrations for a text which does not exist.
The attempt to recoup their meaning through a narrative miming
visual description marks a double falling away from the continuity of
an original textual closure. Roussel ambiguously explains in *How I
Write Certain of My Books* that "the *tableaux vivants* were suggested by
lines from Victor Hugo's Napoleon II (from *Les Chants du Crépuscule*).
But here there are so many lacunae in my memory that I will be
obliged to leave several gaps."[31] Two lines that he does explain are:

1. [Hugo:]   Eut reçu pour hochet la couronne de Rome
2. [Roussel:]   Ursule brochet lac Huronne drome
            (Ursula pike Lake Huron 'drome)
1. [Hugo:]   Un vase tout rempli du vin de l'espérance
2. [Roussel:]   . . . sept houx rampe lit . . . Vesper
            (seven hollies balustrade read . . . Vesper).[32]

Via punning Roussel has transposed Hugo's lines and then depicted
them. His deliberate mis-hearing (misreading) sets off a chain of visu-
al-into-verbal signifieds. Every sign bears a capacity to allude not only
in a "correct" fashion but also by a process of misallusion. In Roussel's
universe every utterance bears the infinity of its meaning and
the infinity of what it might not mean. Thus the tableaus work as
rebuses, pictures that "spell out a message." But Roussel's ironic
device of presenting us with the *writing* of a rebus, not with a rebus
itself, further distances the reader from the final decoding of the
message. If a picture is worth a thousand words, it is through Roussel
that we know that the picture bears the weight of a thousand words
on all sides of its history: at its creation, at its reading, and at every
scene of misapprehension. To be read in words, any tableau must be
given a form of rhetorical organization, must acquire the shape of the
language that will represent it. Thus we see in the depiction of the
tableau the choice of a point of origin and the subsequent *delineation*
of significant aspects in relation to that point. To the right of, to the
left of, next to, behind, before—the language of the tableau moves
continually from center to periphery. What remains ambiguous is the
closed field of the *edges*, for language must remain exterior to this
spatial closure.[33] The irony of language's infinite possibilities in describing a finite spatial field is displayed in Roussel's continual choice

of the minute scene. He writes that his long, final poem, "Nouvelle Impressions d'Afrique" (1932), "was to have contained a descriptive section. It concerned a miniature pair of opera glasses worn as a pendant whose two lenses, two millimetres in diameter and meant to be held up to the eye, contained photographs on glass depicting Cairo bazaars on one side and a bank of the Nile at Luxor on the other."[34] The restricted field (a miniature pair) and the depicted cultural scene (the opera) are further transformed by the still view of the bazaars and the river, nature into culture, into culture, and into culture again by description. Furthermore, the hierarchization of language disappears. Everything seen is equally describable; the point of origin is simply a point of origin, a place to begin in this gliding across the unruffled surface of things.

Visual descriptions have the capacity to portray depth of field, a capacity presented by the invention of perspective. Verbal description must depend upon conventions of subordination in order to portray a sense of perspective, and these conventions rely upon the social process by which significance is simultaneously assigned and denied. In this sense, perspective in narrative is always dependent upon the intrinsically ideological stance of point of view. However, there is a further device which language uses in order to produce an analogous sense of depth of field and that is ambiguity. Here profundity arises through the multivocal aspects of the sign, aspects that speak of the resonance of the sign's history. The word in the word, utterance in the utterance, sentence in the sentence, allusion in the allusion, work in the work, lend depth and the significance of a multiple set of contexts to the functions of language. We see this process at work in Roussel's bilexical inventions:

> Taking the word *palmier* I decided to consider it in two senses: as a *pastry* and as a *tree*. Considering it as a *pastry*, I searched for another word, itself having two meanings which could be linked to it by the preposition *à*; thus I obtained (and it was, I repeat, a long and arduous task) *palmier* (a kind of pastry) *à restauration* (restaurant which serves pastries); the other part gave me *palmier* (palmtree) *à restauration* (restoration of a dynasty). Which yielded the palmtree in Trophies Square commemorating the restoration of the Talou dynasty.[35]

Rayner Heppenstall, following Jean Ferry's analysis of the second canto of "Nouvelle Impressions d'Afrique," says that these typical lexical images confound the great with the small: the confusion of an adjustable spanner with a semiquaver rest, a photographer's tripod with the rejected stalks of a bunch of three cherries, a chamois horn with an eyelash, a stalactite in a cave with the uvula in a throat opened wide for inspection.[36] To this impulse of the representation in the representation should be added Roussel's verse technique of parenthetical sentences, sentences that sometimes involve as many as five parenthetical expressions ((((((!))))))). These parentheses require the reader to move from the temporal edges of the book (beginning to end) toward its center, and once the reader finds himself or herself at that center, there is the intolerable burden of returning to the beginning again in order to capture the original unfolding of the progression of thought.[37]

If Roussel reminds us that the task of describing inevitably leads to exhaustion, Jorge Luis Borges, in "The Aleph," reminds us that such a task—that is, the transportation of vision into temporality and of simultaneity into narrative—inevitably leads to boredom. Following their description of Carlos Argentino Daneri's microcosmic poem, *The Earth*, Borges the character and Borges the author conclude:

> Only once in my life have I had occasion to look into the fifteen thousand alexandrines of the *Polyolbion*, that topographical epic in which Michael Drayton recorded the flora, fauna, hydrography, orography, military and monastic history of England. I am sure, however, that this limited but bulky production is less boring than Carlos Argentino's similar vast undertaking. Daneri had in mind to set to verse the entire face of the planet, and, by 1941, had already dispatched a number of acres of the State of Queensland, nearly a mile of the course run by the River Ob, a gasworks to the north of Veracruz, the leading shops in the Buenos Aires parish of Concepción, the villa of Mariana Cambaceres de Alvear in the Belgrano section of the Argentine capital, and a Turkish baths establishment not far from the well-known Brighton Aquarium.

Like Roussel, Daneri relies upon the "profundity" of allusion in order to accomplish his impossible task of accounting for the planet, and Borges concludes that "Daneri's real work lay not in the poetry but in his invention of reasons why the poetry should be admired."[38]

Despite Daneri's confidence, we find that when language attempts to describe the concrete, it is caught in an infinitely self-effacing gesture of inadequacy, a gesture which speaks to the gaps between our modes of cognition—those gaps between the sensual, the visual, and the linguistic. Thus these attempts to describe the miniature threaten an infinity of detail that becomes translated into an infinity of verbality. Language describing the miniature always displays the inadequacy of the verbal. In contrast, however, *multum in parvo*, the miniaturization of language itself, displays the ability of language to "sum up" the diversity of the sensual, or physical, world of lived experi-

ence. In his book on the place of *multum in parvo* in the poetic imagination, Carl Zigrosser writes:

> Where are prime examples of multum in parvo to be found? Not
> generally in the realm of sound or music, for the sequence of time is an
> integral ingredient in our perception of music, one note after another
> producing the pattern of form. Compression is possible only where
> perception is immediate or nearly so. The appreciation of form through
> touch likewise involves a time factor. As far as other senses are
> concerned, those of taste and smell have never been sufficiently
> developed in man to admit of pointed brevity. At best, the emotive
> stimulus of taste and smell is gained by association. No, the happy
> hunting ground for multum in parvo is through the eye and mind,
> among mathematical formulae and symbols, in the concise and
> epigrammatic forms of poetry, and in the miniature forms of visual art.
> Furthermore, from a purist's point of view, neither a fragment of a
> longer poem nor a detail of a picture can be accepted strictly as
> multum in parvo.[39]

The *multum in parvo* quality of the quotation, the epigram, and the
proverb arises as they each take their place as free-floating pieces of
discourse, pieces of discourse which have been abstracted from the
context at hand in such a way as to seem to transcend lived experience and speak to all times and places. The *multum in parvo* is clearly
rooted in the ideological; its closure is the closure of all ideological
discourse, a discourse which speaks to the human and cultural but
not to the natural except to frame it. Zigrosser articulates this problem
when he writes: "Realistic portraits of people and landscapes (which
are essentially portraits of Nature) do not, as a general rule, provide
apt material for much in little. The basic purpose of both is likeness,
and true likeness precludes imaginative variation. Specific detail is
documentary, referring to the one and not to the many."[40] But one
might add that the *multum in parvo* must offer a kind of univocality, a
form of absolute closure; its function is to close down discourse and
not to open the wounds of its inadequacies. We should remember
that the word *aphorism* comes from the Greek "to set bounds" and
"boundaries." Zigrosser's own predominant choices of pastoral and
religious works speak to the ideological systems, the closed and clear
systems of cultural meaning, from which *multum in parvo* is constructed. Like visual *multum in parvo*, linguistic *multum in parvo* is best
shown in a display mode; hence its place upon home samplers has
now been taken over by posters, cards, bumper stickers, and T-shirts.
Within the frame and without a physical form, the *multum in parvo*
becomes monumental, transcending any limited context of origin and
at the same time neatly containing a universe.

The Secret Life of Things

Let us return to the last lines of the series of tableaus in *Impressions of Africa*. The watercolors give way to this dramatic series and then, "when the usual smooth mechanism which closed the curtains hid this antithetical oddity from view, Carmichael left his post, thus marking the end of the series of scenes without action."[41] In describing the tableau, the writer must address a world of things defined in spatial relation to one another. But with the introduction of action, the task of writing changes toward the description of narrative, the description of events within sequence, and the description of the world of things becomes "mere" context, is supplemental to the description of narrative events. We find this problem over and over again in pastoral and ethnographic writing and in those works of children's literature which create a toy world. In this aspect of the tableau we see the essential *theatricality* of all miniatures. Our transcendent viewpoint makes us perceive the miniature as object and this has a double effect. First, the object in its perfect stasis nevertheless suggests use, implementation, and contextualization. And second, the representative quality of the miniature makes that contextualization an allusive one; the miniature becomes a stage on which we project, by means of association or intertextuality, a deliberately framed series of *actions*.

Foucault writes that in Roussel's "Le Concert," "la petite vignette de papier à en-tête comme la lentille du porte-plume souvenir, comme l'étiquette de la bouteille d'eau d'Evian est un prodigieux labyrinthe—mais vu d'en haut: si bien qu'au lieu de cacher, il met naïvement sous les yeux le lacis des allées, les buis, les longs murs de pierre, les mâts, l'eau, ces hommes miniscules et précis qui vont dans tous les sens d'un même pas immobile. Et le langage n'a plus qu'à se pencher vers toutes ces figures muettes pour tenter par d'infinies accumulations d'en rejoindre la visibilité sans lacune. Celle-ci, à vrai dire, n'a pas a être mise au jour: elle est comme l'offrande d'une ouverture profonde des choses elles-mêmes."[42] That the world of things can open itself to reveal a secret life—indeed, to reveal a set of actions and hence a narrativity and history outside the given field of perception—is a constant daydream that the miniature presents.[43] This is the daydream of the microscope: the daydream of life inside life, of significance multiplied infinitely *within* significance. Thus the state of arrested life that we see in the tableau and in the fixity and exteriority of writing and print always bears the hesitation of a beginning, a hesitation that speaks the movement which is its contrary in the same way that the raised and hesitating baton speaks the bursting action that will result from its fall. It is significant that in manuscript illumination the first letter has borne the ornament.

In children's literature this transition from hesitation to action, from the inanimate to the animate, continually appears in the theme of the toy come to life. The nutcracker theme can be found even on the boundary between didactic and fantastic children's literature. In *The Adventures of a Pincushion,* published in the late 1780's, Mary Jane Kilner felt it necessary to point out that inanimate objects "cannot be sensible of anything which happens, as they can neither hear, see, nor understand; and as I would not willingly mislead your judgement I would, previous to your reading this work, inform you that it is to be understood as an imaginary tale."[44] Pauline Clarke's *Return of the Twelves,* the story of a boy named Max who discovers the Brontë children's toy soldiers and finds that they are alive, presents a good contemporary example of this thematic device. In the beginning of the work, when Max is waiting for the soldiers to show him that they are alive, Clarke slows the action, measuring it to the progressive disappearance of a jawbreaker that Max is sucking: "All the same, he did not give up hope. He had seen them move twice now, and what you saw you believed. (Max also believed many things he did not see, like everyone else.) The jawbreaker was becoming more manageable now, and as he knelt there, Max turned it over and over in his mouth. Suddenly he crunched it all up with determination and impatience. He decided to go in."[45] In the depiction of the still life, attention is devoted to objects, but once the inanimate is animated, the parallel problem of description of action must be placed against the depiction of objects. Max's sister, Jane, sets the table for "the Twelves": "And she began quickly to lay upon the table the set of tiny brass plates she had kept from her dolls' house days. At either end, she put a brass candlestick, and between these, small piled plates, gleaming at the edge, filled with bread crumbs, cake crumbs, biscuit crumbs, dessicated coconut, currants, and silver pills. The plates were milk bottle tops. By each man's own plate she put a tiny wineglass."[46] ". . . The Twelves were not long in accepting the invitation. They fixed a balsawood gangplank, and scrambled or slid down it, according to taste."[47] The problem of scale appears only in relation to the physical world. In the depiction of action there is no need for the constant measurement-by-comparison that we find in the first part of the passage. The profundity of things here arises from those dimensions which come about only through scrutiny.

There are no miniatures in nature; the miniature is a cultural product, the product of an eye performing certain operations, manipulating, and attending in certain ways to, the physical world. Even Max draws the parallel between divine and human creativity and manipulation here: "He thought of all the other small creatures, mice, toads, beetles, some much tinier than Stumps, ants and spiders and furry caterpillars. No doubt to God, he, Max, seemed quite as small and needing help."[48] The miniature assumes an anthropocentric universe for its absolute sense of scale. We see perhaps no better demonstration of this desire to juxtapose the nonhuman and the human than the spectacle of the fleacircus. The flea circus presents a seemingly pure animation, a life-from-death in which the apparatuses of the circus appear to move of their own accord. At the same time, the flea circus provides an explanation of movement; we know that the fleas are there, even though we cannot see them, just as the microscope confirmed the daydream of microcosmic life. Furthermore, the flea circus completes the taming and manipulation of nature which the circus represents. The flea-tamer is the inverse and twin of the lion-tamer: he feeds his animals with his own blood voluntarily, while we marvel that the lion-tamer has evaded the spilling of blood; and the flea-tamer takes control of an invisible nature whose infinity is just as threatening as the jaws of the great beasts.

Problems of the inanimate and the animate here bring us to a consideration of the toy. The toy is the physical embodiment of the fiction: it is a device for fantasy, a point of beginning for narrative. The toy opens an interior world, lending itself to fantasy and privacy in a way that the abstract space, the playground, of social play does not. To toy with something is to manipulate it, to try it out within sets of contexts, none of which is determinative. Henri Allemagne writes in his *Histoire des jouets:* "La différence que l'on peut établir entre le jouet et le jeu, c'ést que le premier est plus particulièrement destiné à diverter l'enfant, tandis que le second peut servir à son instruction et à son développement physique."[49] To *toy* is "to dally with and caress, to compose a fantastic tale, to play a trick or satisfy a whim, to manipulate, and to take fright at," according to the *OED*. Plato, in the *Meno*, writes of the self-moving statues made by Daedalus, small statues of the gods which "if they are not fastened will run away." Socrates explains that "it is not much use possessing one of them if they are at liberty, for they will walk off like runaway slaves: but when fastened, they are of great value, for they are really beautiful works of art. Now this is an illustration of the nature of true opinions: while they abide with us they are beautiful and fruitful, but they run away out of the human soul, and do not remain long, and therefore they are not of much value unless they are fastened by the tie of the cause; and this fastening of them, friend Meno, is recollection, as has been already agreed by us."[50] In these remarks we see the relation between arrested life and absolute, "completed," knowledge which is so important to the notion of the collection. Although the transcendence of such objects allows them to endure beyond flux and history, that very transcendence also links such objects to the world of the dead, the end of organic growth and the beginning of inaccessibility to the living. The desire to animate the toy is the desire not simply to know everything but also to experience everything simultaneously.

The inanimate toy repeats the still life's theme of arrested life, the life of the tableau. But once the toy becomes animated, it initiates another world, the world of the daydream. The beginning of narrative time here is not an extension of the time of everyday life; it is the beginning of an entirely new temporal world, a fantasy world parallel to (and hence never intersecting) the world of everyday reality. On the one hand, we have the mechanical toy speaking a repetition and closure that the everyday world finds impossible. The mechanical toy threatens an infinite pleasure; it does not tire or feel, it simply works or doesn't work. On the other hand, we have the actual place of toys in the world of the dead. As part of the general inversions which that world presents, the inanimate comes to life. But more than this, just as the world of objects is always a kind of "dead among us," the toy ensures the continuation, in miniature, of the world of life "on the other side." It must be remembered that the toy moved late to the nursery, that from the beginning it was adults who made toys, and not only with regard to their other invention, the child. The fashion doll, for example, was the plaything of adult women before it was the plaything of the child. After the death of Catharine de' Medici's husband, eight fashion dolls were found in the inventory of her belongings—all were dressed in elaborate mourning garb and their cost appeared as an entry in her accounting book.[51] Today's catalogs of miniatures often recommend their products as suitable to both the dollhouse and the knickknack shelf.

The toy world presents a projection of the world of everyday life; this real world is miniaturized or giganticized in such a way as to test the relation between materiality and meaning. We are thrilled and frightened by the mechanical toy because it presents the possibility of a self-invoking fiction, a fiction which exists independent of human signifying processes. Here is the dream of the impeccable robot that has haunted the West at least since the advent of the industrial revolution. The eighteenth and nineteenth centuries mark the heyday of the automaton, just as they mark the mechanization of labor: jigging Irishmen, whistling birds, clocks with bleating sheep, and growling dogs guarding baskets of fruit.[52] The theme of death and reversibility reappears in the ambivalent status of toys like the little guillotines that were sold in France during the time of the Revolution. In 1793 Goethe wrote to his mother in Frankfurt requesting that she buy a toy guillotine for his son, August. This was a request she refused, saying that the toy's maker should be put in stocks.

Such automated toys find their strongest modern successors in "models" of ships, trains, airplanes, and automobiles, models of the products of mechanized labor. These toys are nostalgic in a fundamental sense, for they completely transform the mode of production of the original as they miniaturize it: they produce a representation of a product of alienated labor, a representation which itself is constructed by artisanal labor. The triumph of the model-maker is that he or she has produced the object completely by hand, from the beginning assembly to the "finishing touches." As private forms, these models must be contrasted to the public forms of display and recreation which have from the beginning marked the advertisement of industrial products.

Historically, the miniature railway has served both private and public aesthetic functions. Around the middle of the nineteenth century, the utilitarian possibilities of miniature railways were abandoned and such railways came to be used as demonstration or display models. In England in 1874, Arthur Heywood tried to promote a miniature gauge railway for use on country estates and farms, but without success. Later, however, as a pleasure attraction, with its dining and sleeping cars, his railway gained popularity.[53] Early miniature railways found their function in the aesthetic or play sphere whether they were part of private estates or public displays. By the turn of the century, they had been totally given over to amusement. In 1894 four Irish-American brothers, the Cagneys, opened an office in New York City and sold miniature locomotives to amusement parks all over the world. The engines they sold were replicas of standard-gauge locomotives, originally based on the famous No. 999 of the New York Central Railroad, which in 1893 had reached the unprecedented speed of 112 1/2 miles per hour.[54] The names of these early-twentieth-century engines celebrate the distinction between scale and might, materiality and meaning: the Little Giant (Eaton Railway, 1905), the Mighty Atom (Sutton Park Railway, 1907), the Little Elephant (Halifax Zoo Railway, 1910).

The industrial miniature results in amusement. The park here is not just the taming of the natural but the double stamp of culture brought about by introducing the mechanical to the natural and by traversing the natural with the mechanical at the same time that a reduction of scale is effected. Whereas the railroad itself had brought about a new traversal of the landscape, the vision it offered was a partial one, the vision of an observer moving through, not above, the landscape. In the miniature railroad we have a reduction of scale and a corresponding increase in detail and significance, and we are able to transcend the mechanical as well as the natural that forms its context. In the further miniaturization of the table-top train set, we have an access to simultaneity and transcendence completed. Correspondingly, the natural has moved from the forest to the individual trees of the park to the synthetic trees, barns, cows, and farmers of the train set's landscape. For a written account of such a transcendent and transformed view of the natural, we might turn to one of H. G. Wells's books of "floor games," *Little Wars*. Here the frontispiece shows "A Country Prepared for the War Games—the houses are made of wall-paper with painted doors and windows, the roofs are cut out of packing paper, and the houses are filled with wooden toy bricks to make them solid. The castle and the church are made from brown cardboard. There is a river chalked across the centre of the battlefield, which widens to flow past the great rocks in the centre." Comparing his game to the kriegspiel played by the British army, Wells writes: "My game is just as good as their game, and saner by reason of its size. Here is War, done down to rational proportions, and yet out of the way of mankind, even as our fathers turned human sacrifices into the eating of little images and symbolic mouthfuls. . . . Great War is at present, I am convinced, not only the most expensive game in the universe, but it is a game out of all proportion. Not only are the masses of men and material and suffering and inconvenience too monstrously big for reason, but—the available heads we have for it are too small."[55] The movement here is correspondingly one from work to play, from utility to aesthetics, from ends to means. A miniature railway built by a Captain Harvey and Count Louis Zborowski was christened along the Kent coast in the summer of 1927 by Earl Beauchamp, K. G., Lord Warden of the Cinque Ports, who referred to the line as "the most sporting railway in the world, built by sportsmen."[56] What is this erasure of labor, this celebration of the mechanism for its own sake, if not a promise of immortality, the immortal leisure promised by surplus value?

Here it might be useful to contrast the independent meanings of the terms *journey* and *excursion*. The journey belongs to the moral universe of preindustrialism. It marks the passage of the sun through the sky, the concomitant passage of the body's labor through the day, and the pilgrimage or passage of life. It is an allegorical notion, one that suggests a linearity and series of correspondences which link lived experience to the natural world. In contrast, the excursion is an abstract and fictive notion; it emerges from the world of mechanized labor and mechanical reproduction. The excursion is a holiday from that labor, a deviation and superfluity of signification. While the journey encompasses lived experience, the excursion evades it, steps outside and escapes it. The excursion is a carnival mode, but an alienated one; its sense of return is manufactured out of resignation and necessity. Today in America the uses of miniaturized landscapes continue to emphasize this sporting, or play, function. Miniature golf, the fantasy land, the children's zoos, and storybook countries realize the exotic and the fantastic on a miniaturized scale. The image that is produced not only bears the tangible qualities of material reality but also serves as a representation, an image, of a reality which does not exist. The referent here is most often the fantastic, yet the fantastic is in fact given "life" by its miniaturization. Although we cannot miniaturize what has not had material being in the first place, we can align the fantastic to the real and thereby miniaturize it by displacement. For example, the miniature unicorn is a popular gift-shop item, and we must assume that we are expected to read the scale as "miniature unicorn: unicorn :: miniature horse: horse." In these fantastic landscapes, the transformation of the miniature is effected by magic, not by labor. The automaton repeats and thereby displaces the position of its author. And the miniaturized landscape of the amusement park is domesticated by fantasy rather than by lumberjacks, carpenters, architects, and cleaning ladies, those workers who have "really" been its causality.

The amusement park and the historical reconstruction often promise to bring history to life, and it is here that we must pay particular attention once more to the relation between miniature and narrative. For the function of the miniature here is to bring historical events "to life," to immediacy, and thereby to erase their history, to lose us within their presentness. The transcendence presented by the miniature is a spatial transcendence, a transcendence which erases the productive possibilities of understanding through time. Its locus is thereby the nostalgic. The miniature here erases not only labor but causality and effect. Understanding is sacrificed to being in context. Hence the miniature is often a material allusion to a text which is no longer available to us, or which, because of its fictiveness, never *was* available to us except through a second-order fictive world. These "parks" mark the landscape as nostalgic allusions to interiority and fictiveness the way Beatrix Potter figurines mark the nursery or the Toby jug stands on the English mantelpiece, symbol of the interior fire at the heart of the domestic.[57]

The Dollhouse

Transcendence and the interiority of history and narrative are the dominant characteristics of the most consummate of miniatures—the dollhouse. A house within a house, the dollhouse not only presents the house's articulation of the tension between inner and outer spheres, of exteriority and interiority—it also represents the tension between two modes of interiority. Occupying a space within an enclosed space, the dollhouse's aptest analogy is the locket or the secret recesses of the heart: center within center, within within within. The dollhouse is a materialized secret; what we look for is the dollhouse within the dollhouse and its promise of an infinitely profound interiority. In fact, we can see the dollhouse-maker's relative inattention to the exterior of his or her structure as further evidence of this movement inward. Like the fashion doll, the dollhouse was originally (and perhaps still is) an adult amusement. We can see its origins in the crèche, which we find from the Middle Ages on, particularly in Naples and Marseilles. The Neapolitan crèches displayed figures made of wood or terra cotta, with finely finished faces and hands, silk clothing, and silver and pearl ornaments. Surrounding the figures were miniature objects and animals, which, Allemagne writes, "l'on faisait figurer dans ces petites reconstitutions des crèches pour leur donner un plus grand cachet de vérité."[58] In the Sicilian crèche tradition, for example, there seems to be an important movement toward locating the sacred within the secular landscape. At the heart of such crèches are the abstract mythologized figures of the Nativity, but as one moves out from that location, the landscape becomes more familiar: the snail- and herb-gatherers of the Palmeritan hills; the shepherds as Sicilian shepherds. In contrast, the art cabinets of sixteenth- and seventeenth-century Europe focused upon the secular domestic interior as they displayed small objects made of silver, china, glass, and pewter as well as miniature furniture. Dutch miniatures of the time were often exact reproductions of the owner's household furnishings.[59] In 1637 the town of Augsburg bought for presentation to the Swedish king, Gustavus Adolphus, a cabinet from the University of Upsala which contained real toys: a pair of mechanical dolls, a peepshow, and a little falconry after the style of a doll's room.[60]

The dollhouse has two dominant motifs: wealth and nostalgia. It presents a myriad of perfect objects that are, as signifiers, often affordable, whereas the signified is not. Consider the miniature Orkney Island chairs that can be found in the china cupboards of many Island homes. The full-size chairs, handmade of local straw, were once a major furnishing of the peasant house, but because their manufacture is so labor-intensive and because their mode of production has become so esoteric, only the very wealthy can now afford them. Hence the descendants of the peasants who once owned such pieces can afford only the miniature, or "toy," version. Use value is transformed into display value here. Even the most basic use of the toy object—to be "played with"—is not often found in the world of the dollhouse. The dollhouse is consumed by the eye. The most famous dollhouses, such as the Duchess Augusta Dorothea of Schwarzburg-Gotha's reproduction of court life and the dollhouse built for Queen Mary of England in 1920,[61] have been extravagant displays of upper-class ways of life that were meant to stop time and thus present the illusion of a perfectly complete and hermetic world. In his introduction to *The Book of the Queen's Dolls' House* Arthur Benson writes: "The scale of one inch to one foot being precisely maintained throughout, . . . thus there is nothing of the grotesque absurdity of a scene that does not resemble life and has only the interest of caricature. And then there is the *completeness* of the whole. Her majesty [Queen Mary], through all her public life, has realised the extraordinary importance of the small details of life. . . . The Queen's House is a symbol of this."[62] We might suspect that this monument against instability, randomness, and vulgarity speaks all the class relations that are absent from its boundaries. But we need not turn to the most celebrated examples to find these motifs of wealth and nostalgia. In the advertisements for, and catalogs of, miniature articles issued by firms such as the Franklin Mint, the Concord Miniature Collection, and Federal Smallwares Corporation, "period furnishings," "storybook figures," the "charming," the "picturesque," and the "old-fashioned" are presented to a bourgeois public immersed in the discourse of the "petite feminine." The dollhouse is a version of property which is metonymic to the larger set of property relations outside its boundaries. As private property marked by the differentiations of privacy and privatizing functions (bathrooms, maids' rooms, dining rooms, halls, parlors, and chambers) and characterized by attention to ornaments and detail to the point of excruciation (the hand of the artisan, the eye of the beholder), the dollhouse erases all but *the frontal view*; its appearance is the realization of the self as property, the body as container of objects, perpetual and incontaminable.

Here we might briefly link the dollhouse to the house-poem tradition, which also functioned to display and hypostatize the status of the interior world of the ascending and upper classes. For example, Jonson's "To Penshurst" presents a description of lush natural images and their consumption by the eye and the ear. The poem moves from distance to interiority—from "thy walkes and thy Mount" to "thy copps," to "the lower land," "thy ponds," to the espaliered fruit trees, to the scenes within the garden walls (where farmers and peasants bring their goods), to the table, bed, and hearth, and finally to the children of Penshurst, who "may, every day,/Reade, in their vertuous parents noble parts,/The mysteries of manners, armes, and arts." The lyric ramblingness of the poem perhaps belies the parallel that can be seen between the unfolding of the poem in the eye and ear of the reader or audience and the depiction of objects to be consumed in the same manner. And the impulse to describe variety and fecundity can be seen as the same impulse that inspired the Duchess of Schwarzburg-Gotha to include in her dollhouse scenes of a princess at her toilet, a curio closet, a fair with booths, clowns and a quack doctor, and the town crier and a marketplace with the Imperial posting house. Worlds of inversion, of contamination and crudeness, are controlled within the dollhouse by an absolute manipulation and control of the boundaries of time and space.

The house is meant to be viewed from a distance, with attention focused upon one scene and then another, just as it is in Jonson's poem, and, we might add, just as it is in the landscaping tradition that places the house at a remove from the life of the street in proportion to the degree of wealth displayed. Hence what might be seen as a microcosmic tendency is macrocosmic as well: "Thou art not, Penshurst, built to envious show, of touch, or marble." Perfection can be appreciated only through attention to detail and incident; significance bursts the bounds of the physical structure here. Unlike the single miniature object, the miniature universe of the dollhouse cannot be known sensually; it is inaccessible to the languages of the body and thus is the most abstract of all miniature forms. Yet cognitively the dollhouse is gigantic. As Jonson moves from the remote to the domestic, his images become increasingly imbued with refinement. The landscape becomes increasingly detailed and attended to; from rustic humor (where fish and fowl offer themselves to be killed and the fruit clings to walls, just as the ripe country maidens, like "plum, or peare," "add to thye free provisions" as objects to be consumed) we move to the elevated seriousness of the scenes depicting the hospitality extended to King James and the passage on the education of the children. That education enables the children to discern discriminately the separate parts of their parents, their separate features representing the refinement of their behavior.

In contrast, "Upon Appleton House" moves eclectically outward from the structure and history of the house to the garden to the meadow to the forest, where the narrator places himself, and, in conclusion, to a meditation on the merits of Maria Fairfax and an account of how she is responsible for the beauty of the other scenes. But Marvell's poem similarly exhibits a resistance to time, an attention to nature as a panoply of objects for consumption, and a juxtaposition of microcosmic and macrocosmic images. We might draw an analogy between the relative inattention to exterior structure of the poem here and the inattention of the dollhouse-maker to exterior form. Marvell, like Jonson, directs our attention to one location at a time, yet here each scene is marked by a conceit: the battle of Fairfax and the nuns, the garden-fort, the meadow-sea, and the peasantry depicted in a fantastic or toylike manner:

> Where every Mowers wholesome Heat
> Smells like an *Alexanders sweat.*
> Their Females fragrant as the Mead
> Which they in *Fairy Circles* tread:
> When at their Dances End they kiss,
> Their new-made Hay not sweeter is.

We see a similar giganticization of the master of the house—

> Yet thus the laden House does sweat,
> And scarce indures the *Master* great:
> But where he comes the Swelling Hall
> Stirs, and the *Square* grows *Spherical*;
> More by his *Magnitude* distrest,
> Then he is by its straitness prest:—

and a corresponding miniaturization of the villagers:

> They seem within the polisht Grass
> A Landskip drawen in Looking-Glass
> And shrunk in the huge Pasture show
> As spots, so shap'd, on Faces do.
> Such Fleas, ere they approach the Eye
> In Multiplying Glasses lye.
> They feed so wide, so slowly move,
> As *Constellations* do above.

Time and history exist for Fairfax; later generations will wonder at the relation between his physical size and the physical scale of Appleton House, just as the descendants of Penshurst will correlate the expansiveness of the house with that of their ancestors. But the miniature peasant world, the toylike worlds of the farmers and the clowns, takes place in a timelessness that is tableaulike, an arrangement defined by the "picturesque" rather than by history. This mode of description is that of the pastoral up until the late eighteenth century and the advent of the romantics. As Pope wrote in *A Discourse on*

Pastoral Poetry, the author would be most successful if he chose to "expose" only the best side of a shepherd's life and conceal its miseries. The pastoral figures of Pope and his predecessors are more like wind-up toys than the shepherds of romantic pastorals, who sweat and become lonely. They live in fantasy worlds, the literary worlds of a Golden Age or Arcadia, and their stories are imbued with a happy precision that makes them more lyric than narrative.[63] More precisely, they are more dead than alive; for again we find the motif of mechanization with its concomitant immortality as a gesture against organicism and the apparent disorganization of history. The dollhouse, as we know from the political economy as well as from Ibsen, represents a particular form of interiority, an interiority which the subject experiences as its sanctuary (fantasy) and prison (the boundaries or limits of otherness, the inaccessibility of what cannot be lived experience).[64]

Miniature Time

The miniature does not attach itself to lived historical time. Unlike the metonymic world of realism, which attempts to erase the break between the time of everyday life and the time of narrative by mapping one perfectly upon the other, the metaphoric world of the miniature makes everyday life absolutely anterior and exterior to itself. The reduction in scale which the miniature presents skews the time and space relations of the everyday lifeworld, and as an object consumed, the miniature finds its "use value" transformed into the infinite time of reverie. This capacity of the miniature to create an "other" time, a type of transcendent time which negates change and the flux of lived reality, might be seen at work in such projects as the *Museum of Art in Miniature*, which was distributed by the Book-of-the-Month Club in 1948. Here the Metropolitan Museum, that most insistent denial of history and context, is reduced to a series of pictures on stamps that can be pasted into a book. The stamps are presented in a seemingly random arrangement of categories and individual places—Michelangelo, Robert, Homer, Carnevale, Goya, Rembrandt, Fragonard; Italian, Roman, French, Etruscan, Egyptian, and Chinese works. Albums G and J contain, respectively, "the Old Testament in Art" and "the New Testament in Art"—and their detachability presents even more possibilities for manipulation. In this rather remarkable phenomenon we thus find the object at least three degrees of removal from everyday life: the distance between the work of art and what it signifies (itself not necessarily "representational"), the decontextualization of the work of art within the museum context, and the removal of the museum from the constraints of its physical setting into an almost infinite set of possible arrangements and recontextualizations. Like the miniature world of the encyclopedia, where the "arbitrary" order of alphabetization replaces the seemingly determined disorder of history, this "museum of art in miniature" exists in a time particular to its own boundaries.

Interestingly, there may be an actual phenomenological correlation between the experience of scale and the experience of duration. In a recent experiment conducted by the School of Architecture at the University of Tennessee, researchers had adult subjects observe scale-model environments 1/6, 1/12, and 1/24 of full size. The environments represented lounges and included chipboard furniture as well as scale figures. The subjects were asked to move the scale figures through the environment, to imagine humans to be that scale, and to identify activities appropriate for that space. Then they were asked to imagine themselves to be of "lounge scale" and picture themselves engaging in activities in the lounge. Finally, they were asked to tell the researchers when they felt that they had been engaged in such activities for 30 minutes. The experiment showed that "the experience of temporal duration is compressed relative to the clock in the same proportion as scale-model environments being observed are compressed relative to the full-sized environment." In other words, 30 minutes would be experienced in 5 minutes at 1/12 scale and in 2.5 minutes at 1/24 scale.[65] This compressed time of interiority tends to hypostatize the interiority of the subject that consumes it in that it marks the invention of "private time." In other words, miniature time transcends the duration of everyday life in such a way as to create an interior temporality of the subject.

Such a transformation of time, which serves to skew the experience of the social by literally *deferring* it, parallels the miniature's transformation of language. This relation to language is an ironic one at every point. The problem of the miniature described, as we noted above, emphasizes the noniconic nature of language as sign. The miniature always tends toward tableau rather than toward narrative, toward silence and spatial boundaries rather than toward expository closure. Whereas speech unfolds in time, the miniature unfolds in space. The observer is offered a transcendent and simultaneous view of the miniature, yet is trapped outside the possibility of a lived reality of the miniature. Hence the nostalgic desire to present the lower classes, peasant life, or the cultural other within a timeless and uncontaminable miniature form. The miniature is against speech, particularly as speech reveals an inner dialectical, or dialogic, nature. The miniature's fixed form is manipulated by individual fantasy rather than by physical circumstance. Its possible linguistic correlations are the *multum in parvo* of the epigram and the proverb, forms whose function is to put an end to speech and the idiosyncrasies of immediate context. In its tableaulike form, the miniature is a world of arrested time; its stillness emphasizes the activity that is outside its borders. And this effect is reciprocal, for once we attend to the miniature world, the outside world stops and is lost to us. In this it resembles other fantasy structures: the return from Oz, or Narnia, or even sleep.

In Lilliput, Gulliver becomes his body: eating, drinking, defecating, sleeping, and using his muscles are the sum of his social existence within the miniature world. For the Lilliputians, even Gulliver's death has an apparently organic, rather than a cultural or social, meaning: the problem would be how to dispose of his enormous body and the correspondingly enormous stench it would create. The clumsiness of Gulliver, the ways in which new surfaces of his body erupt as he approaches the Lilliputian world, is the clumsiness of the dreamer who approaches the dollhouse. All senses must be reduced to the visual, a sense which in its transcendence remains ironically and tragically remote. Thus, throughout the sojourn among the Lilliputians it is Gulliver's eyes which are continually threatened, from the early arrows that narrowly miss his eyes, to the Blefuscan fleet's attack on them, to the final punishment, which is modified by his friend Reldresal to a request that his eyes, not his life, be put out.

Because Gulliver knows the Lilliputians only through a transcendent visual sense, the narrative voice works within the convention of travel writing and, by déjà vu, within the voice of early anthropology. For what is important here, what is chosen to be *related* and attended to, is detail in juxtaposition with pattern, the broad cliché illustrated by selected example. The very features of the model or automaton become the features of the Lilliputians themselves, a people characterized by a perfect physicality and by values which are mathematical and technocratic. Lilliput is a completely cultural world in Gulliver's description of it; it is marked by a clockwork set of laws and customs and by a language inflated beyond the significance of its referents. Nature is continually transformed into art: "The country round appeared like a continued Garden; and the inclosed Fields, which were generally Forty Foot square, resembled so many Beds of Flowers. These Fields were intermingled with Woods of half a Stang, and the tallest Trees, as I could judge, appeared to be seven Foot high. I viewed the Town on my left Hand, which looked like the painted Scene of a City in a Theatre."[66] What is remarkable about Lilliput, just as what is remarkable about the mechanical toy, is that it works, that it presents movement and change without necessitating a difference of scale. Hence the souvenirs that Gulliver chooses to return with are natural; these cows and sheep exemplify the skewed relation between quality and quantity, significance and amount, presented by the Lilliputian world as a whole.

As is the case with all models, it is absolutely necessary that Lilliput be an island. The miniature world remains perfect and uncontaminated by the grotesque so long as its absolute boundaries are maintained. Consider, for example, the Victorian taste for art (usually transformed relics of nature) under glass or Joseph Cornell's glass bells. The glass eliminates the possibility of contagion, indeed of lived experience, at the same time that it maximizes the possibilities of transcendent vision. Thus the miniature world may always be seen as being overcoded as the cultural. The hearth at Penshurst, the Nuremburg kitchens, the dollhouse, even the interior sky of baroque architecture—all tend to present domesticated space as a model of order, proportion, and balance. Yet, of course, the major function of the enclosed space is always to create a tension or dialectic between inside and outside, between private and public property, between the space of the subject and the space of the social. Trespass, contamination, and the erasure of materiality are the threats presented to the enclosed world. And because the interiority of the enclosed world tends to reify the interiority of the viewer, repetition also presents a threat. It is important to remember that the miniature object, in its absolute (i.e., conventional) representativeness, is "unique" as well. We cannot separate the function of the miniature from a nostalgia for preindustrial labor, a nostalgia for craft. We see a rise in the production of miniature furniture at the same time that the plans of Adam, Chippendale, and Sheraton are becoming reproduced in mass and readily available form.[67] Contemporary dollhouses are distinctly not contemporary; it is probably not accidental that it is the Victorian period which is presently so popular for reproduction in miniature, not only because that period's obsession with detail and materiality is so analogous to the miniature's general functions, but also because Victorian modes of production presented the height of a transformation of nature into culture. Whereas industrial labor is marked by the prevalence of repetition over skill and part over whole, the miniature object represents an antithetical mode of production: production by the hand, a production that is unique and authentic. Today we find the miniature located at a place of origin (the childhood of the self, or even the advertising scheme whereby a miniature of a company's first plant or a miniature of a company's earliest product is put on display in a window or lobby)[68] and at a place of ending (the productions of the hobbyist: knickknacks of the domestic collected by elderly women, or the model trains built by the retired engineer); and both locations are viewed from a transcendent position, a position which is always within the standpoint of present lived reality and which thereby always nostalgically distances its object.

In this chapter I have discussed the miniature in its role as both an experience of interiority and the process by which that interior is constructed. The abstract experiences of fantasy and fictiveness in general, experiences known through representation, have been considered thus far as a dialogue between outside and inside, between partiality and transcendence with regard to authority and authorial knowledge. The miniature, linked to nostalgic versions of childhood and history, presents a diminutive, and thereby manipulatable, version of experience, a version which is domesticated and protected from contamination. It marks the pure body, the inorganic body of the machine and its *repetition* of a death that is thereby not a death. In the next chapter we will move from transcendence to partiality, from the inside to the outside. No longer alone, we will find ourselves within the crowded space below the giant.

3. THE GIGANTIC

t the end of the Book of Job, God asks Job: "Can you draw out Leviathan with a fish hook, or press down his tongue with a cord? Can you put a rope in his nose, or pierce his jaw with a hook? Will he make many supplications to you? Will he speak to you soft words? Will he make a covenant with you to take him for your servant for ever? Will you play with him as with a bird, or will you put him on leash for your maidens?" (41:1–5). The comic image of the monster on a leash, of the domesticated beast, the pet or "friendly" lion, tiger, or dragon, illustrates the absolute inversion of the miniature which the gigantic presents. Whereas the miniature represents closure, interiority, the domestic, and the overly cultural, the gigantic represents infinity, exteriority, the public, and the overly natural. The elephant joke, for example, depends upon this principle, the pink elephant being the most incongruous mixture of nature and culture, a beast dreamed by an interior decorator.

The miniature offers us a transcendent vision which is known only through the visual. In approaching the miniature, our bodies erupt into a confusion of before-unrealized surfaces. We are able to hold the miniature object within our hand, but our hand is no longer in proportion with its world; instead our hand becomes a form of undifferentiated landscape, the body a kind of background. Once the miniature world is self-enclosed, as in the case of the dollhouse, we can only stand outside, looking in, experiencing a type of tragic distance. Here we might think of the paintings of the contemporary folk artist Ralph Fasanella, who paints views of apartment buildings and tenements as if their structures could be sliced open and we could simultaneously examine all the interiors they enclose. Fasanella presents us with an arrangement of simultaneous and unconnected dramas which, as in viewing the dollhouse, we can attend to only one scene at a time.[1] The confrontation of so much life results in an experience of profound aloneness akin to that which Socrates experiences suspended in a basket above *The Clouds;* or, perhaps less abstractly, the loneliness of Frankenstein outside the peasant hut or King Kong as his shadow falls over a sleeping New York City. Although the miniature makes the body gigantic, the gigantic transforms the body into miniature, especially pointing to the body's "toylike" and "insignificant" aspects.

Our most fundamental relation to the gigantic is articulated in our relation to landscape, our immediate and lived relation to nature as it "surrounds" us. Our position here is the antithesis of our position in relation to the miniature; we are enveloped by the gigantic, surrounded by it, enclosed within its shadow. Whereas we know the miniature as a spatial whole or as temporal parts, we know the gigantic only partially. We move through the landscape; it does not move through us. This relation to the landscape is expressed most often through an abstract projection of the body upon the natural world. Consequently, both the miniature and the gigantic may be described through metaphors of containment—the miniature as contained, the gigantic as container.

We find the miniature at the origin of private, individual history, but we find the gigantic at the origin of public and natural history. The gigantic becomes an explanation for the environment, a figure on the interface between the natural and the human. Hence our words for the landscape are often projections of an enormous body upon it: the mouth of the river, the foot-hills, the fingers of the lake, the heartlands, the elbow of the stream. This gigantic reading of the landscape is often supplemented in folklore by accounts of causality: the Giant's Causeway as part of a road constructed by giants between Scotland and Ireland; Stonehenge as the Giant's Dance (*chorea gigantum*); glacial pot-shaped cylindrical holes ascribed as Giants' Kettles; Giant's Leap, the name given in mountainous regions to the rocks separated from each other by large chasms.[2]

In the British Isles many disproportions of landscape or aberrations in the environment are commonly attributed through legend to the activities of giants. For example, Warne's *Ancient Dorset* gives an account of two large boulders in the hills above the Vale of Blackmoor that were positioned when two giants had a contest to see which was the stronger and thereby could throw a weight the greatest distance. Nearby is the Giant's Grave, a large mound of earth said to be the burying place of the unsuccessful of the two. The Scottish giants, called Fomorians, are similarly attributed with the power to throw boulders. In his book on English giants, Harold John Massingham writes of giant figures etched into the turf at the villages of Cerne Abbas in Dorset and Wilmington in Sussex:

> On the slope of a chalk hill surmounted by a small earthwork just outside the village, a rude colossus had been etched into the turf. Like its brother of Wilmington in Sussex, it is the seal of a god-mountain more towering, robust, and grandly moulded than any in its neighborhood; . . . climb the blowing hill and up the causeway of his swelling calves . . . the figure is 180 feet long and carries a great indented club in the right hand. Many of the turf figures on the Downs are, of course, comparatively modern, but the Cerne Giant, the Wilmington Long Man, and the White Horse of White Horse Vale in Berkshire "antiquitate Antiquity."[3]

Massingham concludes that the figures were not simply a form of what we now call "found" art, but rather were deliberately constructed anthropomorphic representations of the gods. He also argues that "it is tenable that the giants of folk-lore are the literary equivalents of the giants incised upon the chalk downs."[4]

In addition to the Cerne Abbas and Wilmington anthropomorphic representations, we find the white horses carved in the turf of the downs in southern England. The White Horse of Uffington Hill in Berkshire, which Massingham mentions, is the most famous of these figures, stretching 335 feet from nose to tail and 120 feet from ear to hoof. Massingham records that the duty of scouring the figure was undertaken by various local parishes. Up until the twentieth century the scouring ceremony was accompanied by a general festival of junketing, horseplay, feasting, and cudgel bouts.[5]

Mary Williams suggests that "belief in giants can easily be accepted. Early invaders to these islands, seeing the gigantic menhirs, stone circles such as Stonehenge, Avebury and many others, would naturally conclude that only giants could have moved such immense masses of stone and set them upright. Again the very large boulders scattered over the countryside would suggest giants at play, hence the many tales of giants, including King Arthur and his Queen, casting huge rocks at one another."[6] In the same vein, large barrows would be attributed as giant's graves. In Germanic tradition we find similar stories in which giants make canals, rivers, lakes, islands, and mountains, or in which lakes and streams are formed from the tears and blood of a giant. Large boulders are described as pebbles shaken from a giant's shoe; large lakes are formed when giants leave their footprints in the earth to be filled by rain; a roaring in the forest, or billowing waves in a field of grain, mark the passage of a giant.[7]

Such explanations of the origins of geographical features often contain corresponding accounts of how the earth was originally inhabited by a giant race of men, present-day man being a fallen descendant of these original figures. We find this idea developed into a philosophy in Blake's prophetic books: "The giants who formed this world into its sensual existence, and now seem to live in it in chains, are in truth the causes of its life and the sources of all activity, but the chains are the cunning of weak and tame minds, which have power to resist energy, according to the proverb, 'The weak in courage is strong in cunning'."[8] Similarly, the children of Uranus represent physical force and lawlessness, a superfluity of nature over culture. The Cyclops—his eye an affront to symmetry and the "correct" view, his cannibalism the ultimate assault upon domesticity and the privatizing functions of the cultural, his labor a mark upon the landscape, yet without cultivation—has his analogues in the one-eyed giants of Bulgaria, Croatia, Slovenia, Ireland, and Wales. Odysseus describes the Cyclopes as "giants, louts, without a law to bless them. . . . Kyklopês have no muster and no meeting, no consultation or old tribal ways, but each one dwells in his own mountain cave dealing out rough justice to wife and child, indifferent to what the others do."[9] The giant, from Leviathan to the sideshow freak, is a mixed category; a violator of boundary and rule; an overabundance of the natural and hence an affront to cultural systems. Here we find the opposite of the clockwork precision of the miniature; for while the miniature "works," coordinating the social, animating a *model* universe, the gigantic unleashes a vast and "natural" creativity that bears within it the capacity for (self-)destruction.

In one Germanic legend, a giant girl comes down from the mountains into a valley. Here she sees a plowman at work in a field. She puts the peasant, the oxen, and the plow in her apron and takes them home as toys. When she shows these playthings to her parents, they are displeased and tell her she must take them back, "for these men are not playthings for giants, but belong to that race of people who will some day do great harm to giants."[10] Typically, the giants are not the gods; they do not inhabit a transcendent space; they inhabit the earth, and it is their movement through the sensual world which gives shape and form to that world, if not meaning. The primordial character of such legendary giants is illustrated in the account Spenser gives us of the birth of the giant fought by the Red Crosse Knight in Canto VII of *The Faerie Queene:*

> The greatest Earth his uncouth mother was,
> And blustering Æolus his boasted sire,
> Who with his breath, which through the world doth pas,
> Her hollow Womb did secretly inspire,
> And fild her hidden caues with stormie yre,
> That she conceiv'd; and trebling the dew time,
> In which the wombes of women do expire,
> Brought forth this monstrous masse of earthly slime,
> Puft up with emptie wind, and fild with sinfull crime.[11]

Here, as elsewhere, the giant is linked to the earth in its most primitive, or natural, state. In Germanic tradition, giants usually wear nothing at all, but sometimes are described as wearing garments made of gray moss, the skins of animals, or the bark of trees.[12] Their merger with the natural is thus further emphasized by their lack of individual dress and, consequently, individual identity. Often such undifferentiated figures are defeated by heroes with names, such as King Arthur,[13] who are "larger than life," yet closer to present-day man in that they are believed to have lived in historical, legendary time and are thus contextualized by the narrative. Giants, like dinosaurs, in their anonymous singularity always seem to be the last of their race.

Just as the miniature presents us with an analogical mode of thought, a mode which matches world within world, so does the gigantic present an analogical mode of thought, world without world. Both involve the selection of elements that will be transformed and displayed in an exaggerated relation to the social construction of reality. But while the miniature represents a mental world of proportion, control, and balance, the gigantic presents a physical world of disorder and disproportion. It is significant that the most typical miniature world is the domestic model of the dollhouse, while the most typical gigantic world is the sky—a vast, undifferentiated space marked only by the constant movement of clouds with their amorphous forms. We can see these contrasting modes of analogy in relation to nature perhaps more clearly if we compare the picturesque and the sublime as historical styles of exaggeration in the depiction and presentation of nature.

Rooted in the *Peri Hupsous* of Longinus, the aesthetic experience of the sublime is characterized by astonishment and surprise: the grandeur of scenery results in a sudden expansion of the soul and the emotions. In the dominant romantic manifesto of the sublime, Edmund Burke's essay "A Philosophical Enquiry into the Origin of Our Ideas of the Sublime and the Beautiful" (1757), we see astonishment elaborated into a profound emotion of terror, an admiration of the destructive forces of nature. The graveyard school of art and poetry and the romantic taste for ruins each contributed to the shape of Burke's conclusions. In his classification of the sublime he outlines the following qualities: obscurity, power, privations, vastness, infinity, difficulty (requiring vast expenditures of labor and effort), and magnificence. What distinguishes the sublime from the beautiful is that the former is individual and painful, while the second is social and pleasant, resting upon love and its attendant emotions.[14]

This description of the beautiful thus appears historically on the interface between the sublime and the picturesque, that rather bourgeois taming of the sublime which emerges at the end of the eighteenth century and flowers during the Victorian period. The terrifying and giganticized nature of the sublime is domesticated into the orderly and cultivated nature of the picturesque. While the sublime is marked by a potential recklessness, a dangerous surrender to disorder in nature, the picturesque is marked by a harmony of form, color, and light, of modulation approached by a distanced viewer. As is apparent in the word itself, the picturesque is formed by the transformation of nature into art and thus the manipulation of flux into form, infinity into frame. Poetry, painting, gardening, architecture, and "the art of travel"[15] make up an art of landscape, an art of meditation and arrangement, rather than an art of the astonishing or the overwhelming. In an essay entitled "Scenery and Mind," printed in 1852 in *The Home Book of the Picturesque*, E. L. Magoon explains:

> Living with supreme delight far above a Lilliputian standard, the mind swells into something of the colossal grandeur it admires. A majestic landscape, often scorned and truly loved, imparts much of its greatness to the mind and heart of the spectator; so that while the species may dwindle in relative worth, the individual is ennobled by the expansion he has received. . . . Wide and dense masses of mankind form the appropriate field whereon superior talents are to be exercised; but, to the aspiring, the distraction and attrition of large cities are rather evils to be shunned, since they vitiate if not destroy that purity and calm which are essential to the best growth of mind.[16]

Here we find the qualities involved in the apprehension of the miniature: the distanced and "over-seeing" viewer, the transcendence of the upper classes, the reduction of labor to the toylike, and the reification of interiority. The distinction made by Arthur Benson in his book on the queen's dollhouse, between the "tasteful harmony" of Queen

Mary's dollhouse and the "coarse and grotesque" qualities of the
contemporary life of the lower classes, is a twentieth-century descendant of these Victorian ideas. "What an admirable picture! exclaim
the tasteful, contemplating a fine landscape from the artist's skill.
Beautiful! exclaim the less tasteful in view of coarser or the coarsest
imitation. How pretty! cries childhood over almost anything,"
warned Warren Burton in his 1844 work, *The Scenery-Shower, with
Word Paintings of the Beautiful, the Picturesque, and the Grand in Nature.*
He urged the unappreciating to seek a "diligent self-culture" that
would consist of surrounding oneself with the picturesque.[17]

In several forms of contemporary postminimalist sculpture we see
a revival of both sublime and picturesque modes of presenting nature. In some cases, such as the work of Carl Andre, Stonehenge and
other earth landmarks of the southern English countryside (as well as
the Indian mounds that stretch through Minnesota) have had a direct
influence on the development of contemporary forms of "earth
art."[18] Works arising from this movement have been characterized by
the particular use of highly textured natural materials on a comparatively large scale in unstructured space; they usually display a
strong relation to immediate context or environment. Furthermore,
most of these works are flexible in the sense that they are designed to
be manipulated by environmental changes. Stonehenge has been
shaped by the rain and wind and sun as much as it has been shaped
by an artistic intention. Similarly, Dennis Oppenheim's project to
mow rings ten miles wide in the wheat fields around an active vol-
cano in Ecuador denies the permanent (and classical) status of the
material art object. The gigantification of contemporary earth art is an
attempt to make marks on or in the landscape on the scale of distanced perception. In other words, earth art attempts to articulate
significance to the same degree that features of the landscape articulate significance. Since such articulation is not a matter of an intrinsic
process of selection on the part of nature, but rather a matter of the
relation between cultural values and the consequent *social* shape of
nature, earth art may be seen as a modern descendant of the sublime
on the one hand and the picturesque on the other. In that earth art
aims to astonish and to confront the viewer with a powerful display
of the natural, it harkens to the sublime. But where the romantics
evoked terror, the minimalists evoke humor and even irony, for contemporary earth art speaks of an immediate intention: its function is
not ascribed to legendary time and remote, more natural, forms of
human life, as is the case with the "earth art" of folk tradition. A
piece like Jan Dibbet's work in Ithaca, New York, where fourteen
trees standing in a row in a forest were selected and painted white

from the ground up to a height of five feet, clearly articulates the trace of culture upon nature. In fact, we might be reminded of the hapless gardeners in *Alice in Wonderland* painting the Queen of Hearts' white roses red. Thus, insofar as the earth art movement centers on a humanistic rearrangement of nature, it may be linked to the picturesque. And, despite its gigantic scale, the enclosure of the earth object within gallery space further links it to the Victorian attempt to domesticate and re-form nature within cultural categories. The earthwork that is displayed out of doors and traveled through is closer to the experience of landscape in the sublime; the viewer is dwarfed by the landscape, which allows him or her a partial vision over time. But the earthwork that is contained becomes an object; the viewer stands away from it in a distanced position approximating a simultaneous and transcendent vision.[19] The contained work of earth art must be linked to landscape arrangement, to the formal garden, and ultimately to nature under cover. Oppenheim's 1968 scale models in fact use grass, flowers, hedges, and furrows in a metaphor of cultivation and hence echo formal garden arrangements.

The critic Sidney Tillim has connected much contemporary earth art to the eighteenth- and nineteenth-century picturesque tradition on semantic grounds. "Less than sublime, yet seeking a surrogate for the ideal, it [the eighteenth- and nineteenth-century picturesque] signalled, by virtue of its resultant sentimentality, the end of the ideals of high art. It substituted the sentimental for nobility of feeling and developed the cult of nature as an antidote to the excessive sophistication of cultivated society. At the same time it was an affectation of cultivated taste at its most refined. As the 20th century form of the picturesque, Earthworks signify an analogous degree of overcultivation of the modernist idiom."[20] Tillim links the earth art movement to the picturesque on the basis of its oversophistication, but he overlooks the strongly "moral" character of both artistic movements. Earth art cannot be separated from the ecological ideals of the 1960's and early 1970's, from the back-to-nature movement and a rejection of institutions, including the institutions of art. Walter DeMaria has lamented, in all seriousness, that "God has created the earth—and we have ignored it."[21] Such a "return to nature" must always be nostalgic. Because the earthwork is a work of the moment of creation and conception, it cannot be returned to in its original form; it exists only through the distance of the photograph. Like other forms of the picturesque, the earthwork is an art of the souvenir or memento insofar as the aesthetic artifact is a trace of an original event[22] now subject to transformations out of the control of the creator and the beholder. But ironically, in its choice of the large scale (i.e., large in relation to the human body), the earthwork itself mimes the distance assumed by the monuments of public space. As Michael Fried has pointed out, literalist or minimalist sculpture's aspirations toward a nonpersonal or public mode have an obvious theatricality: "the largeness of the piece, in conjunction with its non-relational, unitary character, *distances* the beholder—not just physically but psychically. It is, one might say, precisely this distancing that *makes* the beholder a subject and the piece in question . . . an object."[23] The irony of this theatricality is apparent in the double-voiced quality of all manifestations of the sublime. The loneliness of nature spreads out before the solitary figure at the edge of the cliff as the stage of his consequent (and consequential) experience. But this beholder must always remain aware of the frame, aware of the encompassing role of nature. Hence the natural in the sublime is always a tamed beast, is always a transformation of action into object and distance into transcendence, and hence always sublimely ironic.

In this section we have briefly looked at the ways in which the point of view chosen in the presentation of the natural will relate to the prevailing ideology of the natural. The clockwork charm of the pastoral in the Enlightenment, the terror of the romantic sublime, and the sentimental distancing of the picturesque each reflect the historical circumstances of their origin. Thus these forms must always be seen in relation to the modes of production, the perception of distance between classes, and the symbiosis between rural and urban landscapes that prevailed in their times. Furthermore, as can be seen in romanticism, such forms can be considered as reactions against or revivals of their own internal periodization. The gigantification of the natural is approached through cultural categories, nature "herself" being the object of such categorization and thus progressively domesticated and interiorized as an agent of a history invented by narrative.

Exteriority: The City

If we attempt to describe the city from a distanced and transcendent position, to thereby miniaturize it, the tendency is to naturalize the city landscape. As Philip Fisher has noted, "Wordsworth's sonnet on Westminster Bridge landscapes the city with a rural frame, captures the city across from the self as a view or prospect. The city is significantly asleep, still, not itself, and the observer, in order to frame the scene, does not stand within it at all but in midair, on a bridge outside and over against it as a whole."[24] This pastoralizing of the city may be traced to what Bakhtin has called the mode of "experimental fantasticality" in the Menippean satire. Here observation from an experimental or unusual point of view results in a "new perspective" on the object. For example, Lucian's *Ikaromenippos* and Varro's *Endymiones* observe the life of the city from a high altitude.[25] Such a point of view enables the viewer to trivialize the cultural landscape as he or she magnifies and situates the larger natural landscape. At the same time, this view remains radically outside the scene: one cannot enter into the life of the city without experiencing a corresponding change of perspective. Therefore the view from above remains a view from an elsewhere, a view which in making the city *other* must correspondingly employ metaphors of otherness. The view from above could only be a view into a mirror if it were accompanied by a sense of splitting or self-consciousness. For example, there is Burton's citation of Lucian's Menippean dialogue, *Charon, or the Inspectors:* "Charon in Lucian, as he wittily feigns, was conducted by Mercury to such a place, where he might see all the world at once; after he had sufficiently viewed, and looked out, Mercury would needs know of him what he had observed. He told him that he saw a vast multitude and a promiscuous, their habitations like molehills, the men as emmets. . . . Some were brawling, some fighting, riding, running, *sollicite ambientes, callide litigantes* (earnestly suing or cunningly disputing), for toys and trifles. . . . In conclusion, he condemned them all for madmen, fools, idiots, asses."[26] Hence in this view the tendency toward satire, which always, in its critique of affectation and the artificial in society, approximates "the natural stance."

But once we engage in the mode of consciousness offered by existence *within* the city, distance is collapsed into partiality, perception becomes fragmentary and above all temporal. Inside or outside, the typical view of the city is through the window—a view within a definite frame and limited perspective, mediated and refracted through the glass of the city's abstraction of experience. The production of space in the city under industrialism necessarily involves the creation of a space of the family (the biological means of reproduction) in relation to the forms of production and to the state. As Henri Lefebvre has pointed out, these representations of space can be understood only as correspondences to a space of representation, a social space within which and through which ideological formations will be produced.[27] Under capitalism the abstractions of economy produce an abstraction of these spaces; within this abstraction, merchandise (goods/objects) and the social relations that form in contiguity to these commodities can develop. Preindustrial culture locates the gigantic within the surrounding natural landscape. The romantic sublime nostalgically re-creates this location as it simultaneously merges it with the production of interiority (the vastness of the natural world mirrored in the vastness of the individual perceiving consciousness) and the mediation we see at work in the pastoral. But within the rise of industrial capitalism the gigantic becomes located within the abstraction of an exchange economy. The gigantic is moved from a presocial world of the natural to a social world of material production.

In his study of Rabelais, Bakhtin notes that the gigantic figure, as part of the popular imagery of the grotesque, moved from its ascription to the landscape to the festive carnival world. *Gargantua*, as a carnivalesque narrative, displays this tradition of the gigantic features of landscape. For example, Rabelais mentions the gigantic bowl in which the giant ate his gruel, and adds that the bowl can still be seen in Bourges—an immense rock scooped out like a bowl and called *Scutella gigantis*.[28] Under an agrarian economy, the giant became associated with the market and the fair and their attendant feasts. In both statuary and living form, the gigantic appeared as a symbol of surplus and licentiousness, of overabundance and unlimited consumption. Here the giant's consuming image is placed at the center of local civic identity: the hub of the marketplace and its articulation of commodity relations. At the end of the Middle Ages a number of European cities employed "town giants," even "families of giants," along with town jesters, who would take part in all public festivals.[29]

We see this world of feasting and the founding of towns in the opening books of *Gargantua and Pantagruel*. Gargantua is born amid a feast to consume an overabundance of tripe (itself, of course, an image of consumption): "The tripes were plentiful, as you will understand, and so appetizing that everyone licked his fingers. But the devil and all of it was that they could not possibly be kept any longer, for they were tainted, which seemed most improper. So it was resolved that they should be consumed without more ado. For this purpose there were invited all the citizens of Cinais, of Seuilly, of La Roche-Clermault, and of Vaugaudry, not to forget those of Le Coudray-Montpensier and the Gué de Vède, and other neighbors: all strong drinkers, jovial companions, and good skittle players."[30] Because Gargamelle eats too much (sixteen quarters, two bushels, and six pecks), her "fundament" slips out. And thanks to a midwife who stops up Gargamelle's bottom, Gargantua eventually arrives crying "Drink, drink," through his mother's ear. We see Gargantua linked to the life of towns in the account of his trip to Paris. Here he drenches the citizens in his piss, drowning two hundred sixty thousand four hundred eighteen of them. Those who escape swear and curse, saying, "We've been drenched in sport! We've been drenched *par ris*." The narrator explains that although the city was formerly called Leucetia, it is thenceforth called Paris.[31] Gargantua is thus officially the founder of "Paris," but he is a founder by inversion. His narrative reminds us of North American trickster tales, where, by a series of mishaps and mistakes, the trickster comes to establish a vital aspect of culture.[32]

With the development of the bourgeoisie, the marketplace, and the life of towns, we see the gigantic, as part of the grotesque, split into sacred and secular aspects. The gigantic is appropriated by the state and its institutions and put on parade with great seriousness, not as a representative of the material life of the body, but as a symbol of the abstract social formations making up life in the city. On the other hand, the gigantic continues its secular life in the submerged world of the carnival grotesque; its celebrations of licentiousness and lived bodily reality are truly the underbelly of official life. In his book on the processional giants of northern France and Belgium, René Darré writes that the procession of gigantic wooden figures during the Middle Ages contained these two contradictory aspects. On the one hand, great license was allowed in the parading of the figures; festivals of the giants were accompanied by feasting, drinking, and parodying of official institutions. At the time of the Albigensian heresies, "on comprendra plus facilement les prédispositions de certains membres du clergé, de la population, à ridiculiser de plus en plus les moeurs du temps des religieux qui, bien souvent, sombraient dans les plus coupables des abus." For example, in Lyon a giant depicted the Evangelist preaching the domination of Satan over men and nature.[33] On the other hand, in several areas such processions were accompanied by great religious fervor and piety, which, Darré explains, local commerce and industry were able to exploit for a profit by selling goods and exhibiting tributes to local crafts. This double-faceted nature of the giants is emblematic of the conflicts of the time: the giant as symbol of secular town life, vernacular language, and local religious institutions contrasted with the giant as symbol of the institutions of centralized state religion. The brutal suppression of the Albigensians from the crusade of Simon de Montfort to the Inquisition, and the resultant subjection of the provincial church to Rome and of the southern provinces to the central government in Paris, provide the political corollary to this conflict in symbol.[34]

By the fifteenth century the gigantic and grotesque figures of cultural heroes (Renaud dressed as Hector or Hercules, the elder Aymon as Priam, Charlemagne as Agamemnon) are replaced by the local giant, who appears in procession along with figures of saints. The local giant is tied to the vernacular language, to the local dialect, and thus to the affection of the people for their native town. "Demandez à un Douaisien ce qu'il pense des son géant, il vous dira 'Gayant, comme le Beffroi, c'est Douai.'. . . . Le beffroi, le géant, tous deux gigantesque symboles de la grandeur du passé et de l'espérance de l'avenir."[35] Such local giants would often lead the procession, accompanied not only by saints but also by certain anomalous figures. Such figures might include ancient Biblical heroes, Greeks, and Scandinavians. Darré writes that in Aragon a ceremonial cortege was trailed by figures of an American woman, an African king, a woman from the South Sea Islands, a Chinese man, a European woman, Sancho Panza, Dulcinea, and Don Quixote.[36] The humor of the procession is a humor of juxtapositions: sacred and secular, familiar and foreign, inside and outside, male and female, official and vernacular. While the town giant is symbolic of nativity and the vernacular, he or she is also fantastic—an enlargement in the exterior of an "interior" emotion. The giant dances in place beside those other symbols of the fantastic: the literary character and the cultural other. While fantasy in the miniature moves toward an individualized interiority, fantasy in the gigantic exteriorizes and communalizes what might otherwise be considered "the subjective."

For an overview of the ways in which the gigantic can be linked to the spirit of place and commercialism, we might turn to London, which has a particular relationship to the gigantic through legend and procession. In Geoffrey of Monmouth's *Chronicles*, London is founded by giants 1,008 years before the birth of Christ. According to legend, the city was originally called New Troy and was established by Brute, or Brutus, the younger son of Anthenor of Troy, who conquered the giant Albion and his equally gigantic troops. Brute killed Albion in hand-to-hand combat and took Albion's two brothers, Gog and Magog, in chains to the place where London now stands. Here he built a palace and had the two giants chained to the gate as porters. Frederick Fairholt, in his book on the Guild Hall giants, says that effigies of these giants were placed at the entrance to the London Guild Hall, which stands where Brute's palace once was. In Thomas Boreman's "Gigantick History" of the Guild Hall giants (2 volumes, each measuring 2 1/2 inches high and 1 1/2 inches broad), the legend varies slightly: "Corineus and Gogmagog were two brave giants, who nicely valued their honor, and exerted their whole strength and force in defiance of their liberty and country; so the City of London, by placing these their representatives in the Guildhall, emblematically declares that they will, like mighty giants, defend the honor of their country, and liberties of this their city, which excels all others, as much as those huge giants exceed in stature the common bulk of mankind."[37] From the fifteenth to the eighteenth century, accounts were written of the giants Corineus and Gogmagog and other giants being displayed on London Bridge to celebrate the public entry into the city of some distinguished person; they are also recorded as being used in the Lord Mayor's pageants and in Midsummer's Eve festivals. Puttenham, in his *Arte of English Poesie* (1589), writes of "Midsummer pageants in London where, to make the people wonder, are set forth great and uglie gyants, marching as if they were alive, and armed at all points, but within they are stuffed full of brown paper and tow, which the shrewd boyes, underpeeping, do guilefully discover, and turne to a great derision."[38]

Although the English giants frequently were used for occasions of pomp and solemnity, their secularity and profanity also are strongly marked. The pageants in which they appear are performed by trading companies; thus they seem to be descendants of the more ancient feast-day giants. Of all monsters or animals depicted in gigantic form, the dragon was the most popular in England and France; in most cases such dragons conveyed the idea of evil, sorcery, or heresy and were linked in legend to the patron saint of the town, who was said to have defeated the dragon in battle. Here we might be reminded, too, of the founding of Thebes, for the original citizens of that city were giants who sprang up from the ground where Cadmus had sown the teeth of a dragon. The dragon of Norwich was carried in mayoralty processions until 1832. Yet giants in human form were themselves often held to be evil figures associated with the pagan past. *A History of Winchester*, written in 1798, accuses the giants of Dunkirk and Douay of being symbolic of pagan giants who ate the inhabitants of the town until the town's patron saint destroyed them.[39] Thus, as was the case in twelfth- and thirteenth-century France, the giant continued to be associated with the inversion of orthodoxy and allegiance to the vernacular, decentralized, local political structure.

As the gigantic splits into the official parade and the unsanctioned festival, between central and local, sacred and secular respectively, it works to contribute to the creation of the new public spaces necessary to class society: the spaces of reproduction and production within which those classes define themselves by means of an exaggeration of boundaries. Fairholt records that the prosperous traders "rivalled the glories of the old nobility in the palaces they constructed for their Guildhalls: and having no pride of ancestry, they chose the legends of their old cities for display on public occasions."[40] Contrary to a feudal system of allegiances, allegiance here was directed toward the town and the middle class, which sustained the town's economic relations. The giants of Malines and Douai were popularly called Le Grand-Papa and were exhibited on pedestals, while a "family" of smaller giants, consisting of a father and mother, two daughters of different ages, and a young son, marched behind on foot. At Ath, Louvain, and Dunkirk, the town giants appeared as wedded pairs or family groups.[41] The allegiance of the people to this secular "Father" and his family is further illustrated in processions like that at Cassel, where the giant was followed by the tallest humans of the town, who were dressed as babies. The maintenance and presentation of the giants shifted during the Renaissance to secular hands; the gigantic served the functions of free trade and merchandising as it represented the guilds and as the occasions for its celebration became more and more commercial. The giants themselves were sometimes lent by the corporations of one town to another to "swell the public shows."[42]

The appearance of the gigantic within the context of the city must be linked as well to the creation of public *spectacle*. The spectacle provides a clear example of what Tadeusz Kowzan has called the artificialization of the sign: "Le spectacle transforme les signes naturels en signes artificiels, il a donc le pouvoir d''artificialiser' les signes."[43] The appropriation of the gigantic out of the natural landscape and its placement within the urban milieu of market relations marks a transition from the ambivalent (productive and destructive) forces of the natural to the reproductive and productive forces of class societies, forces that are seen as humanly controlled and thereby secularized. Thus social forms such as the culture's particular version of the family are correspondingly naturalized. The gigantic moves away from the magical and religious toward the instrumental and the material life of the body in this transition from sacred to secular folk culture. But with the advent of mechanical reproduction, participation in the spectacle becomes more distanced.

In *The Society of the Spectacle,* Guy Debord suggests:

> The origin of the spectacle is the loss of the unity of the world, and the gigantic expansion of the modern spectacle expresses the totality of this loss: the abstraction of all specific labor and the general abstraction of the entirety of production are perfectly translated in the spectacle, whose *mode of being concrete* is precisely abstraction. In the spectacle, one part of the world *represents itself* before the world and is superior to it. The spectacle is nothing more than the common language of this separation. What ties the spectators together is no more than an irreversible relation at the very center which maintains their isolation. The spectacle reunites the separate, but reunites it *as separate*.[44]

For example, we might say that in contrast to the participatory experience of the carnival world, the parade marks a step away from the time of the body and its labor. The parade is the product of official discourse, the discourse of a history alienated from agrarian time.

Unlike the carnivalistic pageant, where the crowd moves with the image, the image in the parade is exaggerated by the very distance placed between it and its viewer. While the carnival plays on metaphors of display and concealment, on a licentious and sexual shifting between the official and its inverse, between performer as crowd and crowd as performer, the parade seeks a seamless presentation, the smooth movement of official apparatuses toward infinity at either end. We do not see the true origin or conclusion of the parade without experiencing a corresponding disillusionment with its power. Properly viewed, the parade's limits are beyond our own particular moment of viewing, beyond even "the shrewd boyes, underpeeping." And between us and its moving face is the perfectly uniform line of the police barricade, a line designed to perfect the parade's spatial closure as much as to protect the parade from the interruptions of inversion or speech. We might say that the barricade is to the parade as the cover is to the book, providing integrity and an aura of completeness.

Similarly, the spectacle in mass culture exists in a separateness which locates history outside lived reality at the same time that it locates lived reality within the realm of consumer time, outside the time of production. Debord writes that

> time for the consumption of images, the medium of all commodities, is inseparably the field where the instruments of the spectacle fully take over, as well as the goal which these instruments present globally as the place and the central aspect of all particular consumptions: it is known that the saving of time constantly sought by modern society— whether in the form of the speed of transport vehicles or in the use of dried soups—is positively translated for the population of the United States by the fact that merely the contemplation of television occupies an average of three to six hours a day.[45]

Thus a radical transition has taken place, from the separated, yet participatory, time of carnival and its inversions, to the distanced and open-ended historical time of the parade and its official narrative, to the distanced and closed sphere of consumer time, where the gigantic is displaced from the human to the commodity itself. In face-to-face communities the final movement of the giant is that of exposure, the revelation of the machinery of the gigantic. But the appropriation of the gigantic on the part of commodity relations marks the magicalization of the commodity, the final masking of the gigantic apparatus which is the nature of class relations themselves. Here is the complement and the inverse of our view of the miniature, which presented a concrete materiality leading to an abstract (because radically separate) perception. The gigantification of commodity relations is experienced as an abstract materiality that is equally separate from the body: the gigantic sale, the parade of values.

The Gigantic Described

The giant is represented through movement, through being in time. Even in the ascription of the still landscape to the giant, it is the activities of the giant, his or her legendary actions, that have resulted in the observable trace. In contrast to the still and perfect universe of the miniature, the gigantic represents the order and disorder of historical forces. The consumerism of the miniature is the consumerism of the classic; it is only fitting that consumer culture appropriates the gigantic whenever change is desired. We want the antique miniature and the gigantic new. And while our daydream may be to animate the miniature, we admire the fall or the death, the stopping, of the giant.

The preindustrial giant is the giant of natural forces in all their tempestuousness. This is the giant in Blake's prophetic books (the giant without constraints—prolific and producer) and the giant of Goya (both creator and destroyer). The gigantic is viewed as a consuming force, the antithesis of the miniature, whose objects offer themselves to the viewer in a utopia of perfect, because individual, consumption. The giant is frequently seen as a devourer, and even, as in the case of Cyclops, as a cannibal. In Eskimo and other North American Indian mythologies, the giants may be either human, animal, or bird in form; usually they are males, and they are almost always cannibalistically inclined.[46] In Caesar (*De Bello Gallico*, Book VI, Chapter XVI) there is an account of Druid practices of human sacrifice in which large wickerwork images were filled with living men and set on fire, thus allowing the giant to "consume his victims."[47] In his *History of Winchester* Milner railed against the Dunkirk and Douay practice of, on certain holidays, building up an immense figure of basketwork and canvas to the height of forty or fifty feet to represent a huge giant. Inside were placed a number of living men who caused the basket to be moved from place to place.[48] And in Lilliput, Gulliver as giant is similarly "reduced" to his bodily functions, a beast of consumption capable of producing much waste and destruction if unleashed.

The literary depiction of the gigantic involves the same problems of detail and comparison as that of the miniature, but whereas description of the miniature approaches an infinity of relevant detail, description of the gigantic frequently focuses on movement and its attendant consequences. Thus, while the Lilliput section of *Gulliver's*

Travels tends toward the stillness and transcendence of the anthropological model, the Brobdingnag section tends toward the partial and immediate experience of the diary. The description of Lilliput
moves toward scientific discourse in its transcendent concern with
pattern, design, and replicability. The Lilliputian world is trivial in its
comprehensiveness; its time is cyclical time, the time of past and
present meshed, the time of lyric. In contrast, the description of Brobdingnag tends toward narrative suspense in its concern with the immediate, the partial, and the surprising action. Its temporality moves
toward an unknown closure. Because the first-person narrative voice
is in the present looking back, we assume that Gulliver will survive,
yet we don't know how many or what nature of obstacles he will face
before the end of the story. The observer is subjected to manipulation
and misunderstanding, just as Gulliver is condescended to by the
king.

Tragedy in the first book is the threat to Gulliver's vision; tragedy
in the second book is the threat of consumption, of having the entire
body destroyed by being made into an object or small animal. After
his road show in the farmer's box, Gulliver becomes the Queen's pet:
"The Queen giving great Allowance for my Defectiveness in speaking, was however surprised at so much Wit and good Sense in so
diminutive an Animal." He is housed in a traveling closet arranged
with doll-size furnishings, and the King "was strongly bent to get me
a Woman of my own Size, by whom I might propogate the Breed: But
I think I should rather have died than undergone the Disgrace of
leaving a posterity to be kept in cages like tame Canary Birds; and
perhaps in time sold about the Kingdom to Persons of Quality for
Curiosities." We might note that the contemporary science-fiction
story *Land of the Giants* similarly portrays the capture of humans by
giants and the giants' desire to keep the Earth creatures in cages amid
collections of small animals. Just as Gulliver is continually threatened
by the natural in Brobdingnag (among his adversaries are a cat, rats,
hail, a dog, a kite, a frog, a monkey, and an eagle, along with the
uncultured or anomalous human—the baby and the dwarf), so the
Earth creatures in *Land of the Giants* are threatened by a cat, a snake,
rats, and puppies as much as by the high-technology weapons of the
giants. It is significant that the major victories against the giants in the
latter text are made through the use of fire, a quantity and quality
which, like any element, cannot be permanently miniaturized, and
which presents the ultimate image of consumption.

The most horrible images in the Brobdingnag section of *Gulliver's
Travels* have to do with women's bodies as images of the consuming.
Particularly the breast, which often is so overly cultured and literally

disembodied as an image to be consumed, is inverted here into a frightening symbol of growth and contamination. The breast turns from nurturer to destroyer. First, there is the depiction of the nurse's breast: "I must confess no Object ever disgusted me so much as the Sight of her monstrous Breast, which I cannot tell what to compare with, so as to give the curious Reader an Idea of its Bulk, Shape and Colour. It stood prominent six Foot, and could not be less than sixteen in Circumference. The Nipple was about half the Bigness of my Head, and the Hue both of that and the Dug so varified with Spots, Pimples and Freckles, that nothing could appear more nauseous."[49] Later Gulliver sees a group of beggars who exhibit "the most horrible Spectacles that ever an European Eye beheld." Prominent among these "there was a Woman with Cancer in her Breast, swelled to a monstrous Size, full of Holes, in two or three of which I could have easily crept, and covered my whole Body."[50] Similarly, when the Maids of Honor strip him and lay him "at full Length in their Bosoms" he becomes much disgusted by the offensive smell coming from their skins.[51] The breasts represent a superfluity of nature; they will swallow Gulliver in their immediateness. And the Queen, who at this point controls Gulliver's fate, becomes the most horrible of these devouring female giants: "the Queen (who had indeed but a weak Stomach) took up at one Mouthful, as much as a dozen *English* Farmers could eat at a Meal, which to me was for some time a very nauseous Sight. She would craunch the Wing of a Lark, Bones and all, between her Teeth, although it were nine Times as large as that of a full grown Turkey; and put a Bit of Bread in her Mouth, as big as two twelve-penny Loaves. She drank out of a Golden Cup, above a Hogshead at a Draught."[52]

Gulliver of course notes that such disgust is a matter of perspective and that the fairness of English ladies and the perfections of Lilliputian physiognomy are a matter of point of view and its restriction of knowledge. Here we have the basis for the idealization of the miniature, its erasure of disorder, of nature and history, and the basis for the grotesque realism of the gigantic. Microscopic description of the small tends toward the surreal and the fantastic as it both enlarges its object and "makes it strange." Consider the description of the contents of Gulliver's pockets in Book I, the snuff box for example: "In the left Pocket, we saw a huge Silver Chest, with a Cover of the same Metal, which we, the Searchers, were not able to lift. We desired it should be opened; and one of us stepping into it, found himself up to the mid Leg in a sort of Dust, some part whereof flying up to our Faces, set us both a sneezing for several Times together"; or the description of the pistols as a "hollow Pillar of Iron, about the Length of a Man, fastened to a strong Piece of Timber, larger than the Pillar; and upon one side of the Pillar were huge Pieces of Iron sticking out, cut into strange Figures."[53] The modern writer Francis Ponge conducts a similar experiment in his "Notes Toward A Shell":

> A shell is a little thing, but I can make it look bigger by replacing it where I found it, on the vast expanse of sand. For if I take a handful of sand and observe what little remains in my hand after most of it has run out between my fingers, if I observe a few grains, then each grain individually, at the moment none of the grains seems small to me any longer, and soon the shell itself—this oyster shell or limpet or razor clam—will appear to be an enormous monument, both colossal and intricate like the temples of Angkor, or the church of Saint-Maclou, or the Pyramids, and with a meaning far stranger than these unquestioned works of man.[54]

Exaggeration here is not simply a matter of change in scale, for the change in scale and quantity is significant only in relation to a corresponding change in quality and complexity. The more complicated the object, the more intricate, and the more these complications and intricacies are attended to, the "larger" the object is in significance. As Ponge demonstrates, complexity is a matter of context and history as much as it is a matter of number of elements, for the assignation of elements is a cultural process: the description determines the form of the object. The more synecdochic the description, the closer we are to a cultural hierarchy of description. When description moves away from synecdoche toward the "spelled out" and overarticulated, the effect is an exaggeration of the object through estrangement.

What often happens in the depiction of the gigantic is a severing of the synecdoche from its referent, or whole. The breasts of Brobdingnag have a frightening existence as objects or organisms separable from the body. The partial vision of the observer prohibits closure of the object. Our impulse is to create an environment for the miniature, but such an environment is impossible for the gigantic: instead the gigantic becomes our environment, swallowing us as nature or history swallows us. In the representation of the gigantic within public space it is therefore important that the gigantic be situated above and over, that the transcendent position be denied the viewer. Traditionally, this function has been met by public sculpture, a sculpture of commemoration and celebration that looks to a definitive kind of contextualization, a relation between work and environment which we similarly see in earth art's concern with the relation between site and nonsite. In painting and in literature the gigantic is a matter of the readjustment of depicted figure to depicted landscape, but the sculpture's three-dimensionality forces it to account for the immediate relation between its materiality and the human scale of the viewer.

Distinct from the domestic arts and the decontextualized art of the collection/museum, the art of public space is an eternalized parade, a fixing of the symbols of public life, of the state, within a milieu of the abstract authority of the polis. The reduction of the individual viewer in the face of the public monument is all the more evident in the function of the inscription; one is expected to read the instructions for perception of the work—to acknowledge the fallen, the victorious, the heroic, and be taken up in the history of place. All public monuments of this type are monuments to death and the individual's prostration before history and authority. On the other hand, the nineteenth- and twentieth-century obsessions with science, technology, and the occupation of the sky have resulted in a different form of public sculpture and monument. The very fact that you can climb inside and to the top of the Eiffel Tower, the Statue of Liberty, or the statue of William Penn on the tower of Philadelphia's City Hall, simultaneously speaks to an abstract transcendence above and beyond the viewer and the possibility that the viewer can unveil the giant, can find the machinery hidden in the god and approach a transcendent view of the city himself or herself. It is a symbol of the corporate impulse toward absolute authority that the president's office and penthouse suite are often on the top floor of the skyscraper, while the public observatory deck is on the floor immediately below.

The gigantic art of the public space is an art of culture, not an art of nature; its forms and themes are taken from the life of the city that surrounds it. If the unleashed sea is the essential metaphor of the romantic sublime, the orchestrated fountain is the essential metaphor of the art of public space. Thus far in this section we have seen a movement from the legendary figures of natural force and destruction associated with the founding of cities and exhibited in pageant to the "heroic" statues of the public square to the abstract sculpture preferred by the corporate state. The town giant memorializes the imposition of central authority and, at the same time, the persistence of vernacular tradition in the face of and in the service of that authority. And like the town giant, the hero on the horse also symbolizes the reproduction of the social. In this case, a historical narrative, or instructions for the generation of ideology, is presented: the founding fathers, we may be assured, are eternally protecting us from the incursions of the *outside*, be it nature or the cultural other. The hero on the horse memorializes the status difference between those who can afford to ride and those who must walk as much as it celebrates the subjection of nature. In pageant and memorial, the giant states the differences between official and vernacular discourse; differences between state, sacred, and secular, and the system of class relations legitimated by particular versions of history. As we shall see as we turn to the abstractions of pop art, contemporary public forms of the gigantic serve an analogous ideological function as they both memorialize and call into question our relation to the system of commodities.

Leo Lowenthal's studies of popular culture traced a shift from the nineteenth-century hero of the sphere of production—Horatio Alger in the guise of Carnegie, Mellon, and others—to the twentieth-century hero of the sphere of consumption—the hero as an image to be consumed, the movie star or the media personality.[55] Lowenthal correspondingly traces the movement of these aesthetic images, these representative and representational forms of the subject, away from the vernacular and into the abstract space of mass communication. The fact that such subjects are "larger than life" is not a result of their historical acts so much as it is a matter of their medium of presentation; the representation fully effaces its referent; there is only a series of images related to each other in a chainlike, cumulative formation. And that formation, that generation of sign by means of sign, provides the aesthetic corollary for the generative capacity of commodity relations.

This generative capacity of the sign is the phenomenon addressed by Warhol in his 1964 piece *Jackie*, a liquitex and silkscreen reproduction of sixteen familiar photographs of Jacqueline Kennedy at the time of her husband's assassination and funeral. The effect is a neutralization of content, a presentation of the image as gadget or ready-made emotion. As Warhol himself says, "When you see a gruesome picture over and over again it doesn't really have any effect."[56] All experience becomes vicarious experience in spectacle forms, and the possibilities for the exaggeration of scale and significance are multiplied with the distance of each representation from lived reality. The relativizing capacity of context and history and the relativizing capacity of the body are absent to the viewer invented by spectacle.

It is important to remember that the mechanical reproduction of art objects, the movement away from the authenticity of the original that in fact might be seen as *creating* the authenticity of the original, results in the susceptibility of art itself to this mode of exaggeration. As recent psychoanalytic work has told us, repetition, in fact, creates a reproduction which initiates the very aura of the real. In an article on the dearth of modern monumental sculpture, Barbara Rose writes:

> Our idea of the monumentality of Picasso's works is not dependent on actual scale; in fact, in my case an appreciation of their monumentality was largely a result of never having seen the originals, but of having experienced them as slides or photographs. In this way, the comparison

with the human body never came up, so that the epoch-making 1928–29 *Construction in Wire*, although a scant twenty inches high in actuality, was as large as the imagination cared to make it. . . . The photograph, as Michelangelo Antonioni was scarcely the first to realize, permits a blowup to any scale, even the most gargantuan. Through the agency of the photograph, the viewer can mentally transform the intimate living-room art of early modern sculpture into the outdoor monuments Duchamp-Villon envisioned.[57]

We might also consider here the "monumental" small sculptures by Henry Moore. Rose's experience is that of the tourist who finds the representation of culture in the guidebook and the postcard more significant and more attractive than the true culture, contaminated by history and difference, can ever be.

The paradoxes of this problem of the proliferation of images are most clearly articulated in pop art, which has taken its place within the abstract space of mass culture and the mass spectacle at the same time that it has usurped the space of public sculpture. The Oldenburgs that dot the urban landscapes of Chicago and Philadelphia are the legendary giants, the topographical mascots, of those cities. They are relatives of other forms of the architecture-of-the-above, particularly the billboard and the neon sign, those forms which are all façade. And they are representations of mechanical reproduction arrested into authenticity by being "original objects." We see this paradox of "the authentic object" moving out of mechanical reproduction in the phenomenon of people asking Andy Warhol to autograph "real" Campbell's soup cans. Thus, as Lucy Lippard and others have noted, the authenticity of the artist, as well as the authenticity of the artwork, becomes tenuous. In the movement from Jasper Johns's *Ballantine Cans* (1960), which is made of bronze, hand-painted, and displayed on a bronze base, to Warhol's 1964 exhibit of boxes at the Stable Gallery, where piles of wooden boxes silkscreened with various brand insignias represented piled supermarket cartons, the work of art's mode of production has been mapped upon the mode of production of its object—the consumer good. Johns's piece still clearly speaks of its singularity, its marked-off-ness, while Warhol's disappears into a chain of signifiers stretched in both directions toward referent and image. The result is a consumer aesthetic of mechanical reproduction which moves simultaneously toward art and commercial goods: the mechanization of the artwork (Warhol's famous line, "I want to be a machine," and the confusion over whether Rosenquist was in fact a billboard painter or a billboard artist) and the aestheticization of the consumer good.

Pop art's primary qualities of gigantification and novelty, its obsession with the mechanical possibilities of exaggeration, and its anti-classicism, are the modern expression of the qualities of gigantifica-tion we find in previous uses of the spectacle—the articulation of quantity over quality, of "façade" over "content," of materiality and movement over mediation and transcendence. But whereas the gi-gantic in landscape is approached as a relic of a more violent and natural era, and while the town giant eventually loses its ferocity and acquires the sentimental qualities of the vernacular at the same time that it speaks to a historically determined future, the gigantic in pop art celebrates the proliferation of the new. As Lippard has observed about "New York Pop," "Use connotes the past, and the past, even the immediate past, evokes memories. Pop objects determinedly for-go the uniqueness acquired by time. They are not yet worn or left over. Every Campbell's soup can looks like every other Campbell's soup can since it has had no time to acquire character; every TV commercial on one channel at a given moment is the same, whether it is seen in Saugatuck or in Sioux City."[58] The pop gigantic exists in the abstract space of mass production. The human body is not gigantic here; the image is, and the image is an object whether its referent is in fact an object or not. Unlike the use of objects in painting to simulate the interior world of the domestic (the still life), and even unlike the surrealistic collage, which still tends toward the evocative and nostalgic in its choice of objects, the pop object resists the symbolic; it exists in an abstract and autonomous space, a space of the façade, of consumption without "meaning." It is the next-to-the-last stage in the secularization and denaturalization of the gigantic, for in its wholesale rejection of temporality, pop becomes subject to tem-porality, to the process of periodization which attaches symbolic meaning to its context of production. Just as the location of the pop object in space makes it vulnerable to symbolization (e.g., the town mascot), so does its particular form of iconography, as well as its accompanying manifestoes (or lack of them), make it vulnerable to "dating." As we shall see in our final chapter, the nemesis of pop is the nostalgia for novelty which we find in the contradictions of kitsch and camp.

The Lie: Gigantism in Language

The exaggeration of the gigantic in three-dimensional representa-tion is obviously limited by materials and their relation to design. Once the representation is made through language or paint on can-vas, the gap between image and the physical world makes exaggera-tion constrained by social convention rather than by engineering. The work's "internal" system of signs forms a field of relativity within which elements are displayed. But it would be naïve to assume that such aesthetic/social constraints play no part in the determination of scale. When Barbara Rose complains that many artists feel they can "blow up" any design—in her words, "to understand the pitfalls of such speculation, one need only entertain for a moment the nightmarish vision of a fifty-foot Degas bronze dancer"[59]—she is articulating the aesthetic constraints offered by the subject and form of the work. We cannot have a *mammoth* petite and graceful ballerina unless we want a parody, for the history of the depiction of ballerinas has fixed their relation to scale. Indeed, our simultaneous and transcendent view of the clockwork precision of the classical ballet has resulted in a strong tendency toward miniaturization here. Thus we may also begin to ascribe Joseph Cornell's affinity for nineteenth-century ballet to formal as well as nostalgic and thematic considerations.

We have emphasized the skewed relation of language to physical scale, to the fact that description of the miniature and description of the gigantic rely on internal systems of comparisons and social notions of the hierarchy of detail. Describing something small involves the same type of work as describing something enormous: the work of comparison and selection of detail and example. These aesthetic conventions of description arise out of the constraints of making fictions, the constraints of genre. Hence, when Florence Moog publishes an article in *Scientific American* entitled "Why Gulliver is a Bad Biologist,"[60] she misses the point. A human the size of a Brobdingnagian may be a physical impossibility, but a fictive human the size of a Brobdingnagian is absolutely appropriate, particularly in relation to the physical impossibility and fictive possibility of its inverse, the Lilliputian. It was the Lilliputians as much as Swift who made the invention of the Brobdingnagians necessary.

These considerations of aesthetic conventions in relation to exaggeration bring us to the problem of "aesthetic size," the relation between genre and significance. In Chapter 7 of the *Poetics*, Aristotle writes:

> But, besides this, a picture, or any other composite object, if it is to be beautiful, must not only have its parts properly arranged, but be of an appropriate size; for beauty depends on size and structure.
> Accordingly, a minute picture cannot be beautiful (for when our vision has almost lost its sense of time it becomes confused); nor can an immense one (for we cannot take it all in together, and so our vision loses its unity and wholeness)—imagine a picture a thousand miles long! So, just as there is a proper size for bodies and pictures (a size

that can be kept in view), there is also a proper amplitude for fables (what can be kept well in one's mind).[61]

This argument might be seen as a cognitive one, implying that complexity and simplicity are functions of the intellectual capacity of the viewer. Yet it can also be seen as a sociological one, implying that the proper amplitude of a form depends upon the expectations of genre. In a nonliterate culture the qualification "what can be kept well in one's mind" is an aesthetic value serving the particular and necessary functions of memory. Any work composed in such a way that it was unmemorable would, of course, quickly lose its social life. With the advent of mechanical reproduction, the text can acquire a number of properties, from seriality to disjunctiveness, properties that are made possible through its physical form. Repetition forms the most obvious example of this transformation, for whereas repetition may be a major structural and thematic principle of oral art, it tends to be a minor ludic principle in written works. The physical size of a work is dependent upon the social function of the genre; the economy of the proverb and of other forms of *multum in parvo* arises from their situation in the immediate context of conversation and the turn-taking rules prevalent in that context. The structure of *War and Peace* allows for maximum variation and complication at least in part because of the leisure time that is available to its readers and because of the physical status of the book, which permits "dipping," rereading, and the mapping of consecutive chapters onto consecutive situations of reading. Similarly, Bakhtin has traced the divergences between the "banquet dialogue" (through Menippean satire to carnival to the Dostoevskian novel) and the aphoristic thinking of the Enlightenment; he describes the first as a display of tensions between social classes, and the second as an idealization of a unified consciousness and, consequently, a valorization of the notion of individuality.[62] It would be naïve to argue, as Bertram Jessup does in his article "Aesthetic Size," that "size itself can be felt as quality, or yields quality. What is needed is a qualification of the principle of aesthetic size so that it may be maintained that a large work, *otherwise equal in quality*, is superior to a small one."[63] There is no "otherwise equal in quality," no stance in which the social function of the work can be disregarded. We cannot speak of the small, or miniature, work independent of the social values expressed toward private space—particularly, of the ways the domestic and the interior imply the social formation of an interior subject. And we cannot speak of the grand and the gigantic independent of social values expressed toward nature and the public and exterior life of the city. Aesthetic size cannot be divorced from social function and social values.

Aside from their manipulation of length and complexity in relation to scale, works of verbal art can effect what Joyce called the technique of "gigantism" in the position they take with regard to the relation between the world and the word. In the Cyclops chapter of *Ulysses*, for example, Joyce arranges a pageant of language made up of the discourse of bourgeois society; that discourse's legal, medical, parliamentary, and scientific jargon, as well as the exaggerations of popular journalism, is put on display within the scene at Barney Kiernan's. In the schemes he circulated to his friends Linati, Gorman, and Gilbert, Joyce wrote that the scene in the tavern, characterized by the technique of "gigantism," was meant to be symbolic of "nation, state, religion, dynasty, idealism, exaggeration, fanaticism and collectivity."[64] Joyce thus presents the literary equivalent of the gigantic we have seen in other forms of representation. And because of the abstractions of language, the possibilities for the "blowing up" of significance are heightened even further. Such fictions can exaggerate the gap between signified and signifier, and between contexts of firsthand experience and the progressively distanced contexts of fictions. The more fictive the context extablished by the genre, the greater the possibility and potential for exaggeration. The best example of this type of exaggeration is, of course, the hyperbole and its extended form, the tall tale.

In Rabelais's work, language becomes so surfeited that it erupts into the list or the list's double, the collection. In the colloquy between Pantagruel and Panurge on "the virtues of Triboulet" ("A fatal fool/ A high-toned fool/ A natural fool/ A B sharp and B flat fool")[65] there is a threat of an infinite series of juxtaposed adjectives, as if language could clone itself into perpetuity without the necessity of returning "to earth." This hyperbolic language characteristic of the carnival grotesque arises out of folk tradition, and thus the feast of the body in Rabelais has its corollary in the feast of words and images offered during market celebrations. To further examine this earlier (and simultaneous) folk tradition, we might turn to one of the earliest collections of oral tall tales existing in an extant manuscript, "La Nouvelle Fabrique des Excellents Traits de Vérité," assembled by a Norman monk under the pseudonym Philippe d'Alcripe and first published in Paris in 1579, a generation after Rabelais. Although the tall-tale tradition has largely been thought to be a North American phenomenon, Gerald Thomas makes an argument in his translation and analysis of "La Nouvelle Fabrique" that there is a much older European tall-tale tradition. The d'Alcripe manuscript apparently arose from the telling sessions in a local tavern. D'Alcripe addresses his readers: "So, as they say, two useful words are enough, and yet I say quickly that it was not quite a hundred and a half years ago that being in Lyons, in flesh and bones, in the company of many boon companions, my good friends, while having a good feed at Mother Gillette's and drinking the freshest and the best, many merry stories and amusing tales, some fresh and others salty were told: there was as much crying as laughing over them."[66] As in Rabelais, the tall-tale tradition incorporates the themes of the gigantic which we have been enumerating: the grotesque, the body, feasting, leisure, the exterior and the public over the domestic; the vernacular and secular over the official and sacred. In Europe, and later in America, the casual tall-tale session in the tavern becomes formalized into the Liar's Club. Thomas writes that in the eighteenth century, provincial clubs arose in France and the Netherlands for this purpose. In 1783, for example, La Societé des Canaris was founded by men who cultivated songs in the Walloon dialect. This club later became a Cercle des Minteûrs (Liars' Circle) and, in 1834, Li Cabinet des Mintes (The Cabinet of Joyful Lies). In order to join, one had to successfully narrate a tall tale in dialect.[67] Thus the tall-tale session might be seen as the everyday equivalent of the public market days that involved a parading of the gigantic and a concomitant celebration of the vernacular. In both there is an interruption of the temporality of work, an inversion of official values into the vernacular, and a festive display of accumulation over balance.

In folklore, the tall tale bears a particular relation to its context of telling. Unlike the colloquy in the written work, which assumes a standard of exaggeration and remains there, the tall-tale session begins with understatement and proceeds with each narrative element to move farther away from reality as defined by everyday lived experience. A passage describing a hyperbole session from Zora Neale Hurston's study of Afro-American folklore in Florida, *Mules and Men*, might serve as an example:

> [Joe answered:] "Man, he's too ugly. If a spell of sickness ever tried to slip up on him, he'd skeer it into a three weeks' spasm."
> Blue Baby stuck in his oar and said: "He ain't so ugly. Ye all jus' ain't seen no real ugly man. Ah seen a man so ugly till he could get behind a jimpson weed and hatch monkies."
> Everybody laughed and moved closer together. Then Officer Richardson said: "Ah seen a man so ugly till they had to spread a sheet over his head at night so sleep could slip up on him."
> They laughed some more, then Clifford Ulmer said: "Ah'm goin' to talk with my mouth wide open. Those men y'all been talkin' 'bout

wasn't ugly at all. Those was pretty men. Ah knowed one so ugly till you could throw him in the Mississippi river and skim ugly for six months."

"Give Cliff de little dog," Jim Allen said. "He done tole the biggest lie."[68]

On this particular morning the men are waiting for a foreman who never shows up, so they spend the morning *bookooing* (from *beaucoup*, talking loudly and aimlessly) and "telling lies." Clifford moves this passage toward closure because his is the most extreme exaggeration. And yet, like all tall-tale sessions, this set of lies threatens infinity. The context of the tall-tale session works cumulatively. Each lie sets a plateau for the following lie to take as a basis for the possible. (Here we see the appropriateness of Pinocchio's magic nose.) Hence the fiction progressively moves from understatement to the most impossible and improbable of statements. Mostly a male genre, the tall tale is associated with the worker in a period of leisure. In contrast to the lived experience of work, an experience at least traditionally known "firsthand" through the body, the tall tale recounts/invents experiences that are possible only in a fictive universe. The fantastic here is ironically underscored by the juxtaposition of a first-person voice with fabulous events, or by the recounting of an "obvious lie" as legend—that is, true within some historical past. It has been noted in both Europe and North America that those who tell tall tales are often sailors, hunters, fishermen, emigrants, immigrants, soldiers, and, occasionally, farmers.[69] These situations involve considerable distance between the workplace and the home. Often they are typified by solitary outdoor labor. They are "outside" positions in the sense that they are far from the domestic and domesticated modes of sociability. "The one that got away" is all the more credible because we have only the narrator as witness, yet all the more incredible because it is beyond the range of the audience's experience. Thus the narrator plays upon his own credibility in a pattern of understatement and overstatement. Because of this positioning in context, the tall tale presents the generic antithesis of the aphorism. Aphoristic thinking moves toward transcendence and away from the immediate context of situation, seeking to subsume the situation beneath "the rule," but the tall tale is caught up in its own narrative process, a process of invention through progressive stages. The tall tale is nearly unquotable; each of its elements is tied within the narrative structure of the overall tale, and the tale itself is tied into a contextual structure from which it cannot be detached without a considerable loss of effect. Hence the literary tall tale cannot employ the improvisational techniques of the oral tall-tale session.

The idea of a "New World," the enormity of the wilderness and its demand for a type of physical labor correspondingly extraordinary, has been the locus for a particularly strong and widespread tall-tale tradition in North America. The tall tale is both a genre of the frontier, with its expansive form, and a genre of emigration, of experience conveyed second- to thirdhand, of "the report." The tradition of fabulous travel literature, which can be traced to the Middle Ages, via such works as *The Letter from Prester John* and *Mandeville's Travels*, has its North American equivalent in oral travelers' accounts, in occupational tall-tale traditions, and in the written versions of these narratives found in popular literature. Since the settlement of North America came in a postliterate period, oral and written forms of exaggeration arose at the same time. But it was in oral contexts—the leisure contexts of the lumber camp at night, the general store, the community liar's bench—that such tales arose. Once the written form predominantly supplanted the oral form, such tales were viewed nostalgically, even sentimentally.[70] Seventeenth- and early-eighteenth-century settlers' accounts of mythical beasts and vegetation, of Native Americans possessing magic and sorcery, of the richness of the soil and the miraculous powers of the water, were supplanted from the late eighteenth century onward by both oral and written occupational tales centering on the frontiersman (Davy Crockett), the riverboat captain (Mike Fink), the lumberjack (Paul Bunyan), the cowboy (Pecos Bill), the sailor (Old Stormalong), the steelworker (Joe Magarac), the wheat farmer (Febold Feboldson), the oil worker (Gib Morgan), the guide (Jim Bridger), the farmer (Hathaway Jones), the railroad laborer (John Henry), and the engineer (Casey Jones). The historical existence of Crockett, Fink, Henry, and both Hathaway and Casey Jones does not make the cycles of narratives associated with such figures significantly less fantastic, for the tale relies on internal rather than external criteria of realism. These characters are heroes of production, supplanting the Old World giants of the natural. For example, the following literary tall tale of Febold Feboldson is etiological, like the European giants' tales, but it also emphasizes the tremendous productive capacity of the giant:

> Because Nebraska, in those days, was a treeless expanse of prairie, Febold realized that he would have to find trees in another locale if he were to build the log cabin he contemplated. The hardy pioneer started west and walked to the Redwood Forest in California before he found trees which he considered suitable. Febold picked a dozen choice trees, pulled them up by their roots, tied them securely with a huge log chain, and started back to Nebraska. When he got home, he was astounded to discover that the treetops had worn themselves out from

being dragged halfway across the continent. Even to this day, one can still see stretches of red soil and sand between California and Nebraska. Those Redwood trees were ground to powder as Febold dragged them along.

He simply shrugged and said, "Oh, well, live and learn." However, he did regret that he had wasted three days walking to and from California for nothing but a dozen tree stumps.[71]

Thus, although the Old World giants represented the unleashed forces of nature, these North American figures are often famous for taming nature. Feboldson reduces giant redwoods to sawdust, and Pecos Bill is depicted as wearing a ten-foot rattlesnake around his neck for an ornament, riding on the backs of mountain lions and cyclones, and raising his horse Widow Maker from colthood on nitroglycerine and dynamite.[72]

The position of these New World giants within the occupational vernacular of either region or ethnicity makes them symbolic of the collective life. "Paul Bunyan's Day," for example, is held in several logging communities in Minnesota, New Hampshire, and Washington State. Richard Dorson records that "at these ceremonies the carved dummy of a majestic Paul presides over an active scene of logging contests and woodsmen sports, such as birling, canoe-tilting, log-bucking, log-rolling, and log-chopping, or winter pastimes of skiing, bobsledding, and ice skating. Sometimes images of Paul are fashioned from snow or metal, or men of heroic proportions play Bunyan for a day. So fast and far had the 'myth' spiralled upward in the popular imagination that figures of Old Paul adorned both the New York and California World's Fairs of 1939."[73] The legends associated with Paul Bunyan also connect his figure to images of feasting and unlicensed consumption. J. Frank Dobie writes in a story entitled "Royal Feasting": "The immense camps were wonders for good eating and lodging as well as for gigantic labors. Feeding his men well was a mania for Paul. It kept one freighting outfit busy all the time hauling off prime stoves from the cook shack. The men were so fond of bean soup that finally Joe Mufferton had the wagons unload their beans in a geyser, and the geyser stewed up soup for a whole season. A dozen flunkies with sides of bacon strapped to their feet skated over the gridirons to keep them greased for the hot cakes that Paul's men loved so well."[74] Similarly, the most prominent modern urban giant, "Mose the Bowery B'hoy," for sport drank drayloads of beer at one sitting and, with the fumes of his two-foot cigar, blew ships down the East River.[75] Feasting, physical strength, and connection with local tradition are the primary characteristics of these secular and occupational giants. John Henry's tragic battle against the abstract infinity of machine production offers closure to these accounts as a living tradition and marks the beginning of the nostalgic distancing of the gigantic.

The twentieth century has signaled the appropriation of the sphere of the gigantic by a centralized mode of commercial advertising. Whereas the early figures like Crockett are valorized as individual heroes and as symbols of community values, Pecos Bill, Joe Magarac, and Febold Feboldson were invented by "local color writers" to sell more newspapers and magazines. Bunyan was made famous by an advertising executive for the Red River Lumber Company who prepared a pamphlet containing Bunyan stories punctuated with testaments to the company's product.[76] This appropriation of the gigantic away from the vernacular by the domain of commodity advertising marks the gigantic's transition into an abstract space of production. Contemporary giants such as "the Jolly Green Giant" or "Mr. Clean" are nothing more than their products. Behind them we see not labor but frozen peas and the smell of disinfectant; commodities are naturalized and made magically to appear by the narrative of advertising itself. Such giants are symbolic of a transition from production to anonymity, of the transformation of leisure and production into consumption. Similarly, the architecture of the sign (it is possible, for example, in southern New Jersey to give someone the directions "Turn left at the champagne bottle. If you pass the dinosaur you've gone too far") marks the subsuming of lived relations regarding space and shelter to the abstract image of the commodity. The names of grocery chains alone—Giant, Star, Acme—speak to this abstraction of the exchange economy. To complete this process, the local-color hero becomes the symbol of the resort, or "fantasy island," and thus is incorporated into the spectacle of consumption. Disney's worlds become metaspectacles of the spectrum of decontextualized vernacular giants. Thus in late capitalism we see the incorporation of the gigantic into the sphere of private industrial production as it is translated into the pseudo-labor of consumption, and a simultaneous transference of the gigantic's sensual and consuming ethic to the sphere.

Of necessity, our discussion of the miniature took place in the shadow of the gigantic. Now as we conclude our discussion of the gigantic—its relation to landscape, to the exteriority of nature and the city, its place within systems of representation—we find ourselves once again at the place of origin for any investigation of exaggeration: the site of the body. Traditionally, the body has served as our primary mode of understanding and perceiving scale. We have seen earlier in this chapter the ways in which the image of the body can be projected upon the landscape, giving it form and definition. The world in English is measured by the body—spans of hands and feet, a yard the length from nose to fingers at the end of an outstretched arm. Similarly, objects under a use-value economy cannot be defined aside from the terms of the body. The world of tools is a world of handles, arms, blades, and legs. We have only to think of the scythe as it both replaces and graphically represents the bent back of the reaper, or of the fist of the hammer, the clawed hand of the cultivator. This is the image of the body as implement, as moving in and through the environment in such a way that the material world is a physical extension of the needs and purposes of the body. But this relation between the body and the world takes place only in the domain of the physical space actually occupied by the body, the domain of immediate lived experience. The miniature allows us only visual access to surface and texture; it does not allow movement through space. Inversely, the gigantic envelops us, but is inaccessible to lived experience. Both modes of exaggeration tend toward abstraction in proportion to the degree of exaggeration they allow. The most miniature objects cannot be "seen with the naked eye." The body must be clothed in an apparatus, a technological device. The miniature, or microcomputer, is the absolute culmination of the gadget; the transformation of the tool, with its human trace, into a mechanical extension into space. The microcomputer is a further abstraction and distancing of the mind, itself already the most abstract bodily locale. Hence our tendency to mythologize the computer, to see it as robot or machine-made-animate. The gigantic, occurring in a transcendent space, a space above, analogously mirrors the abstractions of institutions—either those of religion, the state, or, as is increasingly the case, the abstractions of technology and corporate power. This space above the body is occupied by the anonymity of corporate architecture and the complementary detached "personalism" of advertising. Whereas the miniature moves from hand to eye to abstraction, the gigantic moves from the occupation of the body's immediate space to transcendence (a transcendence which allows the eye only imperfect and partial vision) to abstraction. Thus nuclear energy can be seen as the most extreme embodiment of technological abstraction, for it incorporates the most miniature abstraction (the split atom) with the most gigantic abstraction (that of a technological apocalypse).

Thus, although the body serves as a "still center," or constant measure, of our articulation of the miniature and the gigantic, we must also remember the ways in which the body is interiorized by the miniature and exteriorized, made public, by the display modes of the gigantic. In the next chapter we will put this center, this measure, into play by outlining a number of its versions. Grotesque or symmetrical, the body's place and privileges are regulated by a social discourse, a discourse which articulates the body's very status as the subjective.

4. THE IMAGINARY BODY

The Grotesque Body

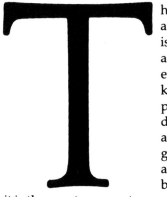he body presents the paradox of contained and container at once. Thus our attention is continually focused upon the boundaries or limits of the body; known from an exterior, the limits of the body as object; known from an interior, the limits of its physical extension into space. Lacan has described "erotogenic" zones of the body as those areas where there are cuts and gaps on the body's surface—the lips, the anus, the tip of the penis, the slit formed by the eyelids, for example. He writes that it is these cuts or apertures on the surface of the body which allow the sense of "edge," borders, or margins by differentiating the body from the organic functions associated with such apertures. Because these cuts or apertures are described on the very surface of the subject, they have no specular image, no outside that they represent; it is this which enables them to be "the 'stuff,' or rather the lining . . . [of] the very subject that one takes to be the subject of consciousness."[1] Thus these apertures of ingestion and emission work to constitute the notion of the subject, of the individual body and ultimately the self. Those products which cross such boundaries thereby become products of great cultural attention. What is both inside and outside the body (feces, spittle, urine, menstrual blood, etc.) tends to become taboo because of its ambiguous and anomalous status.[2] A great deal of cultural regulation is required to privatize the erotogenic zones and to prohibit the projection of their pleasure within the domain of pub-

lic space, and such regulation simultaneously aids in the development not only of the individual subject but also of the "private space" occupied by that subject.

We want to know what is the body and what is not, and it is in the domain of ritual and the carnival grotesque that we see this boundary confused and ultimately redefined. Bakhtin has characterized the grotesque body as a "body in the act of becoming." The grotesque body undergoes a hyperbolization of the bowels, the genital organs, the mouth, and the anus. "All these convexities and orifices have a common characteristic: it is within them that the confines between bodies and between the body and the world are overcome: there is an interchange and an interorientation."[3] The grotesque body, as a form of the gigantic, is a body of parts. Those productive and reproductive organs which are its focus come to live an independent life of their own. The parading of the grotesque is often the isolation and display of the exaggerated part—the mummer hidden by his huge, balloon-filled breasts, or, on a less formal level, the high-school boy substituting a "moon" in the car window for that symbol of balance, proportion, and depth, the face. This scattering and redistribution of bodily parts is the antithesis of the body as a functional tool and of the body as still life, the classical nude. In medieval rhetoric, for example, we find the convention of description specifying that the body should be viewed from head to foot. But the grotesque presents a jumbling of this order, a dismantling and re-presentation of the body according to criteria of production rather than verticality.[4] The free exchange, substitution, and interpenetration of bodily elements during carnival is symptomatic of the exchange of the fair and marketplace which provides its context. In the late Middle Ages and the sixteenth century the presentation of the grotesque image in farces, parades, floats, and street entertainments was accompanied by the collection of money and sweets. Mock coins were distributed during parades by the societies, or "abbeys," of misrule, the "fool-societies" or "play-acting" societies. In nineteenth- and early-twentieth-century America, souvenir coins of the side show were distributed by carnival barkers in an analogous impulse.[5]

The grotesque body thus can be effected by the exaggeration of its internal elements, the turning of the "inside out," the display of orifices and gaps upon the exterior of the body. But in addition to this interpenetration of the exterior and interior of the body, an exchange of sexuality and an exchange between animal and human also can be used to effect the grotesque and its corresponding sense of interchange and disorder. Natalie Zemon Davis, writing about early modern Europe, notes:

The ritual and/or magical functions of sexual inversion were filled in almost all cases by males disguised as grotesque cavorting females. In sections of Germany and Austria, at carnival time male runners, half of these masked as females, half as male, jumped and leaped through the streets. In France it was on St. Stephen's Day or New Year's Day that men dressed as wild beasts or as women and jumped and danced in public (or at least such was the case in the Middle Ages). The saturnalian Feast of Fools, which decorous doctors of theology and prelates were trying to ban from the French cathedrals in the fifteenth and sixteenth centuries, involved both young clerics and laymen, some of them disguised as females, who made wanton and loose gestures.[6]

Similarly, in England and Ireland, the mumming tradition involved men dressed as females, particularly as the grotesque and licentious figures "Bessy" and "Maid Marian." In the Irish St. Stephen's Day custom of the "wren boys," men either disguise themselves as women or wear animal skins and horns.[7]

In anthropological and historical studies considerable attention has been focused on the ways in which such symbolic inversions present the world upside down, the categories and hierarchical arrangement of culture in a recognizable disorder. Theories of inversion have explained these symbolic phenomena as reaffirmations of cultural categories through learning, as mechanisms for change and revolution, and as "safety valves" for an otherwise turbulent populace. Many of these conclusions are based upon cross-cultural studies of trickster characters, for Trickster continually violates the boundary between nature and culture; he is part animal, part human (often a "talking" animal such as the crow or coyote, or a producer such as the spider), part man and part woman (often coupling with either sex indiscriminately), and a violator of cultural taboos (often eating the food that is specific to other animal groups, or eating what should not be food at all). Yet Trickster is also a spirit of creativity, a refuser of rigid systems, and thus is both credited with founding culture and accused of violating the norms of culture. For example, at the conclusion of the Winnebago trickster myth that forms the basis for Paul Radin's classic study of the trickster, Trickster unleashes the Mississippi, allowing it to flood the land, and thereby makes agriculture possible.[8]

It seems clear that the function of such exaggeration in physiology and gesture must be linked to the particular historical context in which it appears. The laity's appropriation of the Feast of Fools and the gigantic in the Renaissance made the carnival grotesque symbolic of a "second life" of the masses, a life of antiorder and vernacular authority as opposed to the official doctrines of religious and state institutions. Such a split perhaps made these forms of festive disorder all the more likely to be taken up in the spirit of revolt when class conflicts arose. And yet rituals of inversion which are clearly framed and circumscribed by religious or state authority (for example, the liminal stages of official puberty rites such as confirmation cere- monies), or phenomena of inversion which are imposed vertically from outside the popular classes (for example, the TV parody show), are far less likely to result in permanent change; these officially sanc- tioned forms would seem to function more to reaffirm cultural catego- ries by forcing participants to articulate such categories from their opposites.

Furthermore, we must also consider these images of the grotesque body precisely as images or representations. Like any art form, they effect a representation and transformation of their subject. Yet to make from the body a work of art involves the creation of a supple- ment or extension. The work of art as costume, mask, and disguise differs significantly from the work of art as external object. The body is paraded, put on display, in time as well as in space; most often those contexts in which it appears are structured so that there is little or no division between participants and audience. The distance be- tween the artwork, the artist, and the audience is thereby collapsed doubly; the body is the work, and there is reciprocity between indi- viduals/works rather than unilinear distance between work and ob- server. The mask and costume are, like the face, apprehended in what Philip Fisher has called "democratic space,"[9] the space immedi- ately in front of our line of perception rather than the space above us, occupied by an authoritative and transcendent architecture; or the space at our feet to which we condescend; or the space directly be- hind us, invisible and threatening. But it is not simply the fact that this space can be directly confronted which makes it democratic; its democracy, its reciprocity, depends upon its *public* quality. It is just beyond the space that each culture variously determines as the pri- vate and just within the space that a culturally determined perception defines as remote. It is space occupied by the other, the space of dialogue. Thus the mask, the costume, and the disguise find their proper context in carnival and festivity, where there is little special- ization of roles and where hierarchy is overturned. Even in ritual uses of mask and disguise, where specialization does occur (say, for exam- ple, kachina clowns at Hopi ceremonial feasts), the performer must engage in face-to-face communication with the audience.

While the grotesque body of carnival engages in this structure of democratic reciprocity, the spectacle of the grotesque involves a dis- tancing of the object and a corresponding "aestheticization" of it. In carnival the grotesque is an exaggeration and celebration of the productive and reproductive capacities of the body, of the natural in its most sensual dimensions. But in spectacle the grotesque appears not in parts but in a whole that is an aberration. The participant in carnival is swept up in the events carnival presents and he or she thereby experiences the possibility of misrule and can thereby envision it as a new order. In contrast, the viewer of the spectacle is absolutely aware of the distance between self and spectacle. The spectacle exists in an outside at both its origin and ending. There is no question that there is a gap between the object and its viewer. The spectacle functions to avoid contamination: "Stand back, ladies and gentlemen, what you are about to see will shock and amaze you." And at the same time, the spectacle assumes a singular direction. In contrast to the reciprocal gaze of carnival and festival, the spectacle assumes that the object is blinded; only the audience sees.

The history of the aberrations of the physical body cannot be separated from this structure of the spectacle. The etymology of the term *monster* is related to *moneo*, "to warn," and *monstro*, "to show forth."[10] From Hellenistic times through the Middle Ages and the Renaissance, dwarfs, midgets, and occasionally gigantic figures were kept as accouterments of court life, as entertainers and pets. In the eighteenth century such figures were put on display in public taverns, and notices posted in local papers or handbills served to advertise them. Gulliver's fate in Brobdingnag (inversely) recapitulates this history: he is first kept in a box and exhibited on market days and in taverns; later he is rescued by an invitation to serve at court. The Queen, who "was however surprised at so much wit and good Sense in so diminutive an Animal," takes him on as a human pet or doll.[11]

In his book *Giants and Dwarfs*, Edward Wood records a handbill advertising a dwarf couple exhibited in "1712 at the Duke of Malborough's Head, over against Salisbury-Court, Fleet-street," and also "a collection of strange and wonderful creatures from most parts of the world, all alive, over against the Mews Gate, at Charing-cross, by her Majesty's permission." The handbill for this exhibition reads:

> The first being a little Black Man being about 3 foot high, and 32 years of age, straight and proportionable every way, who is distinguished by the name of the Black Prince, and has been shewn before most kings and princes in Christendom. The next being his wife, the Little Woman, not 3 foot high, and 30 years of age, straight and proportionable as any woman in the land, which is commonly called the Fairy Queen, she gives a general satisfaction to all that sees her, by diverting them with dancing, being big with child. Likewise their little Turkey horse, being but 2 foot odd inches high, and above 12 years of age, that shews several diverting and surprising actions, at the word of command. The

least man, woman, and horse, that ever was seen in the world alive;
the horse being kept in a box.[12]

Here we have the tragedy of a public miniature: the prince as a mirror
of the princes of Christendom, yet made diminutive, conquered, as
the cultural other; his wife, monstrously "big with child"; and his
horse, miraculously diverting, are the promise of repetition and animation—toys come to a life that is of necessity a death as the box
offers a coffin's promise of eternity. Similarly, in his study *Freaks*,
Leslie Fiedler records that "giants have, ironically, bafflingly (how
hard it is for us to sympathize with them!), played the role of victims
rather than victimizers. Before they became side show attractions,
they were used chiefly as soldiers—parade ground attractions placed
conspicuously in the front ranks—and porters, lofty enough to impress visitors at the gates of kings."[13] The fate of other types of
"freaks," as chronicled by Fiedler—bearded ladies, wild men, feral
children, hermaphrodites, and Siamese twins—was invariably the
spectacle and final ruination.

Often referred to as a "freak of nature," the freak, it must be
emphasized, is a freak of culture. His or her anomalous status is
articulated by the process of the spectacle as it distances the viewer,
and thereby it "normalizes" the viewer as much as it marks the freak
as an aberration. And since the spectacle exists in silence, there is no
dialogue—only the frame of the pitchman or the barker. Even when,
as is sometimes the case in smaller and poorer carnival operations,
the freak delivers his or her own "pitch," there is an absolute separation between the tableaulike silence of the freak's display and the
initial metacommentary of the pitch. This separation is poignantly felt
by the viewer as a hesitation: the pause before the curtain closes or
before the viewer walks on. And the viewer *must* go on; dialogue
across that silence is forbidden, for it is necessary that, like the aberration, the normal be confined to the surface, or appearance, of things.
We find the freak inextricably tied to the cultural other—the Little
Black Man, the Turkish horse, the Siamese twins (Chang and Eng
were, however, the children of Chinese parents living in Siam), the
Irish giants. Accounts of pygmies, for example, date back to Homer
(*Iliad* 3.3), Hesiod, Herodotus (who places them both in Africa and in
Middle India), Ovid (who includes in the *Metamorphoses* the legend of
the battle between the Pygmies and the Cranes), and thus to the
West's earliest encounters with other traditions. We find further ac-
counts of pygmies in *Mandeville's Travels* and in a study of the Outer
Hebrides made by Donald Monro in 1549.[14] The body of the cultural
other is by means of this metaphor both naturalized and domesti-

cated in a process we might consider to be characteristic of colonization in general. For all colonization involves the taming of the beast by bestial methods and hence both the conversion and projection of the animal and human, difference and identity. On display, the freak represents the naming of the frontier and the assurance that the wilderness, the outside, is now territory.

Repeatedly in the history of freaks it has been assumed that the freak is an object. The freak is actually captured and made a present of to the court or to the College of Surgeons, as the case may be. Or the contingencies of the economic system force the freak to sell himself or herself as a spectacle commodity. Except for the famous midget welders of World War II propaganda movies, there are few examples of any other existence made possible to the "prodigy." Thus, Fiedler notes, it is particularly shocking that the Siamese twins Chang and Eng, themselves brought to America in bondage, eventually owned slaves in the period just before the Civil War.[15] The physiological freak represents the problems of the boundary between self and other (Siamese twins), between male and female (the hermaphrodite), between the body and the world outside the body (the *monstré par exces*), and between the animal and the human (feral and wild men). These are the same problems that we see explored in grotesque representation. Ontology is not the point here so much as the necessity of exploring these relations, either through the fantastic or the "real."

It is significant that in the presentation of the freak, language is made object, divorced from communication. Gulliver's native tongue is condescendingly called "his little language" by the Brobdingnagians, and the dwarf as court jester is admired for his wit. Among the earliest recorded Siamese twins were "the Scottish Brothers," who served in the court of James IV. They "won the hearts of the court by playing musical instruments, singing in 'two parts, treble and tenor,' and making witty conversation in Latin, French, Italian, Spanish, Dutch, Danish, and Irish."[16] Similarly, the *London Daily Advertiser* for August 18, 1740, advertised: "To be seen, at the Rummer Tavern, Charing-cross, a Persian dwarf, just arrived, three feet eight inches high, aged 45 years . . . he is justly called the Second Sampson. He also speaks eighteen different languages."[17] The language of the spectacle is properly that of the showman, the hyperbolic pitch which further distances the points of equivalence between audience and object, which presents another layer of surface as it articulates the to-be-presented façade.

The freak must be linked not to lived sexuality but to certain forms of the pornography of distance. The spectacle results only in speculation. Hence, as Fiedler suggests, the actual sexuality of the freak, encumbered by a host of biological limitations, has an independent life from the spectacle sexuality that coexists with it in legend. This sexuality is an imaginary relation, just as, for example, the "girlie" poster on which a woman's body is mapped out, like the body of a steer, into various territories representing cuts of meat is far removed from the festive images of sexuality and consumption found in carnival. As opposed to the "body in the act of becoming" of carnival, the body of the side show offers a horrifying closure. Thus it does not matter whether the freak is alive or dead: John Hunter, the father of British surgery, was just as happy to have the bones of the giant James Byrne as to study him alive. Similarly, Frederick I of Prussia, attempting to kidnap a giant named Zimmerman, smothered him in a coffin, yet was just as satisfied with his skeleton as with the living giants he had brought to his court.[18] Even more crucially, the façade of the pitch or patter makes it of little significance whether the freak is authentic or not. It is the possibility of his or her existence that titillates; it is the imaginary relation, not the lived one, that we seek in the spectacle.

The Body Made Miniature

The handbill advertising the Black Prince and his wife calls attention to her as "the Fairy Queen," "straight and proportionable as any woman in the land." Here is the contrast between dwarf and midget, between the grotesque and the model, which has made quite different the reception of these two varieties of anomaly. The dwarf is assigned to the domain of the grotesque and the underworld, the midget to the world of the fairy—a world of the natural, not in nature's gigantic aspects, but in its attention to the perfection of detail. Like giants, fairies are ascribed to a race that inhabited the earth before men;[19] but unlike giants, they are described as an alternative present reality rather than as a lost generation. The fairies are said to exist contemporaneously in remote nature and to be visible only under certain conditions (under mountains or lakes or caves or caverns within hills) or to those having "second sight."[20] Although the fairies described before 1594 do not seem to be particularly diminutive, it is the convention by the late Renaissance in England to depict them as miniature human beings. And, following an older tradition, they are depicted as figures of great beauty and perfection. In his study of Elizabethan fairy lore, Latham notes that "Elizabeth was the one person in England whose beauty could be compared to that of the fairies."[21] Here again we see Gulliver's discovery that distance creates physical perfection and idealization. The fairies have the attraction of the animate doll, the cultural ideal unencumbered by the natural. While the grotesque erupts into a medley of erotogenic zones, of gaps and orifices, the doll/fairy presents a pure, inpenetrable surface: proportional within a suitably detailed context. As the pioneering psychologist Stanley Hall discovered in his *Study of Dolls,* "Even feared and hated objects excite pleasure when mimicked on a small scale."[22] Thus the early attribution of ambivalence to fairies does not detract from their charm.

The fairies present the animate, human counterpart to the miniature. Unlike the gigantic, which celebrates quantity over quality, the fairies represent minute perfection of detail and a cultured form of nature. Although there are accounts of male fairies (properly called "mannikins"), the fairy world is for the most part depicted as a female one, just as the world of the gigantic is predominantly male. And unlike the singularity of the grotesque in gigantic, dwarf, or elfen form, the fairy is depicted as a socialized being with a culture (dress, ritual organization, economy, and authority structure) particular to fairydom. In his late-seventeenth-century treatise, *The Secret Commonwealth of Elves, Fauns, and Fairies,* the Reverend Robert Kirk writes that fairies "are distributed in Tribes and Orders, and have Children, Nurses, Marriages, Deaths and Burialls, in appearance, even as we,"[23] and that "their apparell and Speech is like that of the People and Countrey under which they live."[24] We are now in a kingdom far from that of the Cyclops, with "no muster and no meeting, no consultation or old tribal ways." Rather, like the miniature world of the dollhouse, the world of the fairies is a world of ornament and detail. Consider, for example, the beginning of this Cornish tale of a miser who tries to catch some fairies:

> Troops of musicians came out, and bands of soldiers, and then servants carrying all kinds of dainties on gold and silver dishes, and then the lords and ladies of the Court came out and ranged themselves in their places, and after them came a band of fairy children in gauzy clothes, who scattered flowers that rooted themselves as they fell; and finally came the King and Queen, who moved up to the high table, glittering with gold, silver and jewels! It was this that drew the miser's greedy eye. The whole exquisite miniature could be covered by his hat, and he went down on his knees and crawled up behind the table.[25]

Like other miniature worlds, the world of the fairies presents a hallucination of detail. Thus, whereas Alfred Nutt held that "the love of neatness and orderly method so characteristic of the fairy world is easily referrable to a time when the operations of rural life formed part of a definite religious ritual, every jot and tittle of which must be carried out with minute precision," such a myth-ritual theory would not seem to be necessary, since the same obsession with detail and order can be seen in other depictions of the miniature and their relation to the order of private space.[26]

The observer of the fairies must "wake up" at the conclusion of his or her encounter with these animated miniatures. Hence the legends of fairies are constructed along the circular lines of fantasy. While the gigantic takes up time and space in history, the fairy lives in a continual present. Fairy rulers are often described as simultaneously ancient and ageless. Elizabethan fairy lore held that the fairies had one ruler; as old as the race itself and of the same nationality as her subjects, she, like the queen bee, was nameless except by her title.[27] Henry Bourne's *Antiquitates Vulgares* (1725) records that "generally they dance in the moonlight, when mortals are asleep, and not capable of seeing them, as may be observed on the following morn, their dancing-places being very distinguishable. For as they dance hand-in-hand, and so make a circle in their dance, so next day there will be seen rings and circles on the grass."[28] Such traces might be seen as a mirror of the structure of the fairy legend, its fantastic and lyric form contrasting with the narrative historical mode we find in the gigantic.

Along with Irish versions, pre-Elizabethan and Elizabethan depictions of the fairies often show them to be powerful and even malevolent figures, but by the Victorian Age, the domestication of the fairy is complete and the English fairy becomes inextricably linked to the enduring creation of the Victorian fantastic: the fairylike child. Although the Victorian child was held to have a near-magical association with nature (think, for example, of Alice and the Fawn in the forest without names), this nature is diminutive and readily transformed into culture. Perhaps the height of this belief in the fairy child is shown in the later Edwardian phenomenon of the Cottingley photographs of fairies. Of great interest to theosophists such as Conan Doyle, these photographs were taken by two young sisters in the Cotswolds after they had developed a long-standing acquaintance with their fairy subjects.[29] Emily Watson's *Fairies of Our Garden* (1862) provides an earlier example of this fantastic mode. In the section entitled "The Fairy Queen's Wardrobe," she explains:

> One season, when the long summer-holidays were over—in which the fairies had lived mostly for their own diversion or in idleness—the queen summoned them, and said they must now prepare for her a new wardrobe. Some were to make linen for the under-garments; others were to make a sort of silken tissue for the dress; another, the stockings; and so on. The fairies who were to make the linen scampered about over hill and dale to gather the thistle-down from which it was to be manufactured. For the silken tissue, armfuls of the

silky pods of the silk-weed were brought; and for the stockings was collected that gossamer-like stuff which floats among the bushes in the autumn days. Then the linen-weavers spread out their bales of thistle-down upon the grass; and in order to break it, and card it into a smooth mat, two fairies seized upon a huge chestnut-burr.[30]

Systematically, each sign of nature is transformed into a sign of culture, just as the domestic arts of the time turned pine cones into picture frames, sea shells into lamps, and enclosed a variety of natural objects, "dried," under glass. It is no accident that undergarments are given much consideration here. Herein lies the Victorian obsession with "the cover." As George Speaight wrote in his *History of the English Toy Theatre*,

> For the next century drawing-rooms were to be submerged beneath a vast accumulation of feminine ingenuity. Objects were coated with gold paper, screens were painted or worked with wool, purses were knitted, tables were painted, samplers were stitched, carpets and rugs were woven, china ornaments were imitated, landscapes were contrived from coloured silks, footstools were covered, windows were obscured with transparencies, artificial flowers were created, filigree baskets were produced from entwined rolls of paper, and scrap books were filled with cyphers and trophies, rhymes and riddles, water-colours and prints.[31]

In concealing nature, the cover, of course, makes nature all the more titillating. The cover invites exposure; it always bears the potential of striptease. The impulse toward control manifested in these Victorian hobbies (which extend backward to the eighteenth century and forward to the twentieth: many elderly American women, for example, crochet small "hoods" for their surplus toilet paper) seems symptomatic of the double nature of Victorian sexuality—the simultaneous urge toward repression and licentiousness which resulted in both a specific moral code and a blossoming taste for pornography and distanced desire.[32]

The Cottingley photographs, which appeared in the early 1920's, are significant not only as an example of the linking of the child with the fantastic/natural; they are also emblematic of the developing importance of the image and its potential for exaggeration. Here the Edwardian image is the culmination of the Victorian fantastic as the photograph becomes more believable than the lived experience. A great deal of attention has been devoted to "scientifically" testing the validity of these photographs. Yet at the same time, such photographs bring the natural into the realm of the cultural. Just as a photograph of a landscape transforms nature into a cultural artifact, so these photographs of the fairies endow them with a "realism" that is aesthetic. The contemporary flapper-type costumes the Cottingley fairies apparently are wearing make them all the more credible; they have joined the transcendent and immortalized present that is the time and space of all photographs. Similarly, although modern skeptics might interpret Charles Dodgson's interest in photographing little girls in the nude as a prurient one, this interest must as well be linked to the place of the photograph in cultivating the natural. The body has become a garden, remote from the uncontrolled sexuality of the natural sublime.

There is only convention in the "realistic" depiction of the body. The body depicted always tends toward exaggeration, either in the convention of the grotesque or the convention of the ideal. There are few images less interesting than an exact anatomical drawing of the human form. This problem arises from the corresponding problem of the absence of stance. Grotesque realism is emblematic of the body's knowledge of itself, a knowledge of pieces and parts, of disassociated limbs and an absent center. The realism of the ideal is emblematic of the body's knowledge of the other, a knowledge of façades, of two dimensions. Only in the embrace is the other's body known as one's own, in parts. Perhaps this is why the grotesque has become the domain of lived sexuality, while the ideal has tended toward the domain of the voyeur and the pornographer.

The point is brought poignantly before us by Joyce in the tableau scenes of the Nausicaä section of *Ulysses*. Odysseus/Bloom, voyeur of the game, gives us a painterly and lingering account of the women by the water. As Cissy Caffrey runs down the beach, "It would have served her just right if she had tripped up over something accidentally on purpose with her high crooked French heels on her to make her look tall and got a fine tumble. *Tableau!* That would have been a very charming exposé for a gentleman like that to witness."[33] Joyce is apparently borrowing here from the parlor game in which participants strike poses meant to symbolize a message and say "Tableau!" to announce that the pose is complete and ready to be observed and interpreted.[34] But he is also obviously borrowing from the photograph's idealization and distancing of an event, a still and perfect, and thereby interpretable and unapproachable, universe whose signified is not the world but desire. Our attention, along with Bloom's, turns to Gerty MacDowell, who echoes yet another exhibition/exhibitionist, Miss Dunne of "Wandering Rocks," who, in echoing the exhibitionism of Maria Kendall "holding up her bit of a skirt" on the Dublin stage, further complicates this picture-in-the-picture that is always promised by the tableau. We should remember that Miss

Dunne is the employee of Blazes Boylan, who later will experience a less mediated form of sexuality in the arms of Molly. Gerty, surrounded by the discourse of the "petite feminine," is presented as a self-conscious commodity; thus, ironically, Bloom's desire for her, a desire which forms an imaginary and thereby complete picture of Gerty as object, will be equally reflexive in its onanism. As this complete picture turns into the partial vision of lived experience—that is, at the moment when the tableau is broken by the movement of Gerty arising and limping—Bloom says: "A defect is ten times worse in a woman. But makes them polite. Glad I didn't know it when she was on show."[35] This phenomenon of the perfect whole broken by the discernment of movement is repeated five pages later, inversely, by Molly: "When I said to Molly the man at the corner of Cuffe street was goodlooking, thought she might like, twigged at once he had a false arm." In these scenes (just as Gerty is only partly whole, so she does not quite merit an entire chapter), Joyce reminds us of the scenic nature of all pornography, indeed the scenic nature of all desire: "Best place for an ad to catch a woman's eye on a mirror." For, in contrast, the lived experience of sexuality shatters—refuses—closure; even the victim of the folie à deux must live and die by imagining the perfect union of some other couple, some other, some eternalized, death.[36]

Indeed, if we combine the structures of these tableaus with the ensuing one inviting our interpretation of the fickleness of women— "Till Mr. Right comes along then meet once in a blue moon. *Tableau!* O, look who it is for the love of God! How are you at all? What have you been doing with yourself? Kiss and delighted to, kiss, to see you. Picking holes in each other's appearance. You're looking splendid. Sister souls showing their teeth to one another. How many have you left? Wouldn't lend each other a pinch of salt"[37]—we see not just the photographic scene but the entire operation of the postcard. The diminutive world of the feminine portrayed in these tableaus makes the reader take the externalized position of Bloom as voyeur, while the caption, the contrasting inside view, is voiced by the narrator, who instructs us in what to see and not see and thereby presents an illusion of totality. Peep show, "dirty" postcard, striptease of the surface of the feminine, "Nausicaä" repeats the uncanny scene whereby the very wholeness of the picture reveals something missing. As Kenneth Clark remarks in his study of the nude, without distortion there cannot be depiction of movement.[38] And yet, on another level, the ideal of the body exists within an illusion of stasis, an illusion that the body does not change and that those conditions and contingencies which shape the ideal are transcendent and "classic" as well. Between the here-and-now of lived experience and this ideal is a distance which creates and maintains desire.

Lacan has linked the child's fascination with "stature, status and statues" to the relationship with the mother, herself an image of harmonius totality at a point when the child is a jumble of drives and functions.[39] During the mirror phase (*stade du miroir*) the child acquires an imaginary identification of the real, corporeal image as a unified image. In this creation of a unified subject, the self begins to be positioned in sociality and is available to the further modifications made possible by language and the symbolic. And at the same time, the other is generated (at first, the mother), an other who can either satisfy or refuse to satisfy the needs of the subject. Lacan borrows from Hegel in saying that desire is based on the gap between need and demand: "The very desire of man (Hegel tells us), is constituted under the sign of mediation; it is desire to make its desire recognised. It has for its object a desire, that of the other, in the sense that there is no object for man's desire which is constituted without some sort of mediation—which appears in his most primitive needs: for example, even his food has to be prepared—and which is found again throughout the development of satisfaction from the moment of the master-slave conflict through the dialectic of labour."[40] This position regarding the necessity of mediation can be generalized to encompass all relations with the imaginary, but our particular focus here will be the mediation of sexuality and the commodification of the body.

The Tom Thumb Wedding

The sexual act itself is antispectacular, erasing the distance between audience and performer; it is an event which cannot be framed from inside as a nonevent. Thus the police were willing to refrain from raiding the cast of *Oh! Calcutta!* so long as there was *no actual penetration*.[41] At the other side of this overly natural center (completely framed by and juxtaposed with a myriad of social accouterments that must remain outside it) is the most cultural mediation of sexuality—the marriage, the cultural imposition of symmetry upon asymmetry. The wedding as marriage ritual marks the transformation of the self from physical body to a network of social and property relations, from play to production, from circularity to linearity. Of all bourgeois rituals, it is the most significant, the most emblematic of class relations; and perhaps this is why, at least since the Renaissance, it has been the ritual most commonly chosen for exaggeration within the realm of the imaginary. A lived tableau, the wedding commonly forms the closure of Renaissance comedies. Out of the grotesque antics of the characters comes the wedding scene, which puts proportion at center stage; the grotesque is forced into the margins at closure. In a similar dialectic, the charivari tradition of publicly mocking disproportionate spouses served the function of ensuring the symmetry of social relations represented by the wedding. Natalie Zemon Davis records that in France, "the rural youth-abbeys had jurisdiction over the behavior of married people—over newlyweds when the wife had failed to become pregnant during the year, over husbands dominated by their wives, sometimes over adulterers. . . . The earliest known French use of the term charivari and the most frequent occasion for it in the villages, however, was in connection with second marriages, especially when there was a gross disparity in age between the bride and groom."[42] Furthermore, Estyn Evans has written that in Ireland "to this day the marriage or remarriage of old men to young women is regarded as unnatural and wrong, perhaps because it complicates the question of succession. In Co. Wexford, and probably elsewhere, unpopular marriages of this kind are marked by noisy gatherings of young men who serenade the married couple with horn-blowing. . . . One of the strangest traditional features of Irish weddings is the visitation of 'strawboys,' that is youths wearing straw masks who attend as uninvited guests and disport themselves at the dance which normally follows the wedding."[43]

In North America we find a tension between the official language of the wedding, including the official social relations it exemplifies, and a similar series of mock rituals that stand opposed to that language. In many Protestant communities, for example, both Anglo- and Afro-American, we find the tradition of the "womanless wedding." In the April 28, 1927, issue of the Virginia newspaper *The Blue Ridge Guide* there is an account of such an event: "Something unique in the wedding line was given last Saturday night at Reynolds Memorial Church, Sperryville. The cast was composed entirely of males— married men, old bachelors, young men and boys, all gowned in the latest female toggery and using powder, lip stick and rouge. Oh, but what a bewildering scene! The groom was very small and the bride around seven feet tall. The church was crowded to its utmost capacity (about 200 people) and then some. Those taking part were from Sperryville, Woodville, Washington, and Flint Hill. The blushing bride was from Washington, D.C. and the happy groom was from Sperryville." In Brogueville, Pennsylvania, such weddings, held in the periods just before and after the Second World War, were called "mock weddings." They were held on the picnic grounds behind the St. James Lutheran Church. Men dressed as women, but instead of wearing contemporary clothing, as was the case in the Sperryville wedding, they wore, in the 1930's, forties, and fifties, long dresses and straw hats evocative of turn-of-the-century styles of women's clothing. It might be argued that just as the Victorian chair is more likely than a modern one to be a signifier of "chairness" in the doll-house, so this antiquated style of dress is more likely to be a signifier of the feminine in the womanless wedding. Such weddings, with their substitution of asymmetry for symmetry, of the festive gro-tesque for the sacred, of improvisational comic dialogue and asides for the linear, fixed-phrase formulas of ceremony, might be seen as a modern version of the charivari tradition. The Brogueville womanless weddings, put on by the "Luther League," a social club for teen-agers at the church, seem particularly close to the charivari.

In contrast to this carnival grotesque exaggeration of the wedding, we also find, in the same communities, an exaggeration of an ideal of the wedding in the ceremony called "the Tom Thumb wedding." Tom Thumb weddings involve the reproduction of an idealized, or model, wedding on a miniature scale, with children "playing" the adult roles. Like the womanless wedding, the Tom Thumb wedding seems to have spread across the country by oral and printed means and perhaps provides our only example of miniaturized ritual. Avery A. Morton of Watertown, Massachusetts, recalled in 1976 that at the turn of the century a woman was hired to direct the Tom Thumb weddings at the Campbellite Church in Bethany, Nebraska. In 1900, when Morton was eight,

> the worst thing was somebody came through puttin' on plays—Tom Thumb's Wedding Affair—and she would pick children and train them and drill them, and then they'd put on a performance. She would do it for pay. Tom Thumb had to sing a love song to the girl—who was that girl now? She was a minister's daughter, and I had to sing that song when I was a small boy. There were quite a number of people acting in the thing, and I had the star role, and the minister's daughter had another star role. It was performed in the church. It was called The Tom Thumb Wedding. She'd be there a couple of weeks and use the kids from the Sunday School. It would be performed for the parents one night.[44]

The professional director speaks to the impulse here toward a fixed text. Correspondingly, W. H. Baker put out *The Tom Thumb Wedding* in 1898 as part of its series Baker's Entertainments for Children. But unlike the other plays in the series, it is not ascribed to an author; rather, it bears the inscription "As originally performed at the Union Tabernacle Church, Philadelphia, Pa." The Baker text specifies that "there should be a minister, bride and groom, maid of honor, groomsman, father and mother, bridesmaids, ushers, guests, and flower girls," and that these participants should be arranged symmetrically on a platform for the ceremony:

Guests Seated	Bridesmaids Standing		Minister				Ushers Standing	Guests Seated
			ô					
			Flower Girls					
			ô ô ô ô					
		Maid of Honor	Bride	Groom	Best Man			
		ô	ô	ô	ô			
			Front of Platform					

DIAGRAM OF ARRANGEMENT OF PLATFORM
DURING CEREMONY

"The costumes should be similar to real wedding costumes. They should be as elaborate as possible. They add largely to the successful effect, and are all easily and inexpensively made. The effect of the costumes is startling; and the outbursts of enthusiasm that invariably greet the little ones in the attire of their elders is scarcely imaginable."[45] The Baker text is designed along the lines of the mock serious. It constructs a model wedding in form, but then turns to hyperbolic parody in its language, effecting a satire of contemporary relations between spouses. For example, the script for the vows is as follows:

> I, Tom Thumb, take thee, Jennie June, to be my lawful partner from this day forward, for better, but not worse, for richer, but not poorer, so long as your cooking does not give me the dyspepsia, and my mother-in-law does not visit oftener than once in a quarter, and then not to remain all night; so long as all bills for millinery shall be paid out of spending money furnished by your beloved father, out of gratitude for not having you left upon his hands in the deplorable station of a helpless spinster. And thereto I give thee my word and honor. Sure enough.

> I, Jennie June, take thee, Tom Thumb, to be my lawful partner from this day forward, for better, but not worse, for richer, but not poorer; provided that you do not smoke or drink; provided that you will never mention how your mother used to cook, or sew on buttons, or make your shirt bosoms shine; provided that you carry up coal three times a

day, put out the ashes once a week, bring up the tub, and put up and take down the clothes-line on wash-day, and perform faithfully all other duties demanded by a "new woman" of the nineteenth century. And thereto I give my word and honor. Sure enough.[46]

Similarly, in a triple Tom Thumb wedding put on by the West Hagert neighborhood of Philadelphia in the summer of 1982 as part of the city's Neighborhood Festivals Day, the boy playing the part of the minister asked each of the grooms: "Do you promise to take her out on the town, to see *E.T.*, and to take her to Roy Rogers' for dinner?" He then asked each of the brides: "Do you promise to take him to Shopping Bag and spend all his money on cakes and cookies?" Other effects that drew laughter from a generally reverent crowd were objections to the marriage expressed by each best man, and the final pronouncement, "You may salute the bride." Furthermore, the text for each of the three ceremonies was varied as the minister addressed the wedding parties by mocking names. The first group was called "Flintstones" ("We are gathered here to marry these Flintstones"); the second, "Smurfs"; and the third, "Jeffersons." Physically a perfect miniature of, as one mother put it, "a big wedding," the Tom Thumb ceremony here is disrupted by the text. The text parodies the cartoonlike nature of this animation. The black community mocks not only the child dressed as adult, the toy come to life, but also the racist caricatures of the mass culture. Such parodies are only heightened by the elaborate and careful attention to exact detail offered in the physical layout of the wedding. As *The Blue Ridge Guide* for April 25, 1928, advertises, "The Wedding of the Midgets or Tom Thumb's Wedding, over 75 children, three to ten years old will give a complete imitation of a 'Society Wedding.' One hundred laughs in 100 minutes." In this case, too, an ideal would seem to be modeled or miniaturized (the "Society" wedding, which we can assume is not typical of the community), only to be transformed by the language of the parody. The community thus has an opportunity to demonstrate its skill and familiarity with upper-class values at the same time that it parodies them by substituting the vernacular on the level of content ("Sure enough").

But it does not seem the case that all Tom Thumb weddings were or are humorous entertainments. If the miniature wedding is simply a reduction of scale with no substitution of content, the effect is one of awe at the most serious and charm at the least solemn. The Brogueville church provides an example. In the mid 1950's there were few real weddings in its congregation and, simultaneously, mock or womanless weddings seemed to be becoming even more popular. In 1956 the church pastor decided that the congregation should hold a

Tom Thumb wedding, not on the picnic grounds where the other mock weddings were held, but in the church building itself. The church's women's group was asked to organize the ceremony, and its Sunday School classes provided the players. The fact that in those classes three sets of twins were available to participate in the ceremony only added to the general emphasis upon symmetry, order, and balance which the minister hoped to present. The wedding party consisted of a bride, groom, two bridesmaids, two flower girls, a ring bearer, a maid of honor, a best man, and an usher. Although the womanless wedding called for dated costumes, this wedding called for contemporary dress. The church's women's organization made long, pink dotted swiss gowns for the girls, and the boys were dressed in white jackets, black pants, and bow ties. Bouquets were made of "miniature" flowers—forget-me-nots and "baby roses"— and a children's choir provided the music. The pastor was the only full-sized participant, and he conducted the wedding ceremony just as he would conduct a "regular wedding." Twenty-four years later, when I interviewed participants and members of the congregation, they remembered the wedding as being "as much as real as possible," and added that "it was a really large wedding. It wasn't small; it was a big affair." Because the wedding was held in the church at a time and within a space in which a full-sized wedding might be held, it was "serious."

Unlike the wedding parodies in the other miniaturized forms we have discussed, this wedding clearly functioned as a *model* wedding. To make an analogy to the Orkney Island chairs or the elaborate dollhouse, we might say that it was more of a wedding than its full-sized representation might be. Its miniature form allowed it to reach perfection of detail. It is significant that this wedding was held at a time when the traditional wedding had fully moved into its contemporary status as a photographic, rather than primarily social, event, the reception of guests being eclipsed by the photography session. Significantly, few of the participants and observers remembered the wedding well (no two people described the number and character of the players in the same way), yet many people had photographs of the event, photographs that narrated the event through the presentation of a tableau. In the photo album of one of the bridesmaids, her own wedding pictures are on the facing page in relation to the Tom Thumb wedding pictures—startlingly, the poses (a rear pose at the altar before the pastor, a frontal pose at the rear of the church) are exactly the same. The parodying Tom Thumb weddings are more truly "plays," in the sense that they subtly flaunt their artifice through physical substitutions (it is recommended, for example, that the costumes be made of cheesecloth, which looks like netting but is much less expensive) and not so subtly flaunt their artifice through a change in discourse; yet the Brogueville wedding is removed from "reality" only on the level of scale. The event in itself is like the photograph—a depiction of an event effected through a reduction of physical dimensions, a picture which becomes both the occasion for the event and a replacement for it. The photographs of the event themselves speak its effort toward transcendence: front is behind, behind is front, and all of history is stopped.

The Tom Thumb wedding would seem to have arisen from the Victorian cult of the child, the child as fairy, and not from the carnival grotesque tradition. This form must be related to the tremendous appeal that Charles Sherwood Stratton, P. T. Barnum's "General Tom Thumb," held for the Victorian public.[47] Stratton was presented by Barnum not as a monster or freak but as an actor. His career with Barnum began while he was a young boy, and so he was in several ways the epitome of the enchanted and enchanting, the toylike, child. In 1863, when he was twenty-six, he married Lavinia Warren, another midget, in an elaborate and highly publicized ceremony at Grace Church in New York City. With the womanless wedding already extant, this event served as a model for the latest type of home-made spectacle, this one having the sanction of religious authority and the traditional women's culture that served that authority.

For the child the wedding is an hour of little more than constraints. At the West Hagert ceremony, several of the boys decided that it looked "more hip" to wear their jacket collars up, but the collars were quickly turned down by the women in charge and the boys were reprimanded. Just as the Brogueville minister hoped that the Tom Thumb wedding would serve as a model, so was the West Hagert wedding, despite its parodying text, accompanied by a general cele-bration of the bourgeois domestic. The ceremony took place in the street: first, a march through several blocks, and then the wedding itself held on a platform *above* the audience. On the day of the wed-ding, the houses of the neighborhood were decorated, *on the outside*, with photographs of married couples and their offspring. Special dis-plays were made at the houses of couples who had been married more than 50 years, displays that included family photographs, art-work by family members, and anniversary gifts. This turning of the inside out is in several ways the reversal of carnivalization. It marks the appropriation of the culture of the street by the domestic culture and thus is the end of licentiousness rather than the beginning of upheaval.[48] It is a refusal of the "outside in," a dissemination of interiority. While the womanless weddings took place within the license of carnival, involving drinking and feasting and improvisation, the Tom Thumb wedding substitutes the "cute" for the dangerous. Such a wedding is manipulated from the outside. As a Brogueville woman said, "There was a rehearsal, I mean there was practice, but there wasn't any reception." Here the body of the child is a body erased of its sexuality—the seamless body of the doll. Dressed in the folds of adult clothing, the child is like the costumed animal or sea shells under glass. And the wedding context further exaggerates this subjugation of nature as an exaggeration of all weddings, their function being to demonstrate the domestication of sexuality, the establishment of symmetrical economic and social relations, and the "saluting" of the bride.

What is, in fact, lost in this idealized miniaturization of the body is sexuality and hence the danger of power. The body becomes an image, and all manifestations of will are transferred to the position of the observer, the voyeur. The body exists not in the domain of lived reality but in the domain of commodity relations. Hall noted in his study of dolls that "a large part of the world's terms of endearment are diminutives, and to its reduced scale the doll world owes much of its charm. The cases of fear of dolls are almost always of large dolls, the charm of which comes out only well on in the doll period and as exceptions to the rule. . . . Smallness indulges children's love of feeling their superiority, their desire to boss something and to gain their desires along lines of least resistance or to vent their reaction to the parental tyranny of anger."[49] This impulse toward transcendence must be juxtaposed with a consideration of the other side of diminutives: their application is especially reserved for children, pets, servants, and women. The diminutive is a term of manipulation and control as much as it is a term of endearment. Similarly, the image of the body as it is presented in commodity advertising—reduced through photography and then projected abstractly before us—has the effect of a generalized sexuality, or, more specifically, a generalized desire, which then becomes focused upon the commodity itself, the only "total" image. Through this process, it becomes appropriate that hazy photographs of lovers are put on the wrappings of ironing boards or on the cardboard backings for auto parts. The relation between the photo and the commodity is not, as it first might seem, an arbitrary one, for the photo's referent is the generalized desire that is the signified of all commodity relations in late capitalism.

If, following Lacan, we say that the recognition of the imaginary during infancy is what begins the process of the constitution of the subject, it is no less the case that the imaginary's function is to continue the process of that constitution through adult life as well. In the play of identity and difference out of which the subject "appears" at any given point, the relation between childhood and the present, a relation which is and is not a repetition, constitutes an imaginary at either end: for the child, the mother as object of desire; for the adult, the image of the past, the dual relation before it was lost, the pure body-within-the-body, which is only approximated in reproduction. And out of this adult desire springs the demand for an object—not an object of use value, but a pure object, an object which will not be taken up in the changing sphere of lived reality but rather will remain complete at a distance. In this way, it resembles childhood, which will not change.

Reading the Body

Since we know our body only in parts, the image is what constitutes the self for us; it is what constitutes our subjectivity. By a process of projection and introjection of the image, the body comes to have the abstract "form," the abstract totality, by which we know it. Anthropomorphism, for example, tells us much more about the shape of the human body than it tells us about an animal other. We continually project the body into the world in order that its image might return to us: onto the other, the mirror, the animal, and the machine, and onto the artistic image. Furthermore, what remains invisible to us becomes the primary subject of figurative art: the head and shoulders of the portrait and the bust. Because it is invisible, the face becomes gigantic with meaning and significance. Hence, in the style of the pornographer, to blindfold someone is enough to make him or her less than human, to make him or her "only a body." The face becomes a text, a space which must be "read" and interpreted in order to exist. The body of a woman, particularly constituted by the mirror and thus particularly subject to an existence constrained by the nexus of external images, is spoken by her face, by the articulation of anothers' reading. Apprehending the face's image becomes a mode of possession. We are surrounded by the image of the woman's face, the obsession of the portrait and the cover girl alike. The face is what belongs to the other; it is unavailable to the woman herself.

Yet in miniature paintings, or limnings, which are almost always portraits, we see this pattern of possession across both sexes. Miniatures from the Renaissance to the eighteenth century were either ornamental miniatures—circular or oval, and worn on the person as ornaments or jewelry—or cabinet miniatures, larger miniatures placed in oval or rectangular frames to hang on a wall. In both cases, the miniature allowed possession of the face of the other. In the first case the other appends the image of the face to his or her own body; in the second the face becomes an object of contemplation independent of the life of the body. Such miniatures are emblematic of a distanced and abstracted sexuality. In his book *On Collecting Miniatures*, Robert Elward writes: "Who does not like miniatures—'portraits in little,' as they used to be called? They appealed to everyone until the daguerrotype and the photograph made them pass out of fashion for a time. Who can resist the charm of these little portraits, so pretty and graceful and full of romance and sentiment meant to be worn on a lady's bosom, or in a bracelet on her arm, or even in a ring on her finger? They speak to us of love, for out of the marriage of art and love was born the miniature."[50] As early as the 1560's, it seems, miniatures had passed from the manuscript to the cabinet to the body. A miniature of Katherine Grey, Countess of Hertford, from this period shows the countess holding her infant son and wearing a miniature of her husband from a ribbon around her neck. In a portrait from 1572, Lady Walsingham displays an open locket in which there is a limning of her husband.[51] Here the miniature serves as both amulet and souvenir.

In this sense the miniature, although a kind of mirror of the world, is the antithesis of the "self-reflecting" mirror, for the mirror's image exists only at the moment the subject projects it. In contrast, the miniature projects an eternalized future-past upon the subject; the miniature image consoles in its status as an "always there." It resembles the crystal ball or Borges's aleph as a surface which provides profundity as well as projection, a glass which "doesn't know when to stop." When Borges looks into the aleph, he says: "I saw, close up, unending eyes watching themselves in me as in a mirror; I saw all the mirrors on earth and none of them reflected me."[52] If the miniature is a kind of mirror, it is a mirror of requited love.[53] Like other forms of magic, it guarantees the presence of an absent other through either contagion or representation. When the miniature exists simply as a representation, it functions as sympathetic magic; when it is enclosed with a lock of hair, a piece of ribbon, or some other object that is "part" of the other, it functions as contagious magic. The symbolism of "ID" bracelets, exchanged by teen-agers, as well as the significance of the wallet photograph, may be seen as descending from such miniatures. In Elizabeth Berkeley Craven Anspach's play *The Miniature Picture: a Comedy in Three Acts*, performed at the Theatre Royal, Drury

Lane, Mr. Comply asks Eliza, "Did he take your picture with him?" and she replies, "Oh yes, he had it hung about his neck; but that is not the worst part of the story: I find he has been ever since with Miss Loveless."[54] This motif of inner feeling versus outer behavior shapes the romantic plot of the play. To carry the other's face in a locket is to create a double interiority, the interiority of the bourgeois marriage encapsulated and surrounded by the ring. Within the body is both the heart and the heart's content—the other. The heart's state of *contentment*, we must remember, exists only in its interior plentitude.

The locket creates an additional secret recess of the body. Such recesses, which depend upon the protective functions of clothing, are always vulnerable to exposure. In contrast to the bursting sexuality of carnival, they typify the restrained and domesticated sexuality of "the private life." In his *Treatise Concerning the Arte of Limning* (1600), in which he describes the techniques used in the miniature portraits the Elizabethans wore in jeweled and enameled lockets, Nicholas Hillyarde wrote: "[limning] is a thing apart from all other *painting* or *drawing* and tendeth not to comon mens vsse."[55] The antithesis of the locket is the tattoo. The tattoo creates not depth but additional surface. It is publicly symbolic; calling on communal symbols and communal values, it is easily read and easily exposed. The locket is always threatened by loss, for its magic is dependent upon possession. But the tattoo is indelible, and in the sense that all ownership proper implies potential separation and loss, it cannot be "owned." It represents incorporation just as other carnival grotesque images do.[56]

If the surface is the location of the body's meaning, it is because that surface is invisible to the body itself. And if the face reveals a depth and profundity which the body itself is not capable of, it is because the eyes and to some degree the mouth are openings onto fathomlessness. Behind the appearance of eyes and mouth lies the interior stripped of appearances. Hence we "read" the expression of the face with trepidation, for this reading is never apparent from the surface alone; it is continually confronted by the correction of the other. The face is a type of "deep" text, a text whose meaning is complicated by change and by a constant series of alterations between a reader and an author who is strangely disembodied, neither present nor absent, found in neither part nor whole, but, in fact, *created* by this reading. Because of this convention of interpretation, it is not surprising that we find that one of the great *topoi* of Western literature has been the notion of the face as book. Curtius traces the metaphor to the Middle Ages and the writings of Alan of Lille and Henry of Settimello, where a man's face is compared to a book in which his thoughts can be read.[57] Dante, following the medieval poet Berthold of Regensburg, expanded the metaphor to include alphabetical symbolism, reading the letters *OMO* in the human face:

> Parean l'occhiaie anella senza gemme;
> Chi nel viso degli uomini legge OMO,
> Bene avria quivi conosciuto l'emme.[58]

Curtius finds other examples in John Heywood's poem to Mary Tudor ("I wish to have non other books /To read or look upon") and in Sidney's poem to Stella, in which he copies "what Nature in her writes," echoing Latin poets of the twelfth century who used the image of the book to describe the beauty of a woman's face. From Shakespeare he cites, among other passages: "Read o'er the volume of young Paris' face / And find delight writ there with beauty's pen . . . / And what obscured in this fair volume lies, / Find written in the margent of his eyes."[59]

The tradition of the face as book should be placed within the more general tradition of the body as microcosm, the tradition that projects the body upon the universe and the universe upon the body in various ways and thus makes the body, as Lévi-Strauss would say, something good to think with. Like other modes of exaggeration, microcosmic thinking involves juxtaposition with relation to scale and detail. Exaggeration is not possible without correspondence and relativity. But whereas miniaturization involves the juxtaposition of object and representation, of everyday and extraordinary scale, microcosmic thought is a matter of the establishment of correspondences between seemingly disparate phenomena in order to demonstrate the sameness of all phenomena. Such thought therefore always tends toward theology and the promulgation of a "grand design." In diversity is unity; all phenomena are miniaturizations of the essential features of the universe.

In Plato we find the broad outlines of a microcosmic theory. The *Timaeus* asserts that the cosmos is a living organism and that, as such, it is a copy of the transitory world of "becoming." And in the *Republic* an analogy is drawn between the tripartite ideal state and the tripartite individual soul: the ruling, military, and producing classes of the state correspond to the reason, enthusiasms, and appetites of the soul.[60] Extensions of this mode of thinking were essential to Neo-Platonism and, throughout the Graeco-Roman period and even earlier, such views were closely connected with the philosophies of the mystery cults, magicians, and astrologers.[61] Platonic and Neo-Platonic microcosmic thought relies upon correspondences between abstract qualities of human "nature" and physical aspects of the universe. In Alan of Lille's *De planctu Naturae* (Complaint of Nature), Nature has created man in the image of the macrocosm, and exactly as the motions of the planets run counter to the revolution of the firmament, so, in man, sense and reason are in conflict.[62] Similarly, recurring theories of the ages of man and of laws of recapitulation must be placed within this mode that compares the abstract qualities of man to the physical phenomena of the universe.

A number of post-Darwinian works, such as Hermann Lotze's *Microcosmus* (1886) and Charles Napier's *The Book of Nature and the Book of Man* (1870), repeat this theme by attempting to link biology and morality within one grand evolutionary design. Lotze contends that "as in the life of the individual, so in the history of the human race, unavoidable changes take place in the definite outlines of the picture in which man's inalienable and highest aspirations are represented."[63] And Napier explains:

> Types of man's character are illustrated in all departments of nature, from the geometric cell-like plants, which float in fluids, all angles and corners, requiring a microscope to bring out their traits of character, to the apes which most resemble man in form. . . . The highest members of the various classes of organisms, like the most elevated among ourselves, show the greatest regard for offspring. The seeds of the highest plants have much protective covering. Among the reptiles, the python, grandest of its order, hatches its eggs; and the crocodile, the largest recent lizard, is said, unlike the lizard tribe in general, to break the shell covering its young.[64]

Napier goes on to discuss "The Moral Significance of Fishes," "The Chemistry of the Mind," and "The Moral Philosophy of Light," among other topics.

In contrast to this establishment of correspondences between the universe and the abstract qualities of man, other microcosmic philosophies work toward correspondences between the physical body of man and the physical features of the universe. Such theories flourished particularly in Renaissance art and architecture. From 1400 to 1650 the term *microcosm* was used in English as a synonym for *man*.[65] Leonard Barkan has written that, in George Herbert's "Man," "the combination of total inclusiveness and miniature proportion represents an essential and typical view of man in the Renaissance: man is a little world. But Herbert does not create this picture in purely abstract terms—when he refers to man as house, tree, beast, sphere, world, palace, he is speaking not of the human condition, but of the human body. Only the human body can be the image of a microcosm which is at once objective, infinite and proportional."[66] Because during the Renaissance the human body was considered to be infinitely proportional and to contain all possible shapes within it, an architecture was developed which relied upon both scientific and allegorical measurements and interpretations of man's body as a perfectly proportioned miniature universe. Giovanni Paolo Lomazzo, in his *Tracte Containing the Artes of Curious Paintings, Carvinge, Buildinge*, says that "from the proportions of man's body (the most absolute of all God's creatures) is that measure taken which is called Brachium, wherewith all things are most exactly measured, being drawn from the similitude of a mans Arme."[67] Yet, whereas microcosmic thought in the Renaissance was used primarily to develop a simultaneously practical and spiritual aesthetic philosophy, other comparisons between the universe and the physical body of man lead toward mysticism. In the Cabala, for example, the human body is considered to be the model for all phenomena. The vault of heaven corresponds to man's skin; the constellations, to the skin's configuration; the four elements, to man's flesh; and the internal forces of the universe (e.g., angels and servants of God), to men's bones and veins.[68] Boehme's theory of signatures propounded that the whole body signifies heaven and earth; the body cavity (or the bladder) signifies the air; the heart signifies fire; and the blood (or liver) signifies water. The arteries signify the course of the stars, and the intestines, their operation and wasting away. The sky is the heart of nature, like the brain in man's head.[69] Similarly, Fechner concluded in the mid nineteenth century that we have rocks in our bones, streams running through our arteries, light penetrating our eyes, and a fine force coursing through our nerves. He developed over fifty numbered points of resemblance between the earth and the human organism.[70]

Like other forms of thought associated with the miniature, microcosmic philosophies are contemplative and aesthetic rather than scientific and historical. Although in Comte we find references to analogies between society and an organism, and although the theory of recapitulation is occasionally used with reference to the state,[71] microcosmic thought usually centers on the notion of the individual "specimen," whether abstract or physical. When such theories do approach the social, they often result in an aestheticization and diminution of the cultural other. For example, Napier's *Book of Nature* explains that "the people of the West Indies have a hot temper because their climate is hot." The alleged hot temper of the Irish gives his theory some difficulty until he realizes that "the warmth and excitability of the Irish are probably occasioned by the rigorous 'stirring up' they have received, which, amongst men as amongst liquids, increases heat. As in chemistry the mixture of two or more substances occasions heat during the process, so amongst human races the greatest amount of excitement follows the union of tribes, whose infusion acts like the addition of fermenting agents. The Irish, if descended from Milesius, would be of Oriental origin, and Asia Minor, from which they are believed to have come, has a particularly fiery climate in the summer."[72] The connection between the processes of stereotyping and caricature is obvious here: both involve the selection and exaggeration of an element of "quality," the distribution of it over quantity, and the invention of a causality to substantiate the original element chosen. Here we can also begin to place the aestheticization of the primitive and the peasant which underlies much of anthropology, particularly ethnography's impulse toward seeing the "primitive," or "peasant," community as a microcosm of larger social principles—the idea that the village is the world. A major historian and modern proponent of microcosmic philosophies, George Conger, has suggested: "Of the persistent motivations which may be expected to keep the microcosmic theories reappearing, there need be no question that the aesthetic motivation has possibilities which are at once the most abundant and the least explored."[73] These forms of projection of the body—the grotesque, the miniature, and the microcosm—reveal the paradoxical status of the body as both mode and object of knowing, and of the self constituted outside its physical being by its image.

5. OBJECTS OF DESIRE

The Selfish

When the body is the primary mode of perceiving scale, exaggeration must take place in relation to the balance of measurement offered as the body extends into the space of immediate experience. But paradoxically, the body itself is necessarily exaggerated as soon as we have an image of the body, an image which is a projection or objectification of the body into the world. Thus the problems in imagining the body are symptomatic of the problems in imagining the self as place, object, and agent at once. We have seen that there are a number of ways in which the body and the world, the experienced and the imagined, mutually articulate and delimit each other. First, the bodily grotesque of carnival offers the possibility of incorporation: the image is not detached from the body here; rather, it moves within the democratic space of carnival, that space of the face-to-face communication of the marketplace. But in the miniaturized world of the freak show, the body is taken from movement into stasis. Through the transcendent viewpoint offered by this variety of spectacle, the body is made an object and, correlatively, is something which offers itself to possession. Hence, while the freak show may seem, at first glance, to be a display of the grotesque, the distance it invokes makes it instead an inverse display of perfection. Through the freak we derive an image of the normal; to know an age's typical freaks is, in fact, to know its points of standardization. Microcosmic thought—the use of the body as a model of the universe and of the universe as a model of the body—is another example of the image's role in the creation of the body. Starting from assumptions of perfection and balance, microcosmic theories make the body metaphoric to the larger "corporeal" universe. It is clear that in order for the body to exist as a standard of measurement, it must itself be exaggerated into an abstraction of an ideal. The *model* is not the realization of a variety of differences. As the word implies, it is an abstraction or image and not a presentation of any lived possibility. Hence, in the case of the human models of advertising, we are given anonymity rather than identity. Indeed, when a model's name becomes known it usually means that he or she is about to become "animate" as an actor or actress. In contrast to this model body, the body of lived experience is subject to change, transformation, and, most importantly, death. The idealized body implicitly denies the possibility of death—it attempts to present a realm of transcendence and immortality, a realm of the classic. This is the body-made-object, and thus the body as potential commodity, *taking place* within the abstract and infinite cycle of exchange.

Within the development of culture under an exchange economy, the search for authentic experience and, correlatively, the search for the authentic object become critical. As experience is increasingly mediated and abstracted, the lived relation of the body to the phenomenological world is replaced by a nostalgic myth of contact and presence. "Authentic" experience becomes both elusive and allusive as it is placed beyond the horizon of present lived experience, the beyond in which the antique, the pastoral, the exotic, and other fictive domains are articulated. In this process of distancing, the memory of the body is replaced by the memory of the object, a memory standing outside the self and thus presenting both a surplus and lack of significance. The experience of the object lies outside the body's experience—it is saturated with meanings that will never be fully revealed to us. Furthermore, the seriality of mechanical modes of production leads us to perceive that outside as a singular and authentic context of which the object is only a trace.

Here we might take Hegel as our model: "The truth is thus the bacchanalian revel, where not a member is sober; and because every member no sooner becomes detached than it *eo ipso* collapses straightway, the revel is just as much a state of transparent unbroken calm. . . . In the entirety of the movement, taken as an unbroken quiescent whole, that which obtains distinctness in the course of its process and secures specific existence, is preserved in the form of a self-recollection, in which existence is self-knowledge, and self-knowledge, again, is immediate existence."[1] The rending of the body of the god takes place in the delirium of immediate experience. In this act of distortion, dismemberment, and ultimately composition, the social is constituted: we have only to think of the authentic con game offered by Chaucer's Pardoner and the fantastic restoration of the relics of the crucifixion as they served to delineate the West from what it was not.[2]

It is no accident that the closing pitch of the freak show is often manifested by the souvenir. Consider this pitch from the end of the giant and half-lady show at Strate's Carnival, Washington, D.C., in 1941. The giant, Mr. Tomainey, says:

> And notice the size of the hands—watch the hand please—and the size
> of the ring I have here, so large you can pass a silver half a dollar
> right through the center of the ring
> Watch this, a silver half a dollar right through the giant lucky ring,
> believe it or not
> Right through the center of the ring
> Now each one of these rings have my name and occupation engraved
> on them, and I'm going to pass them out now for souvenirs, and
> this is how I do it
> I have here a little booklet, tells you all about our married life, has the
> life story, photographs of both of us and ten questions and answers
> pertaining to our married life and
> Now all you care to know about us two is in this booklet
> Now we sell the booklet for 10¢ and for each and every booklet we
> give away one of these giant lucky rings
> Now if you care to take home an interesting souvenir of the circus,
> hold up your dimes and I'll be very glad to wait on you
> 10¢ is all they are.[3]

The souvenir both offers a measurement for the normal and authenticates the experience of the viewer. The giant begins with the two authenticating signs of origin: the graph itself and the mark upon the world made by his labor. As we saw in the discussion of the bodily grotesque, the freak show as spectacle permits a voyeurism which is at once transcendent and distanced. Thus a miniaturization is effected through the viewer's stance no matter what the object is. Furthermore, the marriage of the freaks presents a proportionality of extremes; the cultural sign triumphs over the limits of the natural. This souvenir domesticates the grotesque on the level of content, subsuming the sexual facts to the cultural code. But the souvenir also domesticates on the level of its operation: external experience is internalized; the beast is taken home. The giant's ring is lucky because it has survived, because it marks the transference of origin to trace, moving from event to memory and desire. Like all wedding rings, it is a souvenir of the joining of the circle, the seamless perfection of joined asymmetrical halves. But in this case there is a second displacement of that event in the proportional joining of disproportionate parts. The giant represents excess; the half-lady, impoverishment. And the audience is now witness to this spectacle of culture forcing nature into the harmonic.

We might say that this capacity of objects to serve as traces of authentic experience is, in fact, exemplified by the souvenir. The souvenir distinguishes experiences. We do not need or desire souvenirs of events that are repeatable. Rather we need and desire souvenirs of events that are reportable, events whose materiality has escaped us, events that thereby exist only through the invention of narrative. Through narrative the souvenir substitutes a context of perpetual consumption for its context of origin. It represents not the lived experience of its maker but the "secondhand" experience of its possessor/owner. Like the collection, it always displays the romance of contraband, for its scandal is its removal from its "natural" location. Yet it is only by means of its material relation to that location that it acquires its value. In this is the tradition of "first-day covers" for stamps and the disappointment we feel in receiving a postcard from the sender's home rather than from the depicted sight. The souvenir speaks to a context of origin through a language of longing, for it is not an object arising out of need or use value; it is an object arising out of the necessarily insatiable demands of nostalgia. The souvenir generates a narrative which reaches only "behind," spiraling in a continually inward movement rather than outward toward the future. Here we find the structure of Freud's description of the genesis of the fetish: a part of the body is substituted for the whole, or an object is substituted for the part, until finally, and inversely, the whole body can become object, substituting for the whole. Thus we have the systematic transformation of the object into its own impossibility, its loss and the simultaneous experience of a difference which Freud characterizes as the fetishist's both knowing and not knowing the anatomical distinctions between the sexes. Metaphor, by the partiality of its substituting power, is, in fact, attached to metonymy here. The possession of the metonymic object is a kind of dispossession in that the presence of the object all the more radically speaks to its status as a mere substitution and to its subsequent distance from the self. This distance is not simply experienced as a loss; it is also experienced as a surplus of signification. It is experienced, as is the loss of the dual relation with the mother, as catastrophe and *jouissance* simultaneously.[4]

The souvenir is by definition always incomplete. And this incompleteness works on two levels. First, the object is metonymic to the scene of its original appropriation in the sense that it is a sample. If I save the ribbon from a corsage, the souvenir is, in Eco's terms, a homomaterial replica, a metonymic reference existing between object/part and object/whole in which the part is of the material of the original and thus a "partial double."[5] Within the operation of the souvenir, the sign functions not so much as object to object, but beyond this relation, metonymically, as object to event/experience. The ribbon may be metonymic to the corsage, but the corsage is in turn metonymic to an increasingly abstract, and hence increasingly "lost," set of referents: the gown, the dance, the particular occasion, the particular spring, all springs, romance, etc. Furthermore, a souvenir does not necessarily have to be a homomaterial replica. If I purchase a plastic miniature of the Eiffel Tower as a souvenir of my trip to Paris, the object is not a homomaterial one; it is a representation in another medium. But whether the souvenir is a material sample or not, it will still exist as a sample of the now-distanced experience, an experience which the object can only evoke and resonate to, and can never entirely recoup. In fact, if it *could* recoup the experience, it would erase its own partiality, that partiality which is the very source of its power. Second, the souvenir must remain impoverished and partial so that it can be supplemented by a narrative discourse, a narrative discouse which articulates the play of desire. The plastic replica of the Eiffel Tower does not define and delimit the Eiffel Tower for us in the way that an architect's model would define and delimit a building. The souvenir replica is an allusion and not a model; it comes after the fact and remains both partial to and more expansive than the fact. It will not function without the supplementary narrative discourse that both attaches it to its origins and creates a myth with regard to those origins.

What is this narrative of origins? It is a narrative of interiority and authenticity. It is not a narrative of the object; it is a narrative of the possessor. The souvenir as bibelot or curiosity has little if any value attached to its materiality. Furthermore, the souvenir is often attached to locations and experiences that are not for sale.[6] The substituting power of the souvenir operates within the following analogy: as experience is to an imagined point of authenticity, so narrative is to the souvenir. The souvenir displaces the point of authenticity as it itself becomes the point of origin for narrative. Such a narrative cannot be generalized to encompass the experience of anyone; it pertains only to the possessor of the object. It is a narrative which seeks to reconcile the disparity between interiority and exteriority, subject and object, signifier and signified. We cannot be proud of someone else's souvenir unless the narrative is extended to include our relationship with the object's owner or unless, as we shall see later, we transform the souvenir into the collection. This vicarious position, we might note, is that of the owner of the heirloom. For example, consider the plot of John P. Marquand's novel *The Late George Apley—A Novel in the Form of a Memoir,* in which a family bitterly quarrels over the disputed possession of "a badly worn square of carpet upon which General Lafayette inadvertently spilled a glass of Madeira during his visit to Boston." Such a memento is a souvenir of everyone in the family and of no one in the family. Its possession is a statement of membership, not in the event, but in the prestige generated by the event. The narrative of origins generated is in effect a genealogy, as Veblen suggested when he wrote that anything giving evidence that wealth has been in a family for several generations has particular value to the leisure classes. The function of the heirloom is to weave, quite literally by means of narrative, a significance of blood relation at the expense of a larger view of history and causality. Similarly, the wide availability of high-quality photographs of various tourist sights does not cancel out the attraction of taking one's own pictures of public sights or the continual production of tour books with titles such as "My France."

In his work on tourism, Dean MacCannell notes that while sights and attractions are collected by entire societies, souvenirs are collected by individual tourists.[7] Describing some typical souvenirs, MacCannell writes:

> In addition to matchbooks, postcards, pencils and ashtrays that carry
> the name and/or the picture of a sight, there are the less common items
> such as touristic dish towels and dust cloths overprinted with drawings
> of Betsy Ross' House or Abraham Lincoln's Birthplace. These are not
> intended to serve their original purposes, but are fixed instead so they
> can be hung on kitchen walls. There is also a special type of square
> pillow covered with a white silklike cloth, fringed in gold braid, that is
> made to serve as the canvas for little paintings of sights like Niagara
> Falls. These latter items are spurious elements that have come out of
> the closet, occupying visible places in the domestic environment.[8]

Whether or not such items are "spurious" is beside the point. From a different point of view, what is being effected here is the transformation of exterior into interior. Spatially, as any postcard tells us, this works most often through a reduction of dimensions. The souvenir reduces the public, the monumental, and the three-dimensional into the miniature, that which can be enveloped by the body, or into the two-dimensional representation, that which can be appropriated within the privatized view of the individual subject. The photograph as souvenir is a logical extension of the pressed flower, the preservation of an instant in time through a reduction of physical dimensions and a corresponding increase in significance supplied by means of narrative. The silence of the photograph, its promise of visual intimacy at the expense of the other senses (its glossy surface reflecting us back and refusing us penetration), makes the eruption of that narrative, the telling of its story, all the more poignant. For the narration of the photograph will itself become an object of nostalgia. Without marking, all ancestors become abstractions, losing their proper names; all family trips become the same trip—the formal garden, the waterfall, the picnic site, and the undifferentiated sea become attributes of every country.

Temporally, the souvenir moves history into private time. Hence the absolute appropriateness of the souvenir as *calendar*. Such a souvenir might mark the privatization of a public symbol (say, the Liberty Bell miniaturized), the juxtaposition of history with a personalized present (say, the year 1776 posited against today's date with its concurrent private "dates"), and the concomitant transformation of a generally purchasable, mass-produced object (the material souvenir) into private possession (the referent being "my trip to Philadelphia"). That remarkable souvenir, the postcard, is characterized by a complex process of captioning and display which repeats this transformation of public into private. First, as a mass-produced view of a culturally articulated site, the postcard is purchased. Yet this purchase, taking place within an "authentic" context of the site itself, appears as a kind of private experience as the self recovers the object, inscribing the handwriting of the personal beneath the more uniform caption of the social. Then in a gesture which recapitulates the social's articulation of the self—that is, the gesture of the *gift* by which the subject is positioned as place of production and reception of obligation—the postcard is surrendered to a significant other. The other's reception of the postcard is the receipt, the ticket stub, that validates the experience of the site, which we now can name as the site of the subject himself or herself.

We must distinguish between souvenirs of exterior sights, souvenirs such as those MacCannell lists, which most often are representations and are purchasable, and souvenirs of individual experience, which most often are samples and are not available as general consumer goods. In fact, if children are the major consumers of mass-produced souvenirs, it is most likely because they, unlike adults, have few souvenirs of the second type and thus must be able to instantly purchase a sign of their own life histories. The souvenir of the second type is intimately mapped against the life history of an individual; it tends to be found in connection with rites of passage (birth, initiation, marriage, and death) as the material sign of an abstract referent: transformation of status. Such souvenirs are rarely kept singly; instead they form a compendium which is an autobiography. Scrapbooks, memory quilts, photo albums, and baby books all serve as examples. It is significant that such souvenirs often appropriate certain aspects of the book in general; we might note especially the way in which an exterior of little material value envelops a great "interior significance," and the way both souvenir and book transcend their particular contexts. Yet at the same time, these souvenirs absolutely deny the book's mode of mechanical reproduction. You cannot make a copy of a scrapbook without being painfully aware that you possess a mere representation of the original. The original will always supplant the copy in a way that is not open to the products of mechanical reproduction.[9] Thus, while the personal memento is of little material worth, often arising, for example, amid the salvage crafts such as quilt-making and embroidery, it is of great worth to its possessor. Because of its connection to biography and its place in constituting the notion of the individual life, the memento becomes emblematic of the worth of that life and of the self's capacity to generate worthiness. Here we see also the introduction of the metaphor of texture. From the child's original metonymic displacement to the love-object, the sensual rules souvenirs of this type. The acute sensation of the object—its perception by hand taking precedence over its perception by eye—promises, and yet does not keep the promise of, *reunion*. Perhaps our preference for instant brown-toning of photographs, distressed antiques, and prefaded blue jeans relates to this suffusion of the *worn*.

Distance and Intimacy

The double function of the souvenir is to authenticate a past or otherwise remote experience and, at the same time, to discredit the present. The present is either too impersonal, too looming, or too alienating compared to the intimate and direct experience of contact which the souvenir has as its referent. This referent is authenticity. What lies between here and there is oblivion, a void marking a radical separation between past and present. The nostalgia of the souvenir plays in the distance between the present and an imagined, prelapsarian experience, experience as it might be "directly lived." The location of authenticity becomes whatever is distant to the present time and space; hence we can see the souvenir as attached to the antique and the exotic.

The antique as souvenir always bears the burden of nostalgia for experience impossibly distant in time: the experience of the family, the village, the firsthand community. One can better understand the antique's stake in the creation of an intimate distance if the antique is contrasted to the physical relic, the souvenir of the dead which is the mere material remains of what had possessed human significance. Because they are souvenirs of death, the relic, the hunting trophy, and the scalp are at the same time the most intensely *potential* souvenirs and the most potent antisouvenirs. They mark the horrible transformation of meaning into materiality more than they mark, as other souvenirs do, the transformation of materiality into meaning. If the function of the souvenir proper is to create a continuous and personal narrative of the past, the function of such souvenirs of death is to disrupt and disclaim that continuity. Souvenirs of the mortal body are not so much a nostalgic celebration of the past as they are an erasure of the significance of history. Consider the function of such souvenirs in the contagious and malevolent magic of voodoo. Or consider the enormous display of hunting trophies staged as "The International Competitive Show" by Hermann Göring in 1937 as a premonition of the death camps and their attempted negation of meaning. In contrast to the restoration offered by such gestures as the return of saints' relics, these souvenirs mark the end of sacred narrative and the interjection of the curse. Ironically, such phenomena themselves can later be reframed in an ensuing metonymic displacement such as the punk and kitsch appropriations of fascist material culture.

Cataclysmic and apocalyptic theories of history and personality refuse the continuity of experience. But in antiquarianism we see a theory of history informed by an aesthetics of the souvenir. Antiquarianism always displays a functional ambivalence; we find either the nostalgic desire of romanticism or the political desire of authentication at its base. For the royal antiquarians of Norway, Sweden, and England during the Renaissance, the collection of antiquities was generally politically supported and politically motivated. Such collection was most commonly used to authenticate the history of kingdoms. In the case of John Leyland, for example, who was appointed king's antiquary in 1533, the same year that Henry VIII declared himself head of the Church of England, a survey of British antiquities was to serve the surrogate purpose of secularizing and localizing that history. Camden's *Brittania* (1586) similarly was intended to supplant papal history with national history. However, in the late seventeenth and early eighteenth centuries the motivation of antiquarianism became more complicated. On the one hand, Henry Bourne's *Antiquitates Vulgares* (1725) was designed to expose the pagan and papist relics surviving among the common people in order to ridicule such practices. On the other hand, John Aubrey's *Brief Lives and Miscellanies* and his studies of the "natural histories" and antiquities of Surrey and Wiltshire, all assembled in the 1690's, were, if we can forgive the anachronism, a premonition of a later romanticism, for in Aubrey's works antiquities are symbolic of a dying English past that should be respectfully recorded and studied.

Aubrey's reverence for the past may well have come from the turmoil of the present's revolution. As commercialism and industrialism transformed the British landscape, the artifacts and architecture of a disintegrating rural culture became the objects of middle- and upper-class nostalgia. Early in the nineteenth century, James Storer and I. Greig wrote in the advertisement for their *Antiquarian and Topographical Cabinet, Containing a Series of Elegant Views of the Most Interesting Objects of Curiosity in Great Britain* (1807–1811): "By the continuance of such patronage, the Antiquarian and Topographical Cabinet will be hastening to preserve the lineaments of the most venerable remains of Antiquity which Time is increasingly whittleing away by nearly imperceptible atoms."[10] Antiquarian societies—first appearing in Britain in 1572, suppressed during the reign of James I, and reinstated in 1718—continued to be popular into the late nineteenth century. Yet, as was the case with Aubrey, they were subject to particular historical circumstances that varied the ways in which they formulated their values. Their suppression during the Jacobean period was a consequence of their dangerous capacity to revive the political allegiances of chivalry as they revived a more generalized taste for the chivalric past. Similarly, the specific content of nationalism changed over time and space. Between the time of Camden and the time of the Victorian antiquarians, nationalism became romantic nationalism in England, a veneration of pastoralism, decentralization, and a collective "folk spirit." But in the New World, for example, antiquarianism centered on the discovery of a radical cultural other, the Native American, whose narrative could not easily be made continuous with either the remote past or the present as constructed by non-native historians. The Englishman Joseph Hunter explains in the preface to his *Antiquarian Notices of Lupset, the Heath, Sharlston, and Ackton, in the County of York* (1851):

> There are two sorts of countries that divide the face of the globe, *new countries* and *old.* . . . which of these two sorts of countries would a man of reflection, a man of taste, a man whose heart beats with moral perceptions and feelings, choose to dwell in? . . . I conceive it to be one of the advantages which the fortune of my birth reserved for me, that I was born in an *old country.* . . . I love to dwell in a country where, on whichever side I turn, I find some object connected with a heart-moving tale, or some scene where the deepest interests of a nation for ages to succeed have been strenuously agitated, and emphatically decided [Hunter's ellipses].

In works such as Hunter's, the antique is linked to the childhood of the nation, to the pastoral, and to the origin of narrative.

It is a logical development of the souvenir's capacity for narrative that by 1846 the term *folklore* had replaced the term *antiquity.* As the evolutionist Andrew Lang wrote: "Now when we find widely and evenly distributed in the earth's surface the rude flint tools of men, we regard these as the oldest examples of human skill. Are we not equally justified in regarding the widely and evenly distributed beliefs in ghosts, kelpies, fairies, wild women of the forests (which are precisely the same in Brittany as in New Caledonia) as among the oldest examples of the working of human fancy?"[11] Oral traditions were thus seen as the abstract equivalent to material culture. Whereas oral tradition obviously cannot "age" in the same sense that the physical artifact can, legends and tales were considered by antiquarians of the survivals school as examples of earlier stages of civilization residing amid the discourse of the present. For such a theory of oral traditions to exist, it was necessary that a distinction be made between dialect and standard, between decentralized and centralized languages—what had begun to develop was the abstract language of science and the state. Forsyth's *Antiquary's Portfolio* (1825) promised that within its pages "the philosopher will meet with entertainment of a nobler kind, by being enabled to contrast the deplorable state of the human mind at remote periods, with the present happy triumph of unfettered reason, and of a religion that is comparatively pure and perfect."[12]

Thus the antiquarian seeks to both distance and appropriate the past. In order to entertain an antiquarian sensibility, a rupture in historical consciousness must have occurred, creating a sense that one can make one's own culture *other*—distant and discontinuous. Time must be seen as concomitant with a loss of understanding, a loss which can be relieved through the reawakening of objects and, thereby, a reawakening of narrative. In a poem, "Time's Footsteps," printed in the first volume of *The Antiquarian Magazine and Bibliographer* (1882), H. R. Wadmore wrote:

The book, the picture, helmet with its crest,
The shield, the spear, the sword, the armour bright,
All on the past can shed a flood of light;
The crozier of the bishop now at rest.

All that is past we seek to treasure here,
All that may make the past a thing of life;
And we would save what else in worldly strife
Might perish, though the present hold it dear.

Accompanying this awakening of objects is the objectification of the peasant classes, the aestheticization of rural life which makes that life "quaint," a survival of an elusive and purer, yet diminished, past. In contrast to the historian, who looks for design and causality, the antiquarian searches for material evidence of the past. Yet at the same time, the antiquarian searches for an internal relation between past and present which is made possible by their absolute disruption. Hence his or her search is primarily an aesthetic one, an attempt to erase the actual past in order to create an imagined past which is available for consumption. In order to awaken the dead, the antiquarian must first manage to kill them. Thus, in this aesthetic mode, we see repeated Lacan's formulation that the symbol manifests itself first of all as the murder of the thing and that this death constitutes in the subject the eternalization of his or her desire.[13]

Every aspect of peasant and rural life, from tools to architecture to dialect to "being" itself in the form of "the character," becomes under antiquarianism a potential souvenir. And the impulse of such souvenirs is to simultaneously transform nature into art as they mourn the loss of "pure nature" at a point of origin. By the Romantics, antiquarianism is completely bound up with the picturesque. Francis Grose's journal, *The Antiquarian Repertory*, published between 1775 and 1784, advertised itself as "a miscellany, intended to preserve and illustrate, several valuable remains of old times, adorned with elegant sculptures." Here is status, stasis, statue, once again: the antique is transformed into the tableau through the prints and plates that accompany the texts of such antiquarian works. Indeed, antiquarian books are often billed as "portfolios" or "cabinets." William Henry Pyne's *Microcosm; or, A Picturesque Delineation of the Arts, Agriculture, and Manufactures of Great Britain in a Series of a Thousand Groups of Small Figures for the Embellishment of Landscape* (1845), for example, was designed "to present the student and the amateur with picturesque representations of the scenery of active life in Great Britain." Such a work transforms labor into abstraction, nature into art, and history into still life just as eighteenth-century and Victorian souvenirs of nature (sea shells, leaves, butterflies placed under glass), as well as contemporary "snow balls" (those souvenirs in which representations of locations are placed along with particles of "snow" or glitter within water-filled plastic spheres), eternalize an environment by closing it off from the possibility of lived experience. They deny the moment of death by imposing the stasis of an eternal death.

Because the world of the souvenir offers transcendence to the viewer, it may be seen as a miniaturized one, as a reduction in physical dimensions corresponding to an increase in significance, and as an interiorization of an exterior. But while the miniature object often speaks to the past, it encapsulates the time of production. Miniature objects are most often exaggerations of the attention to detail, precision, and balance that is characteristic of artisanal culture—a culture which, with the possible exception of microtechnology (the major contemporary producer of miniatures), is considered to have been lost at the dawn of industrial production. The antiquarian is nostalgic for use value, for objects that characterized the preindustrial village economy. Such objects, surviving their original contexts, are seen as traces of the way of life that once surrounded them. Hence we see that popular form of restaurant décor in which preindustrial hand tools are tacked on the walls as if they were prints or paintings.

Yet once the miniature becomes souvenir, it speaks not so much to the time of production as to the time of consumption. For example, a traditional basket-maker might make miniatures of his goods to sell as toys just as he makes full-sized baskets for carrying wood or eggs. But as the market for his full-sized baskets decreases because of changes in the economic system, such miniature baskets increase in demand. They are no longer models; rather, they are souvenirs of a mode of consumption which is now extinct. They have moved from the domain of use value to the domain of *gift*, where exchange is abstracted to the level of social relations and away from the level of materials and processes.[14] The opening to *Silas Marner* (1861) articulates the beginning of a similar transition: "In the days when the spinning wheels hummed busily in the farmhouses—and even great ladies, clothed in silk and thread lace, had their toy spinning wheels of polished oak—there might be seen, in districts far away among the lanes, or deep in the bosom of the hills, certain pallid undersized men who, by the side of the brawny countryfolk, looked like the remnants of a disinherited race." For Eliot this transition was, as she had written in *Adam Bede* (1859), the movement from "Old Leisure" to "amusement": "Leisure is gone—gone where the spinning wheels are gone, and the pack-horses, and the slow waggons, and the pedlars, who brought bargains to the door on sunny afternoons. Ingenious philosophers tell you, perhaps, that the great work of the steam-engine is to create leisure for mankind. Do not believe them; it only creates a vacuum for eager thought to rush in."[15] The spinning wheel has split along class lines in the first case, from use value into toy; in the second it has disappeared as a tool entirely. Eliot here offers a premonition of an entire way of life transformed from production to consumption—the specter, foreshadowed in the picturesque, of culture as a commodity: the culture of tourism. We see this same transformation from industrial production to the spectacle over and over again in the current crisis of late capitalism. Flint, Michigan, for example, recently announced that it would solve its Depression-level unemployment problem by creating an Auto-World, a Disneyland of the automobile industry which is expected to draw tourists from all parts of the globe.

Separation and Restoration

The delicate and hermetic world of the souvenir is a world of nature idealized; nature is removed from the domain of struggle into the domestic sphere of the individual and the interior. The souvenir is used most often to evoke a voluntary memory of childhood, a motif we find either in souvenirs, such as scrapbooks, of the individual life history or in the larger antiquarian theme of the childhood of the nation/race. This childhood is not a childhood as lived; it is a childhood voluntarily remembered, a childhood manufactured from its material survivals. Thus it is a collage made of presents rather than a reawakening of a past. As in an album of photographs or a collection of antiquarian relics, the past is constructed from a set of presently existing pieces. There is no continuous identity between these objects and their referents. Only the act of memory constitutes their resemblance. And it is in this gap between resemblance and identity that nostalgic desire arises. The nostalgic is enamored of distance, not of the referent itself. Nostalgia cannot be sustained without loss. For the nostalgic to reach his or her goal of closing the gap between resemblance and identity, *lived* experience would have to take place, an erasure of the gap between sign and signified, an experience which would cancel out the desire that is nostalgia's reason for existence.

In the cultivation of distance which we find in the uses of the souvenir—the distance of childhood and the antique—the third facet is distance in space—the souvenir of the exotic. Just as authenticity and interiority are placed in the remote past, the exotic offers an authenticity of experience tied up with notions of the primitive as child and the primitive as an earlier and purer stage of contemporary civilization. Jean Baudrillard writes in *Le Système des objets* that the exotic object, like the antique, functions to lend authenticity to the abstract system of modern objects, and he suggests that the indigenous object fascinates by means of its anteriority. This anteriority is characteristic both of the exotic object's form and its mode of fabrication and links it to the analogously anterior world of childhood and its toys.[16] Thus the authenticity of the exotic object arises not in the conditions authored by the primitive culture itself but from the analogy between the primitive/exotic and the origin of the possessor, the authentic "nature" of that radical otherness which is the possessor's own childhood. In Baudrillard's terms, modern is "cold" and the antique and the exotic are "warm" because contemporary mythology places the latter objects in a childhood remote from the abstractions of contemporary consumer society. Such objects allow one to be a tourist of one's own life, or allow the tourist to appropriate, consume, and thereby "tame" the cultural other.

Just as in reverie, narrative is used to invent the symbolic, so by a similar process travel writing functions to miniaturize and interiorize those distanced experiences which remain outside contemporary lived relations. The tourist seeks out objects and scenes, and the relation between the object and its sight is continued, indeed articulated, in the operation of the souvenir. Robert Jennings and Company's tourist books from the 1830's are typical of this romantic genre. In *The Tourist in Biscay and the Castilles*, Thomas Roscoe writes of Bayonne: "Being involuntarily detained, we employed the leisure thus created in seeking out the picturesque, which generally lurks, like unassuming characters, in quiet and out-of-the-way places. Nor were we by any means unsuccessful in our pilgrimage, though dire was the number of dirty lanes and alleys, both within and without the walls, which we threaded in search of it. In spite of the spirit of improvement, numbers of antique houses, not at all dilapidated, are still found here, and each of these would form an interesting study for the pencil."[17] While Roscoe emphasizes the picturesque, W. H. Harrison, in *The Tourist in Portugal*, has a more antiquarian focus, concluding that the reader has been presented with "all the objects we deemed worthy of his attention . . . and all we know about them."[18] The function of the tour is the estrangement of objects—to make what is visible, what is surface, reveal a profound interiority through narrative. This interiority is that of the perceiving subject; it is gained at the expense of risking *contamination* (hence the dire and dirty lanes) and the dissolution of the boundary of that subject. The process is later recapitulated more safely within the context of the familiar, the home, by means of the souvenir.

The exotic object represents distance appropriated; it is symptomatic of the more general cultural imperialism that is tourism's stock in trade. To have a souvenir of the exotic is to possess both a specimen and a trophy; on the one hand, the object must be marked as exterior and foreign, on the other it must be marked as arising directly out of an immediate experience of its possessor. It is thus placed within an intimate distance; space is transformed into interiority, into "personal" space, just as time is transformed into interiority in the case of the antique object. Consider Gulliver's souvenirs of his adventures: from Lilliput the cattle, sheep, gold pieces, and "his Majesty's picture at full length"; from Brobdingnag "the small collection of rarities"— "the comb I had contrived out of the stumps of the King's Beard; and another of the same Materials, but fixed into a paring of her Majesty's Thumb-nail, which served for the Back," the collection of needles and pins, some combings from the queen's hair and her rings, a corn cut from a maid of honor's toe, his breeches made of mouse's skin, and a footman's tooth. These souvenirs serve as evidence of Gulliver's experience and as measurements of his own scale just as the giant's ring and booklet serve to authenticate the audience's experience. Like all curiosities, these souvenirs function to generate narrative. More than the souvenirs of Lilliput, which are most often whole and animal and serve as models and representative elements of sets, the souvenirs of Brobdingnag are partial and human; they are samples of the body which simultaneously estrange us from the body. But unlike the souvenirs of mortality discussed earlier, these souvenirs are taboo items collected from the body's refuse. These beard stumps, nail parings, hair combings, and corns do not diminish the body by their absence or appropriation; rather, they speak to its dual capacities of excess and regeneration. They transform the human into the other and yet allow the possessor to intimately know that other in parts. Gulliver's souvenirs of Brobdingnag are not "ordinary": they speak to his degree of involvement with the Brobdingnagians—his partial yet intimate vision. They are "authentic" souvenirs in the same way that the objects of magical tasks in fairy tales ("you must bring me three hairs from the giant's head") are evidence of an experience that is not vicarious but lived within an estranged or dangerous intimacy. They acquire their value only within the context of Gulliver's narrative; without such a narrative, they are not only meaningless, they are also exaggerations of the disposable.

Unlike the ancient object, which, though it arises from the distant past, is endowed with a familiarity more "warm" than the present, the exotic object is to some degree dangerous, even "hot." Removed from its context, the exotic souvenir is a sign of survival—not its own survival, but the survival of the possessor outside his or her own context of familiarity. Its otherness speaks to the possessor's capacity for otherness: it is the possessor, not the souvenir, which is ultimately the curiosity. The danger of the souvenir lies in its unfamiliarity, in our difficulty in subjecting it to interpretation. There is always the possibility that reverie's signification will go out of control here, that the object itself will take charge, awakening some dormant capacity for destruction. This appropriation of reverie by the object forms the basis for certain horror stories: "The Monkey's Paw," or the ghost stories of M. R. James, for example. In such tales curiosity is replaced by understanding only at the expense of the possessor's well-being.

In most souvenirs of the exotic, however, the metaphor in operation is again one of taming; the souvenir retains its signifying capacity only in a generalized sense, losing its specific referent and eventually pointing to an abstracted otherness that describes the possessor. Nelson Graburn, writing on "fourth world arts," has suggested:

> As "civilized societies" come to depend more and more upon standardized mass-produced artifacts, the distinctiveness of classes, families, and individuals disappears, and the importation of foreign exotic arts increases to meet the demand for distinctiveness, especially for the snob or status market. One gains prestige by association with these objects, whether they are souvenirs or expensive imports; there is a cachet connected with international travel, exploration, multiculturalism, etc. that these arts symbolize; at the same time, there is the nostalgic input of the *handmade* in a "plastic world."[19]

Thus such objects satisfy the nostalgic desire for use value at the same time that they provide an exoticism of the self. Ironically, the demand for such objects creates a souvenir market of goods distinct from authentic traditional crafts, that is, crafts designed in light of use value. And these souvenir goods are often characterized by new techniques of mass production. There is thus a directly proportional relationship between the availability of the exotic experience and the availability of "exotic objects." Once the exotic experience is readily purchasable by a large segment of the tourist population, either more and more exotic experiences are sought (consider travel posters advertising the last frontier or the last unspoiled island) or, in a type of reverse snobbery, there is a turning toward "the classic" of the consumer's native culture. In those cities where one finds a wide range of "ethnic" restaurants frequented by those not of the same ethnicity, one is also likely to find restaurants advertising "classic American cuisine," a phrase which itself cannot work without a French deglazing.

For the invention of the exotic object to take place, there must first be separation. It must be clear that the object is estranged from the context in which it will be displayed as a souvenir; it must be clear that use value is separate from display value.[20] There is perhaps no better example of this process than the radical generational separation in America which results in certain nostalgic forms of lawn art. While we see the exotic and the cultural other explored in forms such as pink flamingos and slumbering Mexicans, the most common forms are antiquarian ones such as wagon wheels, donkey carts, sleighs, and oxen yokes. These metonymic forms are the articulation of abandoned use value. Prominently displayed, they speak to the industrialization of the occupants of the house, occupants who have become tourists of their parents' ways of life.

Yet to create "tourist art" is to create display value from the outset and to by-pass this gradual transformation. Separation is accomplished spatially rather than temporally here. Thus it is necessary to invent the pastoral and the primitive through an illusion of a holistic and integrated cultural other. As for tourist souvenirs themselves, they increasingly tend in both form and content to be shaped by the expectations of the tourist market that will consume them. Graburn points out that since makers of souvenirs must compete with imported, manufactured souvenirs, native arts tend toward smaller sizes—not simply small souvenirs, but miniatures of traditional artifacts, as we saw in the basket-maker example earlier. Among the advantages of miniaturized articles are "applicability for decorative use, economy of materials, and a doll-like, folkloristic quality not associated with the real article."[21] Those qualities of the object which link it most closely to its function in native context are emptied and replaced by both display value and the symbolic system of the consumer. William Bascom has found that in African art this tourist influence has resulted in three stylistic trends, all arising out of Western aesthetic principles. First, there is a tendency toward Western ideas of naturalism and realism; traditional modes of stylization were replaced by nineteenth-century European conventions of the picturesque. Second, there is a tendency toward an opposite extreme: the grotesque. Bascom concludes that this work "may reflect both European preconceptions about the savagery or strength of African sculpture as well as the influence of German Expressionism on European artistic taste." The third tendency is toward gigantification. Yoruba carvers, for example, reproduce bells or clappers used in Ifa divination—bells that are normally 8–16 inches long and 1 inch in diameter—in versions that are 3 feet long and 3 inches in diameter. Gigantification allows the maker to charge more for his product, yet at the same time may involve less labor because it requires less attention to detail.[22] Similarly, Graburn writes that "Eskimo soapstone sculptors and Cordova *santeros* calculate that far less time and effort is spent making large, expensive carvings than the more typical small ones."[23] Thus the tourist aesthetic ensures that the object is continually exoticized and estranged. And, ironically, objects that are originally valued by tourists precisely because of their connections to a traditional, holistic, and paradisal culture are transformed, exaggerated, and modified by the fluctuating demands of that same tourist market.

In the uses of the souvenir, the other side of separation is restoration—here the false promise of restoration. The souvenir must be removed from its context in order to serve as a trace of it, but it must also be restored through narrative and/or reverie. What it is restored to is not an "authentic," that is, a native, context of origin but an imaginary context of origin whose chief subject is a projection of the possessor's childhood. Restoration can be seen as a response to an unsatisfactory set of present conditions. Just as the restoration of buildings, often taking place within programs of "gentrification" in contemporary cities, has as its basis the restoration of class relationships that might otherwise be in flux, so the restoration of the souvenir is a conservative idealization of the past and the distanced for the purposes of a present ideology. We thus might say that all souvenirs are souvenirs of a nature which has been invented by ideology. This conclusion speaks not only to the display of Victorian sea shells under glass but also to the broader tendency to place all things natural at one degree of removal from the present flow of events and thereby to objectify them.

The only proper context for the souvenir is the displacement of reverie, the gap between origin/object/subject which fields desire. Whereas the collection is either truly hidden or prominently displayed, the souvenir, so long as it remains "uncollected," is "lost," removed from any context of origin and use value in such a way as to "surprise" and capture its viewer into reverie. The actual locale of the souvenir is often commensurate with its material worthlessness: the attic and the cellar, contexts away from the business and engagement of everyday life. Other rooms of a house are tied to function (kitchen, bath) and presentation (parlor, hall) in such a way that they exist within the temporality of everyday life, but the attic and the cellar are tied to the temporality of the past, and they scramble the past into a simultaneous order which memory is invited to rearrange: heaven

and hell, tool and ornament, ancestor and heir, decay and preservation. The souvenir is destined to be forgotten; its tragedy lies in the
death of memory, the tragedy of all autobiography and the simultaneous erasure of the autograph. And thus we come again to the
powerful metaphor of the unmarked grave, the reunion with the
mother with no corresponding regeneration of the symbolic.

Part II. THE COLLECTION, PARADISE OF CONSUMPTION

Context Destroyed

The souvenir involves the displacement of attention into the past.
The souvenir is not simply an object appearing out of context, an
object from the past incongruously surviving in the present; rather,
its function is to envelop the present within the past. Souvenirs are
magical objects because of this transformation. Yet the magic of the
souvenir is a kind of failed magic. Instrumentality replaces essence
here as it does in the case of all magical objects, but this instrumentality always works an only partial transformation. The place of origin
must remain unavailable in order for desire to be generated.

All souvenirs are souvenirs of nature, yet it is nature in its most
synthetic, its most acculturated, sense which appears here. Nature is
arranged diachronically through the souvenir; its synchrony and
atemporality are manipulated into a human time and order. The
pressed flowers under glass speak to the significance of their owner
in nature and not to themselves in nature. They are a sample of a
larger and more sublime nature, a nature differentiated by human
experience, by human history.

In contrast to the souvenir, the collection offers example rather
than sample, metaphor rather than metonymy. The collection does
not displace attention to the past; rather, the past is at the service of
the collection, for whereas the souvenir lends authenticity to the past,
the past lends authenticity to the collection. The collection seeks a
form of self-enclosure which is possible because of its ahistoricism.
The collection replaces history with *classification*, with order beyond
the realm of temporality. In the collection, time is not something to be
restored to an origin; rather, all time is made simultaneous or synchronous within the collection's world.

The souvenir still bears a trace of use value in its instrumentality,
but the collection represents the total aestheticization of use value.
The collection is a form of art as play, a form involving the reframing
of objects within a world of attention and manipulation of context.

Like other forms of art, its function is not the restoration of context of origin but rather the creation of a new context, a context standing in a metaphorical, rather than a contiguous, relation to the world of everyday life. Yet unlike many forms of art, the collection is not representational. The collection presents a hermetic world: to have a representative collection is to have both the minimum and the complete number of elements necessary for an autonomous world—a world which is both full and singular, which has banished repetition and achieved authority.

We might therefore say, begging forgiveness, that the archetypal collection is Noah's Ark, a world which is representative yet which erases its context of origin. The world of the ark is a world not of nostalgia but of anticipation. While the earth and its redundancies are destroyed, the collection maintains its integrity and boundary. Once the object is completely severed from its origin, it is possible to generate a new series, to start again within a context that is framed by the selectivity of the collector: "And of every living thing of all flesh, you shall bring two of every sort into the ark, to keep them alive with you; they shall be male and female. Of the birds according to their kinds, and of the animals according to their kinds, of every creeping thing of the ground according to its kind, two of every sort shall come in to you, to keep them alive. Also take with you every sort of food that is eaten, and store it up; and it shall serve as food for you and for them." The world of the ark is dependent upon a prior creation: Noah has not invented a world; he is simply God's broker. What he rescues from oblivion is the two that is one plus one, the two that can generate seriality and infinity by the symmetrical joining of asymmetry. While the point of the souvenir may be remembering, or at least the invention of memory, the point of the collection is forgetting—starting again in such a way that a finite number of elements create, by virtue of their combination, an infinite reverie. Whose labor made the ark is not the question: the question is what is inside.

This difference in purpose is the reason why the scrapbook and the memory quilt must properly be seen as souvenirs rather than as collections.[24] In apprehending such objects, we find that the whole dissolves into parts, each of which refers metonymically to a context of origin or acquisition. This is the experience of objects-into-narratives that we saw in the animation of the toy and that becomes, in fact, the "animating" principle of works such as Xavier de Maistre's *Voyage Autour de Ma Chambre:* "Mais il est aussi impossible d'expliquer clairement un tableau que de faire un portrait ressemblant d'après une description."[25] In contrast, each element within the collection is representative and works in combination toward the creation of a new whole that is the context of the collection itself. The spatial whole of the collection supersedes the individual narratives that "lie behind it." In an article on the aesthetics of British mercantilism, James H. Bunn suggests that "in a curio cabinet each cultural remnant has a circumscribed allusiveness among a collection of others. If the unintentional aesthetic of accumulating exotic goods materialized as a side effect of mercantilism, it can be semiologically considered as a special case of eclecticism, which intentionally ignores proprieties of native history and topography."[26] The aesthetics of mercantilism, which Bunn places within the period of 1688–1763, is thus in an important way the antithesis of the aesthetics of antiquarianism. The antiquarian is moved by a nostalgia of origin and presence; his function is to validate the culture of ground, as we see in works such as Camden's *Britannia*. But the mercantilist is not moved by restoration; he is moved by extraction and seriality. He removes the object from context and places it within the play of signifiers that characterize an exchange economy.

Because the collection replaces origin with classification, thereby making temporality a spatial and material phenomenon, its existence is dependent upon principles of organization and categorization. As Baudrillard has suggested, it is necessary to distinguish between the concept of collection and that of accumulation: "Le stade inférieur est celui de l'accumulation de matières: entassement de vieux papiers, stockage de nourriture—à mi-chemin entre l'introjection orale et la rétention anale—puis l'accumulation sérielle d'objets identiques. La collection, elle, émerge vers la culture . . . sans cesser de renvoyer les uns aux autres, ils incluent dans ce jeu une extériorite sociale, des relations humaines."[27] Herein lies the difference between the collections of humans and the collections of pack rats. William James reported that a California wood rat arranges nails in a symmetrical, fortresslike pattern around his nest, but the objects "collected"—silver, tobacco, watches, tools, knives, matches, pieces of glass—are without seriality, without relation to one another or to a context of acquisition. Such accumulation is obviously not connected to the culture and the economy in the same way that the collection proper is connected to such structures. Although the objects of a hobbyist's collection have significance only in relation to one another and to the seriality that such a relation implies, the objects collected by the wood rat are intrinsic objects, objects complete in themselves because of the sensory qualities that have made them attractive to the rat. James found the same propensity for collecting intrinsic objects among "misers" in lunatic asylums: " 'the miser' *par excellence* of the popular imagination and of melodrama, the monster of squalor and misanthropy, is simply one of these mentally deranged persons. His intellect may in many matters be clear, but his instincts, especially that of ownership, are insane, and their insanity has no more to do with the association of ideas than with the precession of the equinoxes."[28] Thus James concludes that hoarders have an uncontrollable impulse to take and keep. Here we might add that this form of insanity is, like anal retentiveness, an urge toward incorporation for its own sake, an attempt to erase the limits of the body that is at the same time an attempt, marked by desperation, to "keep body and soul together."

Although it is clear that there is a correspondence between the productions of art and the productions of insanity in these cases, it is equally clear that the miser's collection depends upon a refusal of differentiation while the hobbyist's collection depends upon an acceptance of differentiation as its very basis for existence. Thus the "proper" collection will always take part in an anticipation of redemption: for example, the eventual coining-in of objects or the eventual acquisition of object status by coins themselves. But the insane collection is a collection for its own sake and for its own movement. It refuses the very *system* of objects and thus metonymically refuses the entire political economy that serves as the foundation for that system and the only domain within which the system acquires meaning. Baudrillard as well concludes that because of the collection's seriality, a "formal" interest always replaces a "real" interest in collected objects.[29] This replacement holds to the extent that aesthetic value replaces use value. But such an aesthetic value is so clearly tied to the cultural (i.e., deferment, redemption, exchange) that its value system is the value system of the cultural; the formalism of the collection is never an "empty" formalism.

Inside and Outside

To ask which principles of organization are used in articulating the collection is to begin to discern what the collection is about. It is not sufficient to say that the collection is organized according to time, space, or internal qualities of the objects themselves, for each of these parameters is divided in a dialectic of inside and outside, public and private, meaning and exchange value. To arrange the objects according to time is to juxtapose personal time with social time, autobiography with history, and thus to create a fiction of the individual life, a time of the individual subject both transcendent to and parallel to historical time. Similarly, the spatial organization of the collection, left to right, front to back, behind and before, depends upon the creation of an individual perceiving and apprehending the collection with eye and hand. The collection's space must move between the public and the private, between display and hiding. Thus the miniature is suitable as an item of collection because it is sized for individual consumption at the same time that its surplus of detail connotes infinity and distance. While we can "see" the entire collection, we cannot possibly "see" each of its elements. We thereby also find at work here the play between identity and difference which characterizes the collection organized in accordance with qualities of the objects themselves. To group objects in a series because they are "the same" is to simultaneously signify their difference. In the collection, the more the objects are similar, the more imperative it is that we make gestures to distinguish them. As an example of this obsession with series, consider Pepys's library:

> Samuel Pepys, who arranged and rearranged his library, finally
> classified his books according to size. In double rows on the shelves the
> larger volumes were placed behind the smaller so that the lettering on
> all could be seen; and in order that the tops might be even with each
> other, this neat collector built wooden stilts where necessary and,
> placing those under the shorter books, gilded them to match the
> bindings! Subject and reference-convenience were secondary in this
> arrangement, except insofar as the sacrosanct diary was concerned, and
> this, which had been written in notebooks of varying size, Mr. Pepys,
> reverting to reason, had bound uniformly so that its parts might be
> kept together without disturbing the library's general arrangement-
> scheme.[30]

Pepys's collection must be displayed as an identical series (the stilt arrangement) and as a set of individual volumes ("so that the lettering on all could be seen"). The necessity of identity at the expense of information here is an example of Baudrillard's suggestion that formal interest replaces real interest. That this is often the motivation of the bibliophile is also made clear by the buying of "books" that are joined cardboard bindings decorated to look like matched sets of volumes, yet in fact are empty.

The collection is not constructed by its elements; rather, it comes to exist by means of its principle of organization. If that principle is bounded at the onset of the collection, the collection will be finite, or at least potentially finite. If that principle tends toward infinity or series itself, the collection will be open-ended. As an example of the first type, William Carew Hazlitt's suggestions for the coin collector hold:

> There are collectors who make their choice and stand by it; others
> who collect different series at different times; others whose scheme is

miscellaneous or desultory. To all these classes increased facility for judging within a convenient compass what constitutes a series, its chronology, its features, its difficulties, ought to be acceptable. To master even the prominent monographs is a task which is sufficient to deter all but the most earnest and indefatigable enthusiasts: and, as usual, no doubt, collections are made on a principle more or less loose and vague. At any rate, the first step should be, we apprehend, to reconnoitre the ground, and measure the space to be traversed, with the approximate cost.[31]

As an example of the second type, consider C. Montiesor's suggestion that children collect clergymen's names: "There were the coloured clergy—Green, Black, White, Gray, etc. The happy clergy, in the state of—Bliss, Peace, Joy, etc. The virtuous clergy—Virtue, Goodenough, Wise, etc. The poor clergy, who possessed only a—Penny, Farthing, Ha'penny. The moneyed clergy; these were—Rich, Money, etc. The bad clergy—Shy, Cunning, etc."[32] Here we might also remember Walter Benjamin's project of collecting quotations, a collection which would illustrate the infinite and regenerative seriality of language itself.

Any intrinsic connection between the principle of organization and the elements themselves is minimized by the collection. We see little difference between collections of stones or butterflies and collections of coins or stamps. In acquiring objects, the collector replaces production with consumption: objects are naturalized into the landscape of the collection itself. Therefore, stones and butterflies are made cultural by classification, and coins and stamps are naturalized by the erasure of labor and the erasure of context of production. This impulse to remove objects from their contexts of origin and production and to replace those contexts with the context of the collection is quite evident in the practices of Floyd E. Nichols of New York City, a collector's collector. Rather than exhibit his many collected items according to type, Nichols would group objects together so that they told a story: "For instance, with miniature cat, mice, whiskey glass, and whiskey bottle, he dramatizes the proverb, 'One drink of moonshine whiskey would make a mouse spit in a cat's face,'" and "To miniature camels he attached a number 5 needle, the wire being shaped so that when it was pulled away from the needle, the camel mounted on the traverse section of the wire passed completely through the eye of the needle."[33] Nichols's practice exemplifies the replacement of the narrative of production by the narrative of the collection, the replacement of the narrative of history with the narrative of the individual subject—that is, the collector himself.

Whereas the space of the souvenir is the body (talisman), the periphery (memory), or the contradiction of private display (reverie), the space of the collection is a complex interplay of exposure and hiding, organization and the chaos of infinity. The collection relies upon the box, the cabinet, the cupboard, the seriality of shelves. It is determined by these boundaries, just as the self is invited to expand within the confines of bourgeois domestic space. For the environment to be an extension of the self, it is necessary not to act upon and transform it, but to declare its essential emptiness by filling it. Ornament, décor, and ultimately decorum define the boundaries of private space by emptying that space of any relevance other than that of the subject. In a suggestive essay on the etymology of the terms *milieu* and *ambience*, Leo Spitzer traces the notion of authentic place as moving from the classical macrocosmic/microcosmic relation between man and nature, in which space is climate, protector, and effecting presence; to the medieval theory of gradations, in which social position becomes the natural place of being; to the late-seventeenth-century notion of the interior: "It is in such descriptions of an interior setting that the idea of the 'milieu' (enclosing and 'filled in') is presented most forcefully; we have the *immediate* milieu of the individual. One may remember the vogue which paintings of the same type enjoyed in the preceding century—intérieurs depicting the coziness and comfort of well-furnished human dwellings. . . . The world-embracing, metaphysical, cupola that once enfolded mankind has disappeared, and man is left to rattle around in an infinite universe. Thus he seeks all the more to fill in his immediate, his physical, environment with things."[34]

If this task of filling in the immediate environment with things were simply one of use value, it would be quite simple. But this filling in is a matter of ornamentation and presentation in which the interior is both a model and a projection of self-fashioning. The contradictions of the aesthetic canon are contradictions of genealogy and personality: harmony and disruption, sequence and combination, pattern and variation. Consider Grace Vallois's extensive advice in *First Steps in Collecting Furniture, Glass, and China*:

> There is to me something distinctly incongruous in seeing a large Welsh dresser (never originally meant for anything but a kitchen) occupying the entire wall of a little jerry-built twentieth century dining room, and adorned with the necessary adjuncts of everyday life, biscuit boxes perhaps, and a Tantalus stand. Sometimes the dresser is promoted to the 'drawing room' so called, and thrusts its grand, simple old lines, among palms in pots, an ugly but convenient Sutherland table for tea, or crowning atrocity, one of those three-tiered stands for cake and bread and butter. These things may be convenient, but they do not go

with the old dresser! . . . It is not necessary to have everything of the
same period, that, to my mind, is dull and uninteresting. An ancestral
home is necessarily built up bit by bit, each generation has added
something and left their impress in the old house. I like to see Jacobean
chairs living amicably with Sheraton cabinets, and old four posters
sharing floor space with 17th century Bridal chests, and 18th century
Hepplewhite chairs. That is as it should be, and appeals to me far more
than a perfect 18th century house, where everything inside and out
seems to speak of Adam.[35]

Ironically, Booth Tarkington's parody of collectors in *The Collector's
Whatnot* contains a similar essay by one "Angustula Thomas" on
"pooning," or arranging, the collection. Angustula advises: "Don't
adhere too closely to periods. If you have acquired a few *good* pieces
of Egyptian furniture of the Shepherd King Period for your living-
room, they may be easily combined with Sheraton or Eastlake by
placing a Mingg vase or an old French fowling-piece between the two
groups; or you may cover the transition by a light scattering of Mexican pottery, or some Java wine-jars."[36] These texts, either "sincere"
or parodying, imply that possession cannot be undertaken independent of collection and arrangement. Each sign is placed in relation to a
chain of signifiers whose ultimate referent is not the interior of the
room—in itself an empty essence—but the interior of the self.

In order to construct this narrative of interiority it is necessary to
obliterate the object's context of origin. In these examples eclecticism
rather than pure seriality is to be admired because, if for no other
reason, it marks the heterogeneous organization of the self, a self
capable of transcending the accidents and dispersions of historical
reality. But eclecticism at the same time depends upon the unstated
seriality it has bounded from. Not simply a consumer of the objects
that fill the décor, the self generates a fantasy in which it becomes
producer of those objects, a producer by arrangement and manipulation. The rather extraordinary confidence with which Vallois addresses her audience, which is assumed to have access to the "controlled variety" of seventeenth- and eighteenth-century antiques
that she "likes to see," is the confidence of the managerial classes,
whose own role in the production of history is dependent upon the
luxury of the collection of surplus value. Here we might consider the
structural meaning of the "flea" market as dependent upon the leisure tastes and discarded fashions of the host culture: the market
economy. Similarly, Balzac's original title for his novel of collecting,
Cousin Pons, was *Le Parasite*. As we know from the antics of that poor
relation, the economy of collecting is a fantastic one, an economy
with its own principles of exchange, substitution, and replicability

despite its dependence upon the larger economic system. Balzac's narrator tells us: "The joy of buying bric-à-brac is a secondary delight; in the give-and-take of barter lies the joy of joys."[37] The term à-bric-à-brac, which we might translate as "by hook or crook," implies the process of acquisition and exchange, which is the (false) labor of the collector. Herein lies the ironic nostalgia of the collection's economic system: although dependent upon, and a mirroring of, the larger economy of surplus value, this smaller economy is self-sufficient and self-generating with regard to its own meanings and principles of exchange. Whereas the larger economy has replaced use value through the translation of labor into exchange value, the economy of the collection translates the monetary system into the system of objects. Indeed, that system of objects is often designed to serve as a stay against the frailties of the very monetary system from which it has sprung. The collection thereby acquires an aura of transcendence and independence that is symptomatic of the middle class's values regarding personality.

When one wants to disparage the souvenir, one says that it is not authentic; when one wants to disparage the collected object, one says "it is not *you*." Thus Spitzer's model of the self as occupying the interior in conjunction with objects is not a completely adequate one, for the contained here *is* the self; the material body is simply one more position within the seriality and diversity of objects. Private space is marked by an exterior material boundary and an interior surplus of signification.

To play with series is to play with the fire of infinity. In the collection the threat of infinity is always met with the articulation of boundary. Simultaneous sets are worked against each other in the same way that attention to the individual object and attention to the whole are worked against each other. The collection thus appears as a mode of control and containment insofar as it is a mode of generation and series. And this function of containment must be taken into account as much as any simple Freudian model when we note the great popularity of collecting objects that are themselves containers: cruets, pitchers, salt-and-pepper shakers, vases, teapots, and boxes, to name a few. The finite boundaries these objects afford are played against the infinite possibility of their collection, and, analogously, their finite use value when filled is played against the measureless emptiness that marks their new aesthetic function.

In other cases, categorization allows the collection to be finite—indeed, this finitude becomes the collector's obsession. The *New York Times* for March 16, 1980, carried an account of a man who was (and probably still is) searching for three antique Tiffany postal scales; he owns six of the nine that are said to exist and has paid a special finding service to look for the missing trio of scales. William Walsh's *Handy-book of Literary Curiosities* recounts a comparable story:

> There is a story of a wealthy English collector who long believed that a certain rare book in his possession was a unique. One day he received a bitter blow. He learned that there was another copy in Paris. But he soon rallied, and, crossing over the Channel, he made his way to the rival's home. "You have such and such a book in your library?" he asked, plunging at once *in medias res.* "Yes." "Well, I want to buy it." "But, my dear sir—" "I will give you a thousand francs for it." "But it isn't for sale; I—" "Two thousand!" "On my word, I don't care to dispose of it." "Ten thousand!" and so on, till at last twenty-five thousand francs was offered; and the Parisian gentleman finally consented to part with this treasure. The Englishman counted out twenty-five thousand-franc bills, examined the purchase carefully, smiled with satisfaction, and cast the book into the fire. "Are you crazy?" cried the Parisian, stooping over to rescue it. "Nay," said the Englishman, detaining his arm. "I am quite in my right mind. I, too, possess a copy of that book. I deemed it a unique."[38]

This story is, by now, a legend of collecting (Baudrillard, via Maurice Rheims, recounts it as happening in New York).[39] It is an account of the replacement of content with classification, an account of the ways in which collection is the antithesis of creation. In its search for a perfect hermeticism, the collection must destroy both labor and history. The bibliomaniac's desire for the possession of the unique object is similarly reflected in the collector's obsession with the aberration. D'Israeli records that Cicero wrote thus to Atticus requesting his help in forming a collection of antiquities: "In the name of our friendship suffer nothing to escape you of whatever you find curious or rare."[40]

The collector can gain control over repetition or series by defining a finite set (the Tiffany postal scales) or by possessing the unique object. The latter object has acquired a particular poignancy since the onset of mechanical reproduction; the aberrant or unique object signifies the flaw in the machine just as the machine once signified the flaws of handmade production. Veblen's critique of conspicuous consumption similarly concluded that the handmade object's crudity was, ironically, a symptom of conspicuous waste. "Hand labor is a more wasteful method of production; hence the goods turned out by this method are more serviceable for the purpose of pecuniary reputability; hence the marks of hand labor come to be honorific, and the goods which exhibit these marks take rank as of higher grade than the corresponding machine product. . . . The appreciation of those evidences of honorific crudeness to which hand-wrought goods owe their superior worth and charm in the eyes of well-bred people is a matter of nice discrimination."[41] Thus a measured crudity of material quality is presented in tension with an overrefinement of significance. This tension is further exaggerated by the juxtaposition of the unique and singular qualities of the individual object against the seriality of the collection as a whole.

The collection is often about containment on the level of its content and on the level of the series, but it is also about containment in a more abstract sense. Like Noah's Ark, those great civic collections, the library and the museum, seek to represent experience within a mode of control and confinement. One cannot know everything about the world, but one can at least approach closed knowledge through the collection. Although transcendent and comprehensive in regard to its own context, such knowledge is both eclectic and eccentric. Thus the ahistoricism of such knowledge makes it particularistic and consequently random. In writings on collecting, one constantly finds discussion of the collection as a mode of knowledge. Alice Van Leer Carrick declares in the preface to *Collector's Luck* that "collecting isn't just a fad; it isn't even just a 'divine madness': properly interpreted, it is a liberal education."[42] Indeed, one might say inversely that the liberal arts education characteristic of the leisure classes is in itself a mode of collection. The notion of the "educational hobby" legitimates the collector's need for control and possession within a world of infinitely consumable objects whose production and consumption are far beyond the ken of the individual subject. Although the library might be seen in a semiotic sense as representing the world, this is not the collector's view; for the collector the library is a representative collection of books just as any collection is representative of its class of objects. Thus, for the collector, the material quality of the book is foregrounded, a feature parodied by Bruyère: "Of such a collector, as soon as I enter his house, I am ready to faint on the staircase, from a strong smell of Morocco leather; in vain he shows me fine editions, gold leaves, Etruscan bindings, and naming them one after another, as if he were showing a gallery of pictures! . . . I thank him for his politeness, and as little as himself care to visit the tan-house, which he calls his library."[43]

Yet it is the museum, not the library, which must serve as the central metaphor of the collection; it is the museum, in its representativeness, which strives for authenticity and for closure of all space and temporality within the context at hand. In an essay on *Bouvard and Pécuchet*, Eugenio Donato has written:

> The set of objects the Museum displays is sustained only by the fiction that they somehow constitute a coherent representational universe. The fiction is that a repeated metonymic displacement of fragment for

totality, object to label, series of objects to series of labels, can still produce a representation which is somehow adequate to a nonlinguistic universe. Such a fiction is the result of an uncritical belief in the notion that ordering and classifying, that is to say, the spatial juxtaposition of fragments, can produce a representational understanding of the world.[44]

Thus there are two movements to the collection's gesture of standing for the world: first, the metonymic displacement of part for whole, item for context; and second, the invention of a classification scheme which will define space and time in such a way that the world is accounted for by the elements of the collection. We can see that what must be suppressed here is the privileging of context of origin, for the elements of the collection are, in fact, already accounted for by the world. And we can consequently see the logic behind the blithe gesture toward decontextualization in museum acquisitions, a gesture which results in the treasures of one culture being stored and displayed in the museums of another. Similarly, the museum of natural history allows nature to exist "all at once" in a way in which it could not otherwise exist. Because of the fiction of such a museum, it is the Linnaean system which articulates the identities of plants, for example, and not the other way around. The popularity of tableau scenes in the natural history museum and the zoo further speaks to the dramatic impulse toward simultaneity and the felicitous reconciliation of opposites which characterize such collections.

In her book on collecting, which she wrote for children, Montiesor recommends that "every house ought to possess a 'Museum,' even if it is only one shelf in a small cupboard; here, carefully dated and named, should be placed the pretty shells you gather on the seashore, the old fossils you find in the rocks, the skeleton leaves you pick up from under the hedges, the strange orchids you find on the downs. Learn what you can about each object before you put it in the museum, and docket it not only with its name, but also with the name of the place in which you found it, and the date."[45] Thus we have directions for the homemade universe; nature is nothing more or less than that group of objects which is articulated by the classification system at hand, in this case a "personal" one. When objects are defined in terms of their use value, they serve as extensions of the body into the environment, but when objects are defined by the collection, such an extension is inverted, serving to subsume the environment to a scenario of the personal. The ultimate term in the series that marks the collection is the "self," the articulation of the collector's own "identity." Yet ironically and by extension, the fetishist's impulse toward accumulation and privacy, hoarding and the secret, serves both to give integrity to the self and at the same time to overload the self with signification. Bunn, in his article on British mercantilist culture, has suggested that this surplus of significance can, in fact, *saturate* the collector: "Although the chance removal of a cultural token cauterizes its source, it also overwhelms unintentionally the semiological substructure of its host."[46] For an example of this process by which the host is overwhelmed, we might remember the haunting picture of Mario Praz at the conclusion of *La Casa della Vita;* gazing into a convex mirror which reflects a room full of collected objects, Praz sees himself as no bigger than a handful of dust, a museum piece among museum pieces, detached and remote.

The boundary between collection and fetishism is mediated by classification and display in tension with accumulation and secrecy. As W. C. Hazlitt wrote, "The formation of Collections of Coins originated, not in the Numismatist, but in the Hoarder. Individuals, from an early stage in the history of coined money, laid pieces aside, as (nearer to our day) Samuel Pepys did, because they were striking or novel, or secreted them in the ground, like Pepys, because they were thought to be insecure."[47] In the hoarder the gesture toward an incomplete replacement (the part-object)—the gesture we saw at work through the substitution of the souvenir for origin—becomes a compulsion, the formation of a repetition or chain of substituting signifiers. Following Lévi-Strauss's work on totems, Baudrillard concludes that the desire and *jouissance* characterizing fetishism result from the systematic quality of objects rather than from the objects themselves: "Ce qui fascine dans l'argent (l'or) n'est ni sa matérialité, ni même l'equivalent capté d'une certaine force (de travail) ou d'un certain pouvoir virtuel, c'est sa *systématicité;* c'est la virtualité, enfermée dans cette matière, de substitutivité totale de toutes les valeurs grâce à leur abstraction définitive."[48] In the collection such systematicity results in the quantification of desire. Desire is ordered, arranged, and manipulated, not fathomless as in the nostalgia of the souvenir. Here we must take into account not only Freud's theory of the fetish but Marx's as well.

The fetishized object must have a reference point within the system of the exchange economy—even the contemporary fetishization of the body in consumer culture is dependent upon the system of images within which the corporeal body has been transformed into another point of representation. As Lacan has noted, the pleasure of possessing an object is dependent upon others. Thus the object's position in a system of referents—a system we may simultaneously and variously characterize as the psychoanalytic life history or as the points of an exchange economy marking the places of "existence"—and not any intrinsic qualities of the object or even its context of origin, determines its fetishistic value. The further the object is removed from use value, the more abstract it becomes and the more multivocal is its referentiality. The dialectic between hand and eye, possession and transcendence, which motivates the fetish, is dependent upon this abstraction. Thus, just as we saw that in its qualities of eclecticism and transcendence the collection can serve as a metaphor for the individual personality, so the collection can also serve as a metaphor for the *social* relations of an exchange economy. The collection replicates Marx's by now familiar account of the objectification of commodities:

> It is a definite social relation between men, that assumes, in their eyes, the fantastic form of a relation between things. In order, therefore, to find an analogy, we must have recourse to the mist-enveloped regions of the religious world. In that world the productions of the human brain appear as independent beings endowed with life, and entering into relation both with one another and the human race. So it is in the world of commodities with the products of men's hands. This I call the Fetishism which attaches itself to the products of labour, so soon as they are produced as commodities, and which is therefore inseparable from the production of commodities.[49]

In this passage we find a description of the process by which the alienation of labor emerges—the abstraction of labor power within the cycle of exchange, an abstraction which makes the work of the body perceivable in terms of its signifying capacity. This estrangement of labor from its location in lived relations is perceivable in the operation of the souvenir as the souvenir both mourns and celebrates the gap between object and context of origin. It is, in other words, by means of the alienation of labor that the object is constituted. Yet Marx's model of the process of fetishization focuses upon the inversion by which the self as producer of meanings is seen as independent of that production. We must extend this description a degree further in order to see the final stage of this alienation, a stage in which the self is constituted by its consumption of goods.

What is the proper labor of the consumer? It is a labor of total magic, a fantastic labor which operates through the manipulation of abstraction rather than through concrete or material means. Thus, in contrast to the souvenir, the collection presents a metaphor of "production" not as "the earned" but as "the captured." The scene of origin is not a scene of the transformation of nature; it is too late for that. Nor is it simply a scene of appropriation, as it might be through the exercise of the body upon the world. We go to the souvenir, but the collection comes to us. The collection says that the world is given; we are inheritors, not producers, of value here. We "luck into" the collection; it might attach itself to particular scenes of acquisition, but the integrity of those scenes is subsumed to the transcendent and ahistorical context of the collection itself. This context destroys the context of origin. In the souvenir, the object is made magical; in the collection, the mode of production is made magical. In this belief in fortune we see a further erasure of labor. As Veblen noted in *The Theory of the Leisure Class*, "The belief in luck is a sense of fortuitous necessity in the sequence of phenomena."[50] The souvenir magically transports us to the scene of origin, but the collection is magically and serially transported to the scene of acquisition, its proper destination. And this scene of acquisition is repeated over and over through the serial arrangement of objects in display space. Thus, collected objects are not the result of the serial operation of labor upon the material environment. Rather, they present the seriality of an animate world; their production appears to be self-motivated and self-realized. If they are "made," it is by a process that seems to invent itself for the pleasure of the acquirer. Once again, an illusion of a relation between things takes the place of a social relation.

The souvenir reconstitutes the scene of acquisition as a merging with the other and thus promises the preimaginary paradise of the self-as-world even as it must use the symbolic, the narrative, as a device to arrive at that reunion. But the collection takes this movement even further. In its erasure of labor, the collection is prelapsarian. One "finds" the elements of the collection much as the prelapsarian Adam and Eve could find the satisfaction of their needs without a necessary articulation of desire. The collector constructs a narrative of luck which replaces the narrative of production. Thus the collection is not only far removed from contexts of material production; it is also the most abstract of all forms of consumption. And in its translation back into the particular cycle of exchange which characterizes the universe of the "collectable," the collected object represents quite simply the ultimate self-referentiality and seriality of money at the same time that it declares its independence from "mere" money. We might remember that of all invisible workers, those who actually make money are the least visible. All collected objects are thereby *objets de lux*, objects abstracted from use value and materiality within a magic cycle of self-referential exchange.

This cycle returns us to Eliot's distinction between "old leisure" and "amusement." Crafts are contiguous to preindustrial modes of production, and thus use value lies at the core of their aesthetic forms; analogously, the production of amusement mimes the seriality and abstraction of postindustrial modes of production. For example, one might think of square dancing, like bluegrass music, as an imitation of the organization of mechanical modes of production in its patterns of seriality, dispersal, and reintegration. Within contemporary consumer society, the collection takes the place of crafts as the prevailing form of domestic pastime. Ironically, such collecting combines a preindustrial aesthetic of the handmade and singular object with a postindustrial mode of acquisition/production: the readymade.

Metaconsumption: The Female Impersonator

This ironic combination of preindustrial content and postindustrial form is only one in a series of contradictions under which the collection operates. We must look more closely at the type of consumerism the collection represents. In presenting a form of aesthetic consumption, the collection creates the conditions for a functional consumption; in marking out the space of the ornament and the superfluous, it defines a mode of necessity. And yet it is not acceptable to simply purchase a collection *in toto;* the collection must be acquired in a serial manner. This seriality provides a means for defining or classifying the collection and the collector's life history, and it also permits a systematic substitution of purchase for labor. "Earning" the collection simply involves *waiting,* creating the pauses that articulate the biography of the collector.

Furthermore, the collection cannot be defined simply in terms of the worth of its elements. Just as the system of exchange depends upon the relative position of the commodity in the chain of signifiers, so the collection as a whole implies a value—aesthetic or otherwise— independent of the simple sum of its individual members. We have emphasized aesthetic value here because a value of manipulation and positioning, not a value of reference to a context of origin, is at work in the collection. Thus, just as we saw that the material value of the souvenir was an ephemeral one juxtaposed with a surplus of value in relation to the individual life history, so the ephemeral quality of the collected object can be displaced by the value of relations and sheer quantity. Every coin dissolves into the infinite meaning of face, the deepest of surfaces, yet every coin also presents a point of enumeration; the accumulation of coins promises the amassing of a cyclical world that could replace the world itself. In the face of an apocalypse, gold and antiques are gathered, just as we earlier saw Crusoe deciding to take the money after all.

And on the other side of this scale of values, we must consider collections of ephemera proper—collections made of disposable items such as beer cans, cast-off clothing, wine bottles, or political buttons.

Such collections might seem to be anticollections in their denial of the values of the antique and the classic as transcendent forms. Yet such collections do more than negate. First, through their accumulation and arrangement they might present an aesthetic tableau which no single element could sustain. For example, collections of wine bottles or cruets placed in a window mark the differentiation of light and space. In this way, they, too, might function as "intrinsic objects" like the nails and glass fragments collected by the wood rat. Second, collections of ephemera serve to exaggerate certain dominant features of the exchange economy: its seriality, novelty, and abstraction. And by means or by virtue of such exaggeration, they are an ultimate form of consumerism; they classicize the novel, enabling mode and fashion to extend in both directions—toward the past as well as toward the future.

Kitsch and camp objects offer a simultaneous popularization of the antique and antiquation of the fad; they destroy the last frontier of intrinsicality. Baudrillard has suggested in a brief passage on kitsch in *La Société de consommation* that kitsch represents a saturation of the object with details.[51] Yet this saturation would be a feature of many valued objects, including both souvenirs and "classic" items for collection. Rather, it would be more accurate to say that the kitsch object offers a saturation of materiality, a saturation which takes place to such a degree that materiality is ironic, split into contrasting voices: past and present, mass production and individual subject, oblivion and reification. Such objects serve to subjectify all of consumer culture, to institute a nostalgia of the populace which in fact makes the populace itself a kind of subject. Kitsch objects are not apprehended as the souvenir proper is apprehended, that is, on the level of the individual autobiography; rather, they are apprehended on the level of collective identity. They are souvenirs of an era and not of a self. Hence they tend to accumulate around that period of intense socialization, adolescence, just as the souvenir proper accumulates around that period of intense subjectivity, childhood. The seriality of kitsch objects is articulated by the constant self-periodization of popular culture. Their value depends upon the fluctuations of a self-referential collector's market, just as all collections do, but with the additional constraint of fashion. Furthermore, whereas objects such as hand tools had an original use value, the original use value of kitsch objects is an elusive one. Their value in their context of origin was most likely their contemporaneousness, their relation to the fluctuating demands of style. Hence kitsch and camp items may be seen as forms of metafashion. Their collection constitutes a discourse on the constant re-creation of novelty within the exchange economy. And in their collapsing of the narrow time and deep space of the popular into the deep time and narrow space of the antique[52] they serve an ideology which would jumble class relations, an ideology which substitutes a labor of perpetual consumption for a labor of production.

The term *kitsch* comes from the German *kitschen*, "to put together sloppily." The kitsch object as collected object thus takes the abstraction from use value a step further. We saw that the collection of handmade objects translates the time of manual labor into the simultaneity of conspicuous waste. The desire for the kitsch object as either souvenir or collected item marks the complete disintegration of materiality through an ironic display of an overmateriality. The inside bursts its bounds and presents a pure surface of outside. The kitsch object symbolizes not transcendence but emergence in the speed of fashion. Its expendability is the expendability of all consumer goods, their dependence upon novelty as the replacement of use value and craftsmanship.

Camp is perhaps a more complex term. *The American Heritage Dictionary* (what title better speaks to a nostalgia for standard?) tells us that the term has obscure origins, but has come to mean "an affectation or appreciation of manners and tastes commonly thought to be outlandish, vulgar or banal . . . to act in an outlandish or effeminate manner."[53] In all their uses, both *kitsch* and *camp* imply the imitation, the inauthentic, the impersonation. Their significance lies in their exaggerated display of the values of consumer culture. Fashion and fad take place within the domain of the feminine not simply because they are emblematic of the trivial. We must move beyond any intrinsic functional argument here that would say that the subject is prior to the feminine. Rather, the feminine-as-impersonation forms a discourse miming the discourse of male productivity, authority, and predication here. And the further impersonation of the feminine which we see in camp marks the radical separation of "feminine discourse" from the subject. This separation has arisen historically as a result of capital's need to place subjects heterogeneously throughout the labor market. And thus this separation has resulted in a denuding of the feminine, making the discourse of the feminine available to parody. The "eternal feminine" presents a notion of the classic, a notion of transcendence necessitated by the political economy: the camp is its parody. And this parody reveals the feminine as surface, showing the deep face of the feminine as a purely material relation, that relation which places women within the cycle of exchange and simultaneously makes their labor invisible. The conception of woman as consumer is no less fantastic or violent than its literalization in the *vagina dentata* myth, for it is a conception which functions to erase the true labor, the true productivity, of women. Yet this erasure forms the very possibility of the cycle of exchange.

If we say that the collection in general marks the final erasure of labor within the abstractions of late capitalism, we must conclude by saying that kitsch and camp, as forms of metaconsumption, have arisen from the contradictions implicit in the operation of the exchange economy; they mark an antisubject whose emergence ironically has been necessitated by the narratives of significance under that economy. It is only by virtue of the imitation that the popular classes have the illusion of *having* at all. The imitation as abstraction, as element of series, as novelty and luxury at once, is necessarily the classic of contemporary consumer culture. This imitation marks the final wresting of the market away from the place we think we know, firsthand, as nature.

CONCLUSION/LITOTES

For both art and life depend wholly on the laws of optics, on perspective and illusion; both, to be blunt, depend on the necessity of error.

—Nietzsche, "A Critical Backward Glance," *The Birth of Tragedy*

hat are the contradictions of camp and kitsch, the proliferation of consumption as a form of magical labor, the overarticulation of the discourse of the feminine here, but the contradictions of a sign in crisis? Thus it is with the disclosure of this sign rather than with the hermeticism promised by the book's materiality that I end my essay. And yet to disclose the machinery behind the god is simply to substitute metaphors—indeed, to place the organic in the position of the before, the position of the façade, where it was situated all along. Refusing the face-to-face, we are talking over the shoulder. This problem of the reification of the organic marks the symptoms of nostalgia in my own discussion: the utopia of use value; the place of alienation in the articulation of a subject more "real" than an unalienated subject could ever be; and, finally, the ideal of a simultaneous consciousness promised by "lived experience."

Even to speak of the miniature is to begin with imitation, with the second-handedness and distance of the model. The miniature comes into the chain of signification at a remove: there is no original miniature; there is only the thing in "itself," which has already been erased, which has disappeared from this scene of arriving-too-late. As we have seen, the miniature typifies the structure of memory, of childhood, and ultimately of narrative's secondary (and at the same time causal) relation to history. It is true that, like all objects, the miniature locates a version of the self, but our attention must be drawn to the particular versions of the self invented by such particular objects. From the privatized and domesticated world of the miniature, from its petite sincerity, arises an "authentic" subject whose transcendence over personal property substitutes for a strongly chronological, and thus radically piecemeal, experience of temporality in everyday life. The narcissistic, even onanistic, view presented by the miniature, its abstraction of the mirror into microcosm, presents the desiring subject with an illusion of mastery, of time into space and heterogeneity into order. The dream of animation here is equally the terror caused by animation, the terror of the doll, for such movement would only cause the obliteration of the subject—the inhuman spectacle of a dream no longer in need of its dreamer.

In contrast, to speak of the giant is to take part in the fiction of an authentic body. The giant, its superfluousness, its oversignification, its simultaneous destruction and creativity, is an exaggeration or lie regarding the social status and social integration of the subject. The giant as the natural is already there. We inherit our giant as we inherit our language, for as the Douaisien knew, they are one and the same. If the giant is not a machine, "he" is yet an object narrated from an increasing distance in the sense of both time (the contemporaneousness of legendary giants becoming the giants of prehistory) and space (the transition from the vernacular giants to the giants of mass spectacle). Just as we have emphasized the relation of the miniature to the invention of the personal, so must we finally emphasize the relation of the gigantic to the invention of the collective. For the authentic body of the giant marks the merger of the self-as-part with an ideological whole. We saw in the rise of the vernacular giants their place in the creation of locality, origin, and mutually experienced identity. Yet we must not underestimate this same function of the gigantic within the exchange economy as well. What better speaks to the subject's desire to participate in a global vernacular than the dedicated pursuit and purchase of commodities whose sign value is articulated entirely by their position within the social realm of exchange?

I have focused upon the operation of certain trivial, or play, forms in this essay, forms that are derivative and secondary in the given social shape of history. I have done so not simply from an aesthetic desire to valorize the marginal, nor from an impulse to trace the real in the outline of the representation, but because any serious study of exaggeration must begin and end with an investigation of the discourse of the childish, the feminine, the mad, and the senile. For the system of signification works by means of a rhetoric of significance; to be marginal to that system is to be cast from the center (authenticity, sincerity, consensus), to live the abstraction of the secondhand. It is not enough simply to relativize the normal in this argument; it becomes apparent that exaggeration—that is, the exaggeration of significance—is an eruption in the economy of consciousness, an eruption which acquires the status of the intolerable and thus must be objectified.

Here Lacan's formulation of the sign over the sign, and thus the sign always suppressing the sign, might serve as our model. In this sense, we can cast a final glance upon the sign as a kind of postcard: description/ideology never quite captioning and thereby never quite capturing the real; the view from one side suppressing the other; an irrecoverable distance arising between the object and its given context of origin; the differentiation or exoticism of the self always articulated beforehand by the cultural determination of the boundaries of experience. Yet the sign, whether stressed or suppressed, historically conscious or unconscious and thus potential, is put into play by its position among differences; like narrative, it is a gesture toward, and therefore against, death. We saw in the lived experience of sexuality a referent with no representation. Analogously, in the subject's desire to experience mortality is issued the simultaneous desire to belie the content of that mortality and hence transcend it: to produce a representation with no referent—each sign as a postcard from the land of the dead, and on the other side, the longing mark that is the proper name.

NOTES

Chapter 1. On Description and the Book

1. "But instead of personality giving the abstractions life, the figure often works the other way around; the excitement comes when we 'conceive' the idea, the person suddenly then becoming charged with meanings of very great depth and extension," writes Rosemond Tuve of allegorical imagery. (See Tuve, *Allegorical Imagery*, p. 26.) Scholes and Kellogg, in *The Nature of Narrative*, quote E. M. Forster's formulation of this disjunction between allegory and chronological realism: "Forster summed up this situation neatly when he contrasted ancient and modern narrative as 'life by values' and 'life by time'" (p. 169).

2. Watt, *The Rise of the Novel*, p. 14.

3. Ibid., p. 25. Writing on Richardson, Watt notes that "in many scenes, the pace of the narrative was slowed down by minute description to something very near that of actual experience." Here we might question Watt's simple formulation, however. Is it the case that everyday life involves minute attention to detail? Instead we might say that the accumulation of concrete detail in writing pays homage to the bourgeois idealization of the concrete as the real, particularly those commodities which mark the *realization* of class relations.

4. Iser writes:

> In our attempts to describe the intersubjective structure of the process through which a text is transferred and translated, our first problem is the fact that the whole text can never be perceived at any one time. In this respect, it differs from given objects, which can generally be viewed or at least conceived as a whole. The "object" of the text can only be imagined by way of different consecutive phases of reading. We always stand outside the given object, whereas we are situated inside the literary text. The relation between text and reader is therefore quite different from that between object and observer: instead of a subject-object relationship, there is a moving viewpoint which travels along inside that which it has to apprehend.

Iser, *The Act of Reading*, pp. 108–109. In a recent article, Suzanne Brown has suggested (borrowing from Bakhtin's notion of the chronotope) that it is the length of the novel that permits character development, and that forms such as the short story (from Ovid on) present a notion of "character essence," that is, each character embodying a fundamental cultural trait which is then tested in a

controlled situation. (See Brown, "The Chronotope of the Short Story.") This is a suggestive idea and might be linked more closely to the historical construction of notions of the self and to generic changes as they respond to that construction.
5. Defoe, *Robinson Crusoe*, p. 122.
6. MacCannell, *The Tourist*, p. 20.
7. Eco, *A Theory of Semiotics*, pp. 24–25.
8. Vološinov, *Marxism and the Philosophy of Language*, p. 184.
9. Abrahams, "The Complex Relations of Simple Forms," p. 126.
10. Benjamin, *Illuminations*, p. 239.
11. O'Súilleabhain, *Storytelling in Irish Tradition*, p. 11.
12. Butor, *Inventory*, pp. 20–21.
13. See Doležel, "A Scheme of Narrative Time," pp. 209–217, for a discussion of the differences between authorial time, reader's time, the story time, the time of the storytelling act, and the time of the text's representation.
14. Benjamin, *Illuminations*, p. 228.
15. Recounted in David Cook, *History of Narrative Film*, p. 11. Of course, the other interruption of surface which results in terror is the production of the absent object à la Hitchcock. For observations and insights on the theory of film in this section I am indebted to Timothy Corrigan.
16. See Aronowitz, "Film—the Art Form of Late Capitalism," p. 114. For a complementary view see Bazin, *What is Cinema?*
17. K. Burke, *Counterstatement*, p. 143.
18. This popular and intrinsically *social* assumption regarding the solitude of reading must be linked, however, to the ideology of individual self-improvement. Theorists of reading and writing from Coleridge to Sollers have noted the social and dialogic relation between readers and writers. See Corrigan, *Coleridge, Language, and Criticism*. And actual social practice regarding reading may have been, and may still be, quite different. On the place of reading in the workplace and other group situations in early modern France, see Davis, *Society and Culture in Early Modern France*, 189–226. For a notion of collaborative literacy, see Shuman, *Retellings*.
19. *Robinson Crusoe*, p. 107.
20. Marx, *Capital*, p. 90.
21. *Robinson Crusoe*, pp. 170–171.
22. See Wilgus, *Anglo-American Folksong Scholarship since 1898*, p. 4.
23. Marx, *Capital*, p. 43.
24. Vološinov, *Marxism and the Philosophy of Language*, pp. 23–24.
25. See, for example, Lefebvre, *Critique de la Vie Quotidienne*, 1:340: "La répétition des cycles et rythmes cycliques diffère de la répétition des gestes mécaniques: le premier type fait partie des processus non-cumulatifs, avec leur temporalité propre, le second fait partie de processus cumulatifs, avec leur temporalité linéaire, tantôt continue, tantôt discontinue."
26. Ibid., p. 216.
27. See Jankélévitch, *L'Irréversible et la nostalgie*, pp. 46–47:

Celui qui a déjà vécu l'expérience de la première fois accueille la répétition de cette fois non pas comme si c'était la "fois" précédente ou la "fois" initiale, mais comme si c'était une nouvelle première fois; dans la deuxième expérience il éprouve, sous forme d'appréhension, d'ennui ou de familiarité, le sentiment du déjà-vu et du déjà-vécu: mais le sentiment du déjà vu implique lui'même que la seconde fois n'est pas identique à la première; l'homme de la seconde fois est celui qui a connu la première fois, et par conséquent la "reconnaît" dans la deuxième: mais la re-connaissance est une toute nouvelle connaissance, un savoir spécifique, et non pas un redoublement ne varietur de la connaissance première.

28. This privileging of immediate experience is what Gadamer called "the naïve assumption of historicism, namely that we must set ourselves within the spirit of the age, and think with its ideas and its thoughts, not with our own." See Gadamer, "The Historicity of Understanding," pp. 117-133 (p. 123).

29. See Jankélévitch, *L'Irréversible et la nostalgie,* p. 288: "La nostalgie, comme l'amour, est prévenante, et les justifications qu'elle se donne sont rétrospectives; mais secondairement ces justifications, qui sont un effet et un rayonnement de l'amour, confirment le sentiment et lui donnent un statut légal."

30. Derrida has noted this nostalgic strain in the work of Lévi-Strauss, saying that passages like the following one from *Structural Anthropology* define "writing as the condition of social inauthenticity":

> *In this respect it is, rather, modern societies that should be defined by a privative character. Our relations with one another are now only occasionally and fragmentarily based upon global experience, the concrete "apprehension," of one person by another. They are largely the result of an (indirect) construction, through written documents. We are no longer linked to our past by an oral tradition which implies direct (vécu) contact with others (storytellers, priests, wise men, or elders), but by books amassed in libraries, books from which criticism endeavors— with extreme difficulty—to form a picture of their authors. And we communicate with the immense majority of our contemporaries by all kinds of intermediaries— written documents or administrative machinery—which undoubtedly vastly extend our contacts but at the same time make those contexts somewhat "unauthentic."*

See Derrida, *Of Grammatology,* pp. 136-137 (emphasis added by Derrida).

31. See Lotman, "Primary and Secondary Communication-Modeling Systems," pp. 95-98 (p. 98); see also p. 7, for a discussion of the concept of modeling systems.

32. See Lotman, "Point of View in a Text."

33. Pratt, *Toward a Speech Act Theory of Literary Discourse,* p. 143, n. 13.

34. Iser has written of the novel: "If the limitations of the novel are such that one cannot reveal a complete character, it is even more impossible to try to transcribe complete reality. And so even a novel that is called realistic can present no more than particular aspects of a given reality, although the selection must remain implicit in order to cloak the author's ideology." (See Iser, *The Implied Reader,* p. 103.) But this is a rather naïve way of looking at the problem, for the "real" is just as much a matter of the processes of fictions as it is an outside which the fiction can only approximate. Iser's formulation of the reading act, which follows rather closely a Protestant model of conversion, depends upon a conceit of hidden intentions and privatized revelations.

35. Butor, *Inventory,* p. 21.

36. Riffaterre, *Semiotics of Poetry,* p. 87.

37. Debord, *The Society of the Spectacle,* p. 6.

38. Baudrillard, *Le Système des objets,* p. 43.

39. Marin, *Etudes sémiologiques, écritures, peintures,* p. 89.

40. See R. Williams, *Marxism and Literature,* p. 41.

41. Eco, *A Theory of Semiotics,* pp. 71-72. Eco contends that "a sign is everything which can be taken as significantly substituting for something else. . . . Thus *semiotics is in principle the discipline studying everything which can be used in order to lie*" (p. 7).

42. Similarly, in his essay on Proust, Deleuze writes:

What is the superiority of the signs of art over all the others? It is [for Proust] that the others are material. Material, first of all, by their emission: they are half sheathed in the object bearing them. Sensuous qualities, loved faces, are still matter. (It is no accident that the significant sensuous qualities are above all odors and flavors: the most material of qualities.) Only the signs of art are immaterial. . . . The other signs are material not only by their origin and by the way they remain half sheathed in the object, but also by their development or their "explication". . . . Proust often speaks of the necessity which weighs upon him: that something always reminds him of or makes him imagine something else. But whatever the importance of this process of analogy in art, art does not find its profoundest formula here. As long as we discover a sign's meaning in something else, matter still subsists, refractory to spirit. On the contrary, art gives us the true unity: unity of an immaterial sign and of an entirely spiritual meaning.

Deleuze, *Proust and Signs*, pp. 39–40.
43. Butor, *Inventory*, p. 42.
44. D'Israeli, *Curiosities of Literature*, 1:1.
45. Ibid., p. 3.
46. Ibid., p. 5.
47. Valéry, *Aesthetics*, pp. 218–219.
48. Ibid., p. 218.
49. Bombaugh, *Gleanings for the Curious*, p. 722.

Chapter 2. The Miniature

1. Derrida, *Of Grammatology*, p. 18.
2. See Sokol, "Portraits of Modern Masters." These portraits were originally shown at the Gotham Book Mart Gallery from February 20 to March 10, 1978. For more Sokol portraits, see the Summer 1982 issue of *Antaeus*.
3. D'Israeli, *Curiosities of Literature*, 1:231–232.
4. Curtius, *European Literature and the Latin Middle Ages*, p. 328.
5. McMurtie, *Miniature Incunabula*, pp. 5–6.
6. Stone, *An Unusual Collection of Miniature Books*, foreword.
7. Avery, *A Short List of Microscopic Books*, p. 121.
8. *A Miniature Almanack*, 1820/1821.
9. Hooke, *Micrographia*. See also Nicholson's studies: *The Microscope and English Imagination; Mountain Gloom and Mountain Glory;* and *Science and Imagination.*
10. See Henderson, *Newsletter*, February 1, 1928.
11. Ibid.
12. Avery, *A Short List of Microscopic Books*, no. 129.
13. Henderson, *Newsletter*, July 15, 1928.
14. The 1841 edition of "Schloss's English Bijou Almanac" is "poetically illustrated by the Hon. Mrs. Norton." It measures 13/16 by 9/16 of an inch, with beautifully engraved portraits and views. In its 62 pages it includes "6 poems, the almanac, the Royal Family, Sovereigns of Europe, the Queen's Ministers, Ladies of the Court, and H. R. H. Prince Albert's Household." (See Avery, *A Short List of Microscopic Books*, no. 127.) Holy books, of course, become the other side of the miniature as amulet. In 1900 David Bryce, a Glasgow publisher, printed 100,000 New Testaments measuring 3/4 of an inch by 1/2 an inch, and at the advent of World War I he printed several hundred thousand copies of the Koran the size of postage stamps. These were enclosed in small metal cases with magnifying glass

covers and were given by the British government to its Moslem soldiers, who suspended them about their necks as talismans. (See Henderson, *Miniature Books*, p. 21.)

15. *Miniature Books*, p. 13.
16. Ibid., pp. 15–16.
17. Stone, *A Snuff-boxful of Bibles*, p. 12.
18. Janes, *Miniature Bible*, pp. 7–10.
19. *Wisdom in Miniature*, p. iv.
20. See Ariés, *Centuries of Childhood*.
21. Henderson, *Newsletter*, February 1, 1928.
22. Solomon Grildrig [pseud.], *The Miniature*, pp. 3–4. Although we are particularly interested here in the problems of describing the miniature, we cannot separate these problems from the notion of "standard scale" more generally. Here we might follow Gombrich's argument in *Art and Illusion*, p. 303:

> If we still assign a size in our mind to images of pennies or houses this is due to the same habit, as Professor Osgood has suggested, of thinking of things in some standard situation in which we usually inspect them. We compare the penny in the hand with the house across the road. It is this imaginary standard distance which will influence the scale at which a child draws such objects and which will also determine our descriptions of ants and men. The notorious question whether the moon looks as large as a dime or a dollar, to which I have alluded before, may not allow of a clear-cut answer, but most of us would protest if anyone suggested that it looks like a pinhead or an ocean steamer, easy though it would be to devise a situation where these statements would be true.

23. Halliwell, *The Metrical History of Tom Thumb the Little*, preface. Wood, in *Giants and Dwarfs*, pp. 242–243, adds:

> Tom Hearne, in his appendix to Benedictus Abbas, states that the fiction of Tom Thumb was founded upon an authentic account of King Edgar's dwarf. Some lines written in 1630, and entitled Tom Thumbe, his Life and Death, say:
>
> > In Arthur's court Tom Thumbe did live,
> > A man of mickle might
> > The best of all the table round,
> > And eke a doughty knight:
> > His stature but an inch in height,
> > Or quarter of a span;
> > Then think you not this little knight
> > Was prov'd a valiant man?
>
> An almanack for 1697 tells us that, one hundred and four years before that date, Tom Thumb and Gargantua fought a duel on Salisbury Plain.

24. Yonge, *The History of Sir Thomas Thumb*, pp. 21, 23.
25. Swift, *Gulliver's Travels*, pp. 38–39.
26. Bachelard, *The Poetics of Space*, p. 160.
27. Lévi-Strauss, *The Savage Mind*, pp. 24–25.
28. Olrik, "Epic Laws of Folk Narrative," pp. 129–141 (p. 138).
29. Roussel, *How I Write Certain of My Books*, p. 50.
30. Roussel, *Impressions of Africa*, pp. 12–13.
31. Roussel, *How I Write Certain of My Books*, p. 10.
32. Ibid.
33. In his book on Roussel, Foucault has written: "Il n'y a pas de point pri-

vilégié autour duquel le paysage s'organiserait, puis en s'éloignant s'effacerait peu à peu; mais toute une série de petites cellules spatiales de dimensions à peu près semblables qui sont posées les unes à côté des autres, sans proportions réciproques (telles étaient à peu près les loges à résurrection de *Locus Solus*). Leur position n'est jamais définie par rapport à l'ensemble, mais selon un repère de voisinage qui permet de passer de l'une à l'autre comme on suit les maillons d'une chaîne." Foucault, *Raymond Roussel*, pp. 138–139.

34. Roussel, *How I Write Certain of My Books*, p. 18.

35. Ibid., p. 5.

36. Heppenstall, *Raymond Roussel*, p. 69. Similarly, Joyce's use of multivocal signs opens the text of *Finnegans Wake* into a series of layered and interconnecting thematic systems that ultimately speak the world.

37. See Heppenstall, *Raymond Roussel*, pp. 64–65:

> J. B. Brunius devised "a machine for reading Roussel" which was exhibited at the big surréaliste *exhibition in 1938. This was a table on a tripod, about which the reader was required to walk. Others since, have constructed things with handles. The idea was in all cases to make it possible quickly to by-pass brackets. Roussel himself had apparently toyed with the idea not of multiplied brackets but of differently coloured printer's inks. . . . The important thing was not to cut the pages. . . . For Roussel had decided, in the first place, that the volume would be too slim. He almost quadrupled its thickness by, first, commissioning a fixed number of whole page illustrations and second, by having nothing printed on left-hand pages, so that, with the* Nouvelle Impressions *proper . . . the text appears on only one page in four. . . . The book was so printed that you could read the whole text without cutting the pages and need not then see the illustrations at all. The precise instructions sent to the illustrator result at one point in the drawing of a man peering curiously between uncut pages.*

This conjunction of stasis, tableau, and voyeurism is one we will meet again in our discussion of "The Imaginary Body" (Chapter 4).

38. Borges, *"The Aleph" and Other Stories*, pp. 19–20. In his commentary on "The Aleph," Borges writes: "My chief problem in writing the story lay in what Walt Whitman had very successfully achieved—the setting down of a limited catalog of endless things. The task, as is evident, is impossible, for such chaotic enumeration can only be simulated, and every apparently haphazard element has to be linked to its neighbor either by secret association or by contrast" (p. 264).

39. Zigrosser, *Multum in parvo*, pp. 11–12. An exception to the impossibility of miniaturization in music might be works such as Powell's "Miniatures for Baroque Ensemble" (Opus 8) for flute, one violin, viola, violocello, and harpsichord. Composed of several 10-minute pieces, it compresses the ornamentation of the baroque mode into a comparatively limited temporal frame.

40. Zigrosser, *Multum in parvo*, p. 52. See also the section on *multum in parvo* in Bombaugh's *Gleanings for the Curious*, pp. 823–826. That Bombaugh's examples ("The boxes which govern the world are the cartridge-box, the ballot-box, the jury-box, and the band-box") seem strangely dated to us speaks to the fact that *multum in parvo* is effective only within a particular ideological matrix.

41. Roussel, *Impressions of Africa*, p. 81.

42. Foucault, *Raymond Roussel*, p. 135.

43. Riffaterre, in a passage in his *Semiotics of Poetry* on the capacity of this metaphor for text production, has remarked: "The rule of polarization applies: the moment it is stylistically emphasized, any statement of motionlessness will gener-

ate a statement of motion. The more natural and permanent the movelessness, the more striking the mobilization, and the more suggestive of fantasy. Consequently, the very immobility of furniture or of the knickknacks sitting on this furniture, or of the deck of cards, can be the proof of their unseen mobility, and unseen mobility equals secret life" (p. 69).

44. Quoted in Townsend, *Written for Children*, p. 47.

45. Clarke, *The Return of the Twelves*, pp. 19–20. The Brontë children's own "Young Men's Play," which invented four kingdoms known as "The Glasstown Confederation," we might note, is recorded in micrographia. See Ratchford, *The Brontës' Web of Childhood*, p. xiii: "I have studied in originals or in copies more than a hundred manuscripts by Charlotte and her brother Bramwell, equaling in mass the published works of the Brontë family. Nearly all of them are in the minute hand printing described by Mrs. Gaskell. The earlier manuscripts have the appearance of printed books varying in size from miniatures of 1 1/2–1 1/4" to small octaves, with elaborate title pages, prefaces and colophons containing signatures and dates." See also Ratchford's edition of Emily Brontë's *Gondal's Queen*. Perhaps beside these remarkable childhood writings of the Brontës is the place to mention the remarkable artistic productions of the contemporary artist Donald Evans, who died in 1977 at the age of thirty-one. From the age of ten until his death Evans painted, and catalogued in what he called "The Catalogue of the World," over 4,000 stamps. These were miniature watercolors in which "he commemorated everything that was special to him, disguised in a code of stamps from his own imaginary countries—each detailed with its own history, geography, climate, currency and customs." Souvenirs of his life and of the life of his imagination, the stamps depict landscapes, fruits, vegetables, plants, animals, windmills, the work of Gertrude Stein, Chinese ceramics, airplanes, his friends, and much more. Each stamp was linked to an imaginary place and registered in "The Catalogue of the World," a 330-page volume in three languages listing all issues with their dates, denominations, and colors, as well as prices in the appropriate imaginary currency for mint-condition and canceled stamps. See Eisenhart, *The World of Donald Evans*, pp. 10–12.

46. Clarke, *The Return of the Twelves*, p. 123.

47. Ibid., p. 124.

48. Ibid., p. 66.

49. Allemagne, *Histoire des jouets*, p. 17.

50. Plato, "Meno: The Immortality of the Soul," in *Works*, 3:3–55 (52).

51. Jackson, *Toys of Other Days*, p. 19. For further discussion of toys in relation to adults, see Ariés, *Centuries of Childhood*, pp. 67–71. In *Las miniaturas en el arte popular Mexicano*, p. 9, Mauricio Charpenal briefly outlines ritual and ornamental functions of miniatures in Mexican folk art.

52. See Daiken, *Children's Toys Throughout the Ages*, p. 58.

53. Clayton, *Miniature Railways*, p. 6.

54. Ibid., p. 19.

55. Wells, *Little Wars*, pp. 105–106.

56. Clayton, *Miniature Railways*, p. 94.

57. See "The Toby Jug."

58. Allemagne, *Histoire des jouets*, pp. 145–147. For examples of Sicilian crèches, see the holdings of the Museo Etnografico Pitré, Palermo, and, on a smaller scale, the extensive crèche made by the monk who is the tour guide at the Basilica and Catacombe di San Giovanni, Siracusa. This microcosmic pattern of comparing the sacred to the secular also appears to be typical of (at least nineteenth-century examples of) Sicilian herders' carvings:

The figures and decorations appearing on all these sculptures and carvings run within a restricted circle of subjects, and never or rarely appear outside it. The Saints, protectors of herds and single animals dear and useful to man, are in the first row: St. Pascal, St. George, St. Eloi, St. Anthony Abbot, St. Vitus, etc. In second place come the Saints that enjoy universal adoration and devotion: the Crucifix, Mary of Sorrows, Mary Immaculate, St. Joseph, St. Francis of Paola, etc., and the Saints who are special patrons of the town in which the herder was born or lives. There are often added animals that surround the herder and are important to him: the dog, the ox, the sheep, etc., then the sun and moon and stars, and not rarely some fine bird, or even a soldier whose uniform and pose have struck the fancy of the solitary and simple artist.

Salomone-Marino, *Customs and Habits of the Sicilian Peasants*, p. 232.

59. McClinton, *Antiques in Miniature*, p. 5.

60. Gröber, *Children's Toys of Bygone Ages*, p. 20.

61. Ibid., p. 23.

62. Benson, *The Book of the Queen's Dolls' House*, p. 5.

63. See Price's discussion of the work of Pope in relation to problems of scale in *To the Palace of Wisdom*, pp. 143–163.

64. Here, of course, we are reminded of *Hamlet* II, 2:

Ham.:   *Denmark's a prison.*

Ros.:   *Then is the world one.*

Ham.:   *A goodly one; in which there are many confines, wards and dungeons, Denmark being one o' the worst.*

Ros.:   *We think not so, my lord.*

Ham.:   *Why, then, 'tis none to you; for there is nothing either good or bad, but thinking makes it so: to me it is a prison.*

Ros.:   *Why then, your ambition makes it one; 'tis too narrow for your mind.*

Ham.:   *O God, I could be bounded in a nutshell and count myself a king of infinite space, were it not that I have bad dreams.*

65. DeLong, "Phenomenological Space-Time." The Tennessee experiment is described in detail, and various constraints on its conclusions, such as investigator bias and auditory interference, are discussed. The relationship of experience to scale and time, the researchers conclude, can be stated as $E = X (T)$, where X is the reciprocal of the scale of the environment being used. "It should be equally obvious, however, that spatial scale is relative to the size of the observer," they add (p. 682). One factor that is not discussed is the obvious choice of the lounge, a leisure area which would as an environment tend to "elongate" the notion of everyday duration. For another example of the way in which the "standards" of scale cannot be discussed independently of our experience of scale, see the discussion of geographers' conventions of depiction in Gombrich, *Art and Illusion*, p. 311: "There is one type of scientific illustration in which this effect of scale on impression is acknowledged officially, as it were. Geographers who draw sections of mountain ranges will exaggerate the relation of height to width according to a stated proportion. They have found that a true rendering of vertical relationship looks false. Our mind refuses to accept the fact that the distance of 28,000 feet to which Mount Everest soars from sea level is no more than the distance of just over 5 miles which a car traverses in a matter of minutes."

66. Swift, *Gulliver's Travels*, p. 12.

67. McClinton, *Antiques in Miniature*, p. 8.

68. See Henderson, *Lilliputian Newspapers*.

Chapter 3. The Gigantic

1. See P. Watson, *Fasanella's City.*
2. Brewer, *Dictionary of Phrase and Fable,* p. 460.
3. Massingham, *Fee, fi, fo, fum,* pp. 57–66 (pp. 65–66).
4. Ibid., p. 70. See also M. Williams, "Folklore and Placenames."
5. Massingham, *Fee, fi, fo, fum,* pp. 103–105.
6. M. Williams, "Folklore and Placenames," p. 365.
7. Broderius, *The Giant in Germanic Tradition,* pp. 43–91.
8. Blake, *Poems,* p. 186.
9. Homer, *Odyssey,* p. 148.
10. Broderius, *The Giant in Germanic Tradition,* p. 140.
11. Spenser, *The Poetical Works of Edmund Spenser,* p. 35.
12. Broderius, *The Giant in Germanic Tradition,* p. 188.
13. M. Williams, "Folklore and Placenames," p. 366.
14. Longinus, *On the Sublime;* E. Burke, "Inquiry into the Origin of Our Ideas of the Sublime and Beautiful." For discussions of these modes, see also Monk, "The Sublime," and Sypher, "Baroque Afterpiece: The Picturesque."
15. Hussey, *The Picturesque,* p. 4.
16. Magoon, "Scenery and Mind," pp. 1–48 (pp. 8–10).
17. W. Burton, *The Scenery-Shower,* pp. 25, 4.
18. See "Notes Toward an Understanding," in *Earth Art.*
19. See Fried, "Art and Objecthood," for a description of the theatrical nature of minimalist sculpture, a theatricality which makes the observer part of the setting.
20. Tillim, "Earthworks and the New Picturesque," p. 43.
21. See *Earth Art.*
22. But the modernist impulse here can also tend toward irony. Consider, for example, Smithson's tour of the "monuments" of Passaic, New Jersey, a photographic record of the detritus of industrialism. See Smithson, "The Monuments of Passaic."
23. Fried, "Art and Objecthood," p. 15.
24. Fisher, "City Matters: City Minds," p. 372.
25. Bakhtin, *Problems of Dostoevsky's Poetics,* p. 95.
26. R. Burton, *The Anatomy of Melancholy,* p. 47. I am indebted to Philip Holland for calling my attention to this citation. In his study "Robert Burton's *Anatomy of Melancholy* and Menippean Satire," p. 272, Holland writes:

> Whatever particular dramatic setting the view-from-above is given, its import is always the same in the menippea, of whose structural doubleness it provides a concrete image. It opposes the point of view (the version of "truth") prevailing in the realm that is being surveyed, not from another point of view (another particular "truth" as for example, a contrary ideology), but from a position that is indeterminate of itself, whose truth rests in its very unfixity or unapproachable transcendence. The view-from-above represents a principle of otherness. An overseer may engage the work below in dialogue, but may never be absorbed into it.

27. See Lefebvre, *La Production de l'espace.*
28. Bakhtin, *Rabelais and His World,* pp. 342–343.
29. Ibid., p. 343.
30. Rabelais, *Gargantua and Pantagruel,* pp. 47–48.
31. Ibid., pp. 74–75.

32. See, for example, Radin's analysis of the Winnebago trickster myth in *The Trickster*.

33. Darré, *Géants d'hier et d'aujourd'hui*, p. 32.

34. An early-fourteenth-century Inquisitor wrote of the Albigensians: "Moreover they read from the Gospels and the Epistles in the vulgar tongue, applying and expounding them in their favor and against the condition of the Roman Church." See Cantor, *The Medieval World, 300–1300*, pp. 279–280. Dawson notes in *Religion and the Rise of Western Culture*, pp. 208–209, that "the Catharist or Albigensian heresy was not a reformist movement or even an unorthodox form of Christianity. It marked the reappearance of an ancient oriental religion as far or farther removed from Christianity than the religion of Islam. Consequently the Papacy used the same methods as it had employed against the Moslems—the method of the Crusade, and of an appeal to Christian princes to use their power in defense of the faith; a method which was supplemented by a missionary compaign for the reconversion of the affected regions and finally by a code of repressive legislation which gave birth to the Inquisition."

35. Darré, *Géants d'hier et d'aujourd'hui*, p. 83.

36. Ibid., p. 36.

37. Fairholt, *Gog and Magog, the Giants in Guildhall*, p. 15–17.

38. Ibid., pp. 51–52.

39. Ibid., pp. 100–101. Fairholt does tell of one saintly giant, St. Christopher, who was converted to Christianity and devoted his life to carrying travelers across a dangerous stream. One night, according to legend, a child asked to be carried over, but the child was so heavy and the waters rose so high that Christopher was nearly drowned. The child then tells him it was Christ he had borne across (ibid., pp. 103–104).

40. Ibid., p. 64.

41. Ibid., pp. 89–90.

42. Ibid., p. 65.

43. Kowzan, *Littérature et spectacle*, p. 180.

44. Debord, *The Society of the Spectacle*, p. 29.

45. Ibid., p. 153.

46. See M. Leach, *Standard Dictionary of Folklore, Mythology, and Legend*, 1:453.

47. Squire, *Celtic Myth and Legend*, p. 38.

48. Fairholt, *Gog and Magog, the Giants in Guildhall*, pp. 100–101.

49. Swift, *Gulliver's Travels*, p. 71.

50. Ibid., p. 90.

51. Ibid., p. 95.

52. Ibid., p. 84.

53. Ibid., p. 17.

54. Ponge, *The Voice of Things*, pp. 58–59.

55. See Lowenthal, *Literature, Popular Culture, and Society*, pp. 109–136.

56. Lippard, *Pop Art*, p. 98.

57. Rose, "Blow-Up—the Problem of Scale in Sculpture," p. 83. For a discussion of phenomena of reproduction in relation to film, see Metz, *Le Signifiant Imaginaire;* and Baudry, "Cinéma: Effets idéologiques."

58. Lippard, *Pop Art*, p. 78.

59. Rose, "Blow-Up—the Problem of Scale in Sculpture," p. 83.

60. Moog, "Gulliver Was a Bad Biologist."

61. Aristotle, *On the Art of Fiction*, p. 27. An argument of this type has been made by Jessup in his article "Aesthetic Size," pp. 34–35: "When over-crowding

or over-loading occurs, the result is blurred structure, lack of clarity, and a consequent perceptual discomfort leading to loss of interest. Nothing is sufficiently followed through or held together, and the effect is one of perceptual and aesthetic frustration." A solution to the ethnocentrism and lack of historical perspective here might be found in Bakhtin's notion of the *chronotope*. According to Bakhtin, the literary work's projection of time and space is a concrete whole determined by social values. The developmental novel, for example, relies upon culture-specific notions of time and space and their relation to ideas of progression and character. See Bakhtin, *The Dialogic Imagination*. For suggestive analyses of the relations between seventeenth- and eighteenth-century conceptions of time and space and literary genres, see Kawasaki, "Donne's Microcosm"; and Stevick, "Miniaturization in Eighteenth-Century English Literature."

62. See Bakhtin, *Problems in Dostoevsky's Poetics*, pp. 63–82.

63. See Jessup, "Aesthetic Size," p. 32.

64. See the appendix to Ellman's *Ulysses on the Liffey*, "The Linati and Gorman-Gilbert Schemas Compared," pp. 186–199 (p. 195).

65. Rabelais, *Gargantua and Pantagruel*, p. 393.

66. Thomas, *The Tall Tale and Philippe d'Alcripe*, p. 79.

67. Ibid., p. 26.

68. Hurston, *Mules and Men*, p. 73.

69. Thomas, *The Tall Tale and Philippe d'Alcripe*, p. 7.

70. See Dorson, *American Folklore*, pp. 199–243.

71. Beath, *Febold Feboldson: Tall Tales* p. 19. See also Beath, *Legends of Febold Feboldson*.

72. Dobie, "Giants of the Southwest," p. 71.

73. Dorson, *American Folklore*, p. 224.

74. Dobie, "Giants of the Southwest," p. 11.

75. Dorson, "Mose the Far-Famed and World Renowned."

76. Dorson, *American Folklore*, pp. 216–226.

Chapter 4. The Imaginary Body

1. Lacan, *Ecrits* (trans. Sheridan), pp. 314–315.

2. See E. Leach, "Anthropological Aspects of Language."

3. Bakhtin, *Rabelais and His World*, p. 317.

4. See Robertson, *Preface to Chaucer*, for a discussion of how Chaucer's portraits in *The Canterbury Tales* are mock descriptions in the same way that Gothic portrayals of the vices in the late-thirteenth and fourteenth centuries parodied official modes of representation.

5. See Davis, *Society and Culture in Early Modern France*, pp. 97–99. Amanda Dargan has recorded examples of such souvenir coins from carnival pitchmen. See her forthcoming Ph.D. diss., University of Pennsylvania, Department of Folklore and Folklife Studies.

6. Davis, *Society and Culture in Early Modern France*, p. 137.

7. Evans, *Irish Folk Ways*, p. 279.

8. Radin, *The Trickster*. For a recent anthology of approaches to symbolic inversion, see Babcock, *The Reversible World*. In addition, see the author's survey of several approaches to reversal and inversion in chapter 3 of *Nonsense*.

9. Fisher, "The Construction of the Body," p. 8; see also idem, "The Recovery of the Body."

10. Fiedler, *Freaks*, p. 20.

11. Swift, *Gulliver's Travels*, p. 81.

12. Wood, *Giants and Dwarfs*, pp. 313–314.

13. Fiedler, *Freaks*, p. 107.

14. Ritson, *Fairy Tales, Legends, and Romances*, p. 6, note.

15. Fiedler, *Freaks*, p. 214.

16. Ibid., p. 201.

17. Wood, *Giants and Dwarfs*, pp. 310–311.

18. Fiedler, *Freaks*, pp. 113 and 108.

19. See MacRitchie, *Fians, Fairies, and Picts*, p. vii, for an elaboration of J. F. Campbell's claim, in *Popular Tales of the West Highlands* (Edinburgh: Edmonston, 1860), that "there once was a small race of people in these islands, who are remembered as fairies, for the fairy belief is not confined to the Highlanders of Scotland." W. Y. Evans Wentz's *The Fairy Faith in Celtic Countries* (London: Frowde, 1911) contains "An Irish Mystic's Testimony" "as to the character of Irish fairies, the sidhe who live in a parallel world and who enjoy a relative immortality, their space of life being much greater" (p. 64). Wentz's book has been reprinted with a foreword by Kathleen Raine (Gerrards Cross: Colin Smythe, 1977).

20. Kirk, *The Secret Commonwealth*, p. xxiv.

21. Latham, *The Elizabethan Fairies*, p. 82. The Irish tradition held that the fairies were shape-shifters, appearing at will as stately full-sized or giant figures or as small figures. This distinction from the English tradition of diminutive fairies was important to the writers of the Irish Renaissance. See Hirsch, "Yeats and the Commonwealth of Faery" (forthcoming). Yet, Hirsch notes, Yeats's friend Dermot Macmanus wrote that "the word 'fairy' has shifted away completely from its medieval concept of a powerful spirit in human form which should be treated with respect, if not with a little fear, and has now become attached to dainty little winged figures flitting like butterflies from flower to flower. . . . [the word has] come to be associated with everything that is unreal and childish." See Macmanus, *The Middle Kingdom*, p. 23.

22. Hall, *A Study of Dolls*, p. 48. This convention of distanced and diminutive sexuality must be distinguished from the medieval attribution of a demonic sexuality to the full-sized otherworld of the fairies, or fallen angels. See Duffy, *The Erotic World of Fairy*, for a discussion of this medieval view.

23. Kirk, *The Secret Commonwealth*, p. 8.

24. Ibid., p. 14.

25. Briggs, *The Fairies in English Tradition and Literature*, p. 21.

26. *Folk-Lore* 32:47; quoted in Spence, *British Fairy Origins*, p. 174.

27. Latham, *The Elizabethan Fairies*, p. 104.

28. See Ritson, *Fairy Tales, Legends, and Romances*, p. 25.

29. See Doyle, *The Coming of the Fairies*.

30. E. Watson, *Fairies of Our Garden*, pp. 141–142.

31. Speaight, *The History of the English Toy Theatre*, p. 89.

32. Here we should also note the persistence of the metaphor of the cover in the limericks of Edward Lear, in which characters are continually noteworthy or exposed in relation to their wigs, hats, furs, muffs, and fluffs. Baudrillard gives a different reading of the cover in his essay "Sign Function and Class Logic," in *Critique of the Political Economy of the Sign*: "Here we consider redundancy, the whole baroque and theatrical covering of domestic property. The table is covered with a table cloth which itself is protected by a plastic table cloth. Drapes and double drapes are at the windows. We have carpets, slipcovers, coasters, wainscoting, lampshades. Each trinket sits on a doily, each flower in its pot, and each pot in its saucer . . . the obsession of the cottage owner and small capitalist is not merely to possess, but to underline what he possesses two or three times"

(p. 42). He adds that "the overworking of signs of possession, which here act as demonstration, can be analyzed as not only the intention to possess, but to show how *well* one possesses," and at the same time, because the middle class is a class which has had to resign itself to a compromise with its class destiny, such overworking emphasizes "the limits of what it [the middle class] has attained and . . . the implicit consciousness that this is all it will ever be able to attain" (pp. 42–43).

33. Joyce, *Ulysses*, p. 359.

34. For a note on the parlor game of tableau, see Gifford and Seidman, *Notes for Joyce*, p. 321.

35. Joyce, *Ulysses*, p. 368.

36. See Bersani's distinction between sublimated and scenic desire in *A Future for Astyanax.*

37. Joyce, *Ulysses*, p. 369.

38. Clark, *The Nude*, p. 234.

39. Lacan, *The Language of the Self*, p. 174.

40. Lacan, *Ecrits*, p. 111; quoted in Coward and Ellis, *Language and Materialism*, p. 118 (translation by Coward and Ellis).

41. See Kowzan, *Littérature et spectacle.*

42. Davis, *Society and Culture in Early Modern France*, p. 105.

43. Evans, *Irish Folk Ways*, p. 286.

44. Interview by Alvin Schwartz with Avery Morton, Watertown, Massachusetts, 1976; Alvin Schwartz, letter to author, December 30, 1979. For information about the Brogueville weddings, I am particularly grateful to Elsie Downs, Darlene M. Williams, the late Ruth Crawford, my grandmother Nellie Brown, and my mother, Delores Brown Stewart. For information about the West Hagert ceremony, I am grateful to Dorsha Mason, Eva Johnson, and Sarah Atkins. I would also like to thank Debora Kodish for her insightful observations during this fieldwork. Professor Charles L. Perdue, Jr., of the University of Virginia's Department of Anthropology graciously sent me the Virginia Tom Thumb wedding accounts described here. The persistence of Tom Thumb weddings in southeastern Pennsylvania and southern New Jersey seems attested to by the numerous students I have had in my classes who have participated in such ceremonies. Mable Frazier and Kelly Meashey are two of those students who generously shared information and photographs regarding Tom Thumb weddings with me. For an account of preparations for a Tom Thumb wedding, see the autobiography of Charlie Mingus, *Beneath the Underdog*, pp. 18–23. A more recent example is the Tom Thumb wedding held by the Holy Trinity Armenian Church of Cheltenham, Pennsylvania, on September 26, 1982. Here a member of the church who makes wedding clothes professionally made the children's costumes. Although the ceremony itself followed a typical format for an Armenian wedding, including a crowning ceremony, the children were all given parodying names. Norpie Balboosian ("Cold Ice") was the bride; Massis Dakshoonian ("Hot Dog") was the groom, the flower girl and ring-bearer both had the surname Tootzarian, or "mulberry tree" (source of a favorite hard liquor). Finally, the minister's name was Hyre Yerginkian ("Father Heaven").

45. *The Tom Thumb Wedding*, p. 5. Later editions of this work include the following warning: "Persons in Jacksonville, Florida, and in Kansas City, Missouri, who put out similar entertainments under the titles, 'The Marriage of the Tots,' 'The Jennie June Wedding' and 'The Marriage of the Midgets, or the Tom Thumb Wedding' have been calling the attention of our customers to what they

describe as an 'infringement' of their 'rights' through such a performance, basing their claim upon copyrights issued in 1911 and 1914, thirteen to sixteen years later than the date under which we claim."

46. Ibid., pp. 9–10.

47. See also Barnum, *Struggles and Triumphs*, 1:240–258, 284–290. For a discussion of the place of midgets in Victorian exhibitions in England, see Altick, *The Shows of London*, pp. 255–256.

48. See Abrahams and Bauman, "Ranges of Festival Behavior."

49. Hall, *A Study of Dolls*, p. 48.

50. Elward, *On Collecting Miniatures*, p. 8.

51. Murdoch et al., *The English Miniature*, pp. 76–77. See "From Manuscript to Miniature," pp. 25–84.

52. Borges, *"The Aleph" and Other Stories*, p. 27.

53. Here it seems appropriate to quote the suggested forms for sending and receiving miniatures to a suitor as outlined in Tousey's *How to Write Letters*, pp. 38–39:

> *From a Lady, on Sending her Miniature to her Suitor.*
> *Boston, July 11, 18—.*
>
> *Dear Sir:—Accept my very best thanks for your kind inquiries regarding my health, which I am happy to say is as good as usual. My thoughts often recur to the happy hours which we have passed together—hours which I have thought passed like minutes, so full were they of the pleasure which I ever feel in your company. While I feel that my personal pretensions are but humble, I believe that you will be pleased with the enclosed miniature, the view of which, in my absence, may call to your mind a remembrance of me. While I feel that the likeness is rather a flattering one, still, should it but serve to bring me to your remembrance, the skill of the artist will not have been exercised in vain. Pray accept it as a friendly memento from,*
>
> > *My dear sir,*
> > *Ever sincerely yours*
> > *(_____)*
>
> *On Receiving a Miniature from her Suitor.*
> *Main Street, Chicago, June 3d, 18—.*
>
> *My Dear _____:—I never thought that any fresh proof of your attachment was needed, nevertheless, I have this day received another, and that one of the most acceptable I could have desired, viz.: the portrait of him whom of all others I am most desirous to keep in recollection. In contemplating this specimen of the artist's skill, I feel that it will ever recall you forcibly to my recollection, and in so doing will be a constant source of delight to my mind, and will afford me some kind of solace during your absence. I need scarcely add that I accept your gift with unspeakable delight, although, at present, I have nothing better to send you in return than a fresh assurance of my most constant attachment, which I trust may prove as welcome to you as your treasured miniature has proved to me, and in this hope I remain,*
>
> > *My dear_____,*
> > *Ever yours, affectionately,*
> > *(_____)*

54. Anspach, *The Miniature Picture*, pp. 16–17.

55. Hilliard, *A Treatise*, p. 62. We might note that Blake's resistance to painting miniatures came from a strong criticism of their materiality, a materiality which overrides any symbolic and historical content they might possess. Thus he writes in "A Pretty Epigram for the Entertainment of Those Who Have Paid Great Sums in the Venetian and Flemish Ooze":

> Nature and Art in this together Suit
> What is most Grand is always most Minute
> Rubens thinks Tables Chairs and Stools are Grand
> But Rafael thinks A Head a foot a hand.

Blake, *The Poetry and Prose of William Blake*, p. 505. See also Erdman, *Blake: Prophet Against Empire*, p. 384.

56. Making a similar point, Simmel writes: "Everything that 'adorns' man can be ordered along a scale in terms of its closeness to the physical body. The 'closest' adornment is typical of nature peoples: tattooing. The opposite extreme is represented by metal and stone adornments, which are entirely unindividual and can be put on by everybody." See "Adornment," in *The Sociology of Georg Simmel*, pp. 338–344 (quotation on p. 340).

57. Curtius, *European Literature and the Latin Middle Ages*, p. 316.

58. Ibid., p. 330.

59. Ibid., pp. 332–336.

60. For a discussion, see Barkan, *Nature's Work of Art*, p. 9; and Conger, *Theories of Macrocosms and Microcosms*, p. 7. Boas explains in "The Microcosm," chap. 10 of *The History of Ideas*, pp. 219–220:

> The actual word "microcosm" (little world) was first used by Plato's pupil, Aristotle, in his Physics (252b, 26). He is arguing in this passage about the cause of motion in the cosmos. His sentence reads, "If [self-initiated] motion can occur in an animal, the little world, why not in the larger one?" There are at least three things to be noticed about this sentence: (1) the animal is for the first time called a microcosm; (2) an animal trait is projected into the cosmos, which later, in Stoicism, was to be called a great animal (mega zoon); (3) the microcosm is not specifically man. Oddly enough, the third of these was not developed. When one comes upon the word "microcosm," one can be sure it means "man."

61. Conger, *Theories of Macrocosms and Microcosms*, p. 28.

62. Curtius, *European Literature and the Latin Middle Ages*, p. 118.

63. Lotze, *Microcosmus*, 1:xiv.

64. Napier, *The Book of Nature and the Book of Man*, pp. 12–13.

65. Conger, *Theories of Macrocosms and Microcosms*, p. 71.

66. Barkan, *Nature's Work of Art*, p. 2.

67. Quoted in Barkan, p. 126.

68. Conger, *Theories of Macrocosms and Microcosms*, p. 45.

69. Ibid., p. 64.

70. Ibid., p. 88.

71. Ibid., pp. 111, 110.

72. Napier, *The Book of Nature and the Book of Man*, p. 25.

73. Conger, *Theories of Macrocosms and Microcosms*, p. 136. See also Conger's own treatise on microcosmic philosophy, *Synoptic Naturalism*.

Chapter 5. Objects of Desire

1. Hegel, *The Phenomenology of Mind*, pp. 105–106.

2. For a discussion of reliquism, both religious and "sweet domestic," see

Mackay, *Extraordinary Popular Delusions*, pp. 695–702. One of the most tragic, and humorous, accounts of reliquism may be found in the final chapter of Giuseppe di Lampedusa's novel on the decline of the Sicilian nobility, *The Leopard*, pp. 295–320.

3. Recording from Strate's Carnival, Washington, D.C., 1941, Archive of Folk Culture, Smithsonian Institution, AFS #4699-4705. I would like to thank Amanda Dargan and Steve Zeitlin for this transcription. The custom of receiving a souvenir (or purchasing one) of participation in or viewing of the spectacle is, of course, not limited to the freak show. In an article on mechanics' institute exhibitions before 1851 in England, Kusamitsu writes: "Specimen products from these model working machines were sold to the visitors. Pieces of woven fabrics and calico were in general demand, and the girls of the Lady's Jubilee Charity School of Manchester in 1838 were 'highly delighted at being allowed to take home with a piece of calico, which was printed in their presence, as a memento of this their *first* visit to any popular exhibition.'" See Kusamitsu, "Great Exhibitions before 1851" p. 79; and *Manchester Guardian*, January 31, 1838.

4. Freud, *Standard Works*, 7:153–155 and 21:150–157. See also Schafer, *Aspects of Internalization*, pp. 98–99.

5. Eco, *Theory of Semiotics*, p. 227.

6. MacCannell, *The Tourist*, p. 158.

7. Ibid., p. 42.

8. Ibid., pp. 148–149.

9. As an example, consider *The Souvenir: By the Ladies Literary Union of Hillsdale College, Hillsdale Michigan*, August 1860:

> During the year, the accumulation of articles written by members of the Union in fulfillment of Institutional and Society appointments is considerable: and, although dear Mr. Public, it may be difficult for you to discover anything very remarkable in these ephemeral productions, some of them have, to us, a real value. They are the offspring of the heart—incidents which, in other days, we shall remember with a smile and a tear, possibly with both; and as we separate, there is a natural desire to take with us copies of them, as we do of each other's faces, as daguerrotypes of scenes in which, alas, we shall mingle together no more! . . . as the fountain of school-time recollections is unsealed by its talismanic touch.

10. Storer and Greig, *Antiquarian and Topographical Cabinet*, vol. 1, advertisement.

11. Andrew Lang, preface to *The Folk-lore Record*, vol. 2, p. iii; quoted in Gomme, *Folk-lore Relics of Early Village Life*, p. 4.

12. Forsyth, *The Antiquary's Portfolio*, 1:i. The introduction to Forsyth's book presents a concise history of antiquarianism in the British Isles to the beginning of the nineteenth century (1:v–xi).

13. Lacan, *Ecrits* (trans. Sheridan), p. 104.

14. See Marshall, "Mr. Westfall's Baskets," pp. 168–191.

15. Eliot, *Adam Bede*, p. 543.

16. "Et, encore une fois, par extension, les objets exotiques: le dépaysement et la différance de latitude équivaut de toute façon pour l'homme moderne à une plongée dans le passé (cf. le tourisme). Objets faits main, indigènes, bimbeloterie de tous les pays, c'est moins la multiplicité pittoresque qui fascine que l'antériorite des formes et des modes de fabrication, l'allusion à un monde antérieur, toujours relayé par celui de l'enfance et de ses jouets." Baudrillard, *Le système des objets*, p. 106, note.

17. Roscoe, *The Tourist in Spain*, 3:5.

18. Harrison, *The Tourist in Portugal*, p. 289.

19. Graburn, *Ethnic and Tourist Arts*, pp. 2–3.

20. We also find the curious inversion of native use value replaced by a simultaneous touristic use/display value when an ancestral figure is miniaturized and made into a bottle opener, or, in the case of the antique, when a candlestick is wired for electricity.

21. Graburn, *Ethnic and Tourist Arts*, p. 15.

22. Bascom, "Changing African Art," pp. 313–314.

23. Graburn, *Ethnic and Tourist Arts*, p. 15.

24. In her book, *Some Hobby Horses*, Montiesor concludes: "For, after all, the greatest delight which a collection of any kind can afford is the memory of the days in which it was formed; the happy holidays spent in 'arranging'; the bright birthdays, which added as a gift some longed for specimen; the little squabbles and arguments over doubtful treasures; the new ideas gleaned in 'reading it up'" (p. 193). This might be considered an instance of the use of the collection as souvenir, particularly since Montiesor's work is addressed to children and is suffused with a nostalgia for the pastimes of her own childhood.

25. De Maistre, *Voyage autour de ma chambre*, p. 51.

26. Bunn, "The Aesthetics of British Mercantilism," p. 304.

27. Baudrillard, *Le Système des objets*, p. 146.

28. James, *Principles of Psychology*, 2:424.

29. Baudrillard, *Le Système des objets*, pp. 147–148.

30. Rigby, *Lock, Stock, and Barrel*, p. 79.

31. Hazlitt, *The Coin Collector*, p. 15.

32. Montiesor, *Some Hobby Horses*, pp. 190–191.

33. O'Donnell, *Miniaturia*, pp. 163, 165.

34. Spitzer, "Milieu and Ambiance," p. 195. See also Praz, *History of Interior Decoration*.

35. Vallois, *First Steps in Collecting*, pp. 3–4.

36. Van Loot, Kilgallen, and Elphinstone [pseud. of Booth Tarkington] *The Collector's Whatnot*, pp. 144–145.

37. De Balzac, *Cousin Pons*, p. 9.

38. Walsh, *Handy-book of Literary Curiosities*, pp. 95–96.

39. Baudrillard, *Le Système des objets*, p. 131.

40. D'Israeli, *Curiosities of Literature*, 2:343. Similarly, Walsh quotes the Marquis d'Argenson:

> "I remember," he says, "once paying a visit to a well-known bibliomaniac who had just purchased an extremely scarce volume quoted at a fabulous price. Having been graciously permitted by its owner to inspect the treasure, I ventured innocently to remark that he had probably bought it with the philanthropic intention of having it reprinted." "Heaven forbid!" he exclaimed, in a horrified tone; "how could you suppose me capable of such an act of folly? If I were, the book would be no longer scarce, and would have no value whatever. Besides," he added, "I doubt, between ourselves, if it be worth reprinting." "In that case," said I, "its rarity appears to be its only attraction." "Just so," he complacently replied; "and that is quite enough for me."

Walsh, *Handy-book of Literary Curiosities*, p. 95.

41. Veblen, *The Theory of the Leisure Class*, p. 114.

42. Carrick, *Collector's Luck*, preface (n.p.).

43. Quoted in D'Israeli, *Curiosities of Literature*, 1:7.

44. Donato, "The Museum's Furnace," p. 223.
45. Montiesor, *Some Hobby Horses*, p. 192.
46. Bunn, "The Aesthetics of British Mercantilism," p. 317.
47. Hazlitt, *The Coin Collector*, p. 19.
48. Baudrillard, "Fétichisme et idéologie," p. 217.
49. Marx, *Capital*, p. 83.
50. Veblen, p. 184.
51. Baudrillard, *La Société de consommation*, pp. 166–168.
52. See Glassie, *Patterns in the Material Folk Culture of the Eastern United States*, p. 33: "In general, folk material exhibits major variation over space and minor variation through time, while the products of popular or academic culture exhibit minor variation over space and major variation through time."
53. For a classic analysis of the dimensions of camp, see Sontag, "Notes on Camp."

SELECTED BIBLIOGRAPHY

Abrahams, Roger D. "The Complex Relations of Simple Forms." *Genre* 2 (1969): 104–128.

Abrahams, Roger D., and Richard Bauman. "Ranges of Festival Behavior." In *The Reversible World: Symbolic Inversion in Art and Society*, edited by Barbara A. Babock, pp. 193–208. Ithaca, N.Y.: Cornell University Press, 1978.

Allemagne, Henri. *Histoire des jouets*. Paris: Librairie Hachette, n.d.

Altick, Robert. *The Shows of London*. Cambridge: Harvard University Press, 1978.

Anspach, Elizabeth Berkeley Craven. *The Miniature Picture: A Comedy in Three Acts*. London: G. Riley, 1781.

Ariés, Philippe. *Centuries of Childhood: A Social History of Family Life*. Translated by Robert Baldick. New York: Alfred A. Knopf and Random House, Vintage Books, 1962.

Aristotle. *On the Art of Fiction: "The Poetics."* Translated by L. J. Potts. 1953. Reprint. Cambridge: Cambridge University Press, 1968.

Aronowitz, Stanley. "Film—The Art Form of Late Capitalism." *Social Text* 1 (1979): 110–129.

Avery, Samuel P. *A Short List of Microscopic Books in the Library of the Grolier Club, Mostly Presented by Samuel P. Avery*. New York: The Grolier Club, 1911.

Babcock, Barbara A., ed. *The Reversible World: Symbolic Inversion in Art and Society*. Ithaca, N.Y.: Cornell University Press, 1978.

Bachelard, Gaston. *The Poetics of Space*. Translated by Maria Jolas. Boston: Beacon Press, 1969.

Bakhtin, Mikhail. *The Dialogic Imagination*. Translated by Caryl Emerson and Michael Holquist. Edited by Michael Holquist. Austin: University of Texas Press, 1981.

———. *Problems of Dostoevsky's Poetics*. Translated by R. W. Rotsel. Ann Arbor, Mich.: Ardis, 1973.

————. *Rabelais and His World*. Translated by Helene Iswolsky. Cambridge: MIT Press, 1968.

Balzac, Honoré de. *Cousin Pons*. Translated by Ellen Marriage. New York: Merrill and Baker, 1901.

Barkan, Leonard. *Nature's Work of Art: The Human Body as Image of the World*. New Haven: Yale University Press, 1975.

Barnum, P. T. *Struggles and Triumphs; or, The Life of P. T. Barnum, Written by Himself*. Edited by George S. Bryant. 2 vols. New York: Alfred A. Knopf, 1927.

Bascom, William. "Changing African Art." In *Ethnic and Tourist Arts*, edited by Nelson Graburn, pp. 303–319. Berkeley: University of California Press, 1979.

Baudrillard, Jean. "Fétichisme et idéologie: La Réduction sémiologique." *Nouvelle Revue de Psychanalyse* 2 (1970): 213–224.

————. *For a Critique of the Political Economy of the Sign*. Translated by Charles Levin. St. Louis: Telos Press, 1981.

————. *La Société de consommation, ses mythes, ses structures*. Paris: Le Point de la Question, 1970.

————. *Le Système des objets*. Paris: Gallimard, 1968.

Baudry, Jean-Louis. "Cinéma: Effets idéologiques produits par l'appareil de base." *Cinéthique* 7–8 (1970): 1–8.

Bazin, André. *What Is Cinema?* Translated by ˙Hugh Gray. Berkeley: University of California Press, 1967.

Beath, Paul R. *Febold Feboldson: Tall Tales fro˙n the Great Plains*. Lincoln: University of Nebraska Press, 1948.

————. *Legends of Febold Feboldson*. Lincoln: Federal Writers Project in Nebraska, 1937.

Benjamin, Walter. *Illuminations*. Translated by Harry Zohn. Edited by Hannah Arendt. New York: Schocken Books, 1976.

Benson, Arthur. *The Book of the Queen's Dolls' House*. London: Methuen, 1924.

Bersani, Leo. *A Future for Astyanax: Character and Desire in Literature*. Boston: Little, Brown, and Co., 1976.

Blake, William. *Poems of William Blake*. Edited by William Butler Yeats. New York: Boni and Liveright, n.d.

————. *The Poetry and Prose of William Blake*. Edited by David V. Erdman, with a commentary by Harold Bloom. Garden City, N.Y.: Doubleday, 1965.

Boas, George. *The History of Ideas*. New York: Charles Scribner's Sons, 1969.

Bombaugh, C. C. *Gleanings for the Curious from the Harvest Fields of Literature*. Hartford, Conn.: A. D. Worthington, 1875.

Borges, Jorge Luis. *"The Aleph" and Other Stories, 1933–1969*. Translated by Norman Thomas Di Giovanni in collaboration with the author. New York: E. P. Dutton, 1978.

Brewer, Ebenezer Cobham. *Dictionary of Phrase and Fable*. Edited by Ivor Evans. New York: Harper and Row, 1970.

Briggs, Katharine M. *The Fairies in English Tradition and Literature*. Chicago: University of Chicago Press, 1967.

Broderius, John P. *The Giant in Germanic Tradition*. Chicago: University of Chicago Libraries, 1932.

Brontë, Emily. *Gondal's Queen: A Novel in Verse*. Edited by Fannie Ratchford. Austin: University of Texas Press, 1955.

Brown, Suzanne Hunter. "The Chronotope of the Short Story: Time, Character, and Brevity" (1982). Department of English, Dartmouth College. Photocopy.

Bunn, James H. "The Aesthetics of British Mercantilism." *New Literary History* 11 (1980): 303–321.

Burke, Edmund. "A Philosophical Inquiry into the Origin of Our Ideas of the Sublime and Beautiful; with an Introductory Discourse Concerning Taste." In *Works*, 1: 55–219. London: Oxford University Press, 1925.

Burke, Kenneth. *Counterstatement*. Chicago: University of Chicago Press, Phoenix Books, 1957.

Burton, Robert. *The Anatomy of Melancholy*. Edited by Holbrook Jackson. New York: Random House, 1977.

Burton, Warren. *The Scenery-Shower, with Word Paintings of the Beautiful, the Picturesque, and the Grand in Nature*. Boston: William Ticknor, 1844.

Butor, Michel. *Inventory*. Translated by Richard Howard. New York: Simon and Schuster, 1961.

Cantor, Norman F., ed. *The Medieval World, 300–1300*. London: Macmillan, 1970.

Carrick, Alice Van Leer. *Collector's Luck; or, A Repository of Pleasant and Profitable Discourses Descriptive of the Household Furniture and Ornaments of Olden Time*. Boston: Atlantic Monthly Press, 1919.

Charpenel, Mauricio. *Las miniaturas en el arte popular Mexicano*. Latin American Folklore Series, no. 1. Austin: University of Texas Center for Intercultural Studies in Folklore and Oral History, 1970.

Clark, Kenneth. *The Nude*. Garden City, N.Y.: Doubleday, 1956.

Clarke, Pauline. *The Return of the Twelves*. New York: Coward, McCann, 1963.

Clayton, Howard. *Miniature Railways*. Lingfield, Surrey: Oakwood Press, 1971.

Conger, George P. *Synoptic Naturalism*. Minneapolis: University of Minnesota Library, 1960.

———. *Theories of Macrocosms and Microcosms in the History of Philosophy*. New York: Russell and Russell, 1967.

Cook, David. *History of Narrative Film*. New York: W. W. Norton, 1981.

Corrigan, Timothy. *Coleridge, Language, and Criticism*. Athens: University of Georgia Press, 1982.

Coward, Rosalind, and John Ellis. *Language and Materialism: Developments in Semiology and the Theory of the Subject*. London and Boston: Routledge and Kegan Paul, 1977.

Craven, Elizabeth Berkeley. *See* Anspach, Elizabeth Berkeley Craven.

Curtius, Ernst Robert. *European Literature and the Latin Middle Ages*. New York: Harper and Row, 1953.

Daiken, Leslie. *Children's Toys Throughout the Ages*. London: B. T. Batsford, 1953.

Darré, René. *Géants d'hier et d'aujourd'hui*. Arras: Imprimerie de la Nouvelle Société anonyme du Pas-de-Calais, 1944.

Davis, Natalie Zemon. *Society and Culture in Early Modern France*. Stanford: Stanford University Press, 1975.

Dawson, Christopher. *Religion and the Rise of Western Culture*. Garden City, N.Y.: Doubleday, 1958.

Debord, Guy. *The Society of the Spectacle*. Anonymous translation. Detroit: Black and Red, 1970.

Defoe, Daniel. *Robinson Crusoe*. Edited by Michael Shinagel. New York: W. W. Norton, 1975.

Deleuze, Gilles. *Proust and Signs*. Translated by Richard Howard. New York: George Braziller, 1972.

DeLong, Alton J. "Phenomenological Space-Time: Toward an Experiential Relativity." *Science* 213 (1981): 681–683.

Derrida, Jacques. *Of Grammatology*. Translated by Gayatri Chakravorty Spivak. Baltimore: Johns Hopkins University Press, 1976.

D'Israeli, Isaac. *Curiosities of Literature*. 2 vols. Paris: Baudry's European Library, 1835.

Dobie, J. Frank. "Giants of the Southwest." *Country Gentleman* 91 (1926): 11, 71–72.

Dolĕzel, Lubomir. "A Scheme of Narrative Time." In *The Semiotics of Art*, edited by Ladislav Matejka and Irwin R. Titunik, pp. 209–217. Cambridge: MIT Press, 1976.

Donato, Eugenio. "The Museum's Furnace: Notes Toward a Contextual Reading of *Bouvard and Pécuchet*." In *Textual Strategies: Perspectives in Post-Structuralist Criticism*, edited by Josué Harari, pp. 213–238. Ithaca, N.Y.: Cornell University Press, 1979.

Dorson, Richard. *American Folklore*. Chicago: University of Chicago Press, 1973.

———. "Mose the Far-Famed and World Renowned." *American Literature* 15 (1943): 288–300.

Doyle, Sir Arthur Conan. *The Coming of the Fairies*. Toronto: Hodder and Stoughton, 1922.

DuBois, W. E. B. *The Souls of Black Folk*. New York: Blue Heron Press, 1953.

Duffy, Maureen. *The Erotic World of Fairy*. London: Hodder and Stoughton, 1972.

Earth Art. Catalog of an exhibition at the Andrew Dickson White Museum of Art, January 11–March 16, 1969. Ithaca, N.Y.: Cornell University Press, 1970.

Eco, Umberto. *A Theory of Semiotics*. Bloomington: Indiana University Press, 1976.

Eisenhart, Willy. *The World of Donald Evans*. New York: Dial/Delacorte, A Harlin Quist Book. 1980.

Eliot, George. *Adam Bede*. New York: Washington Square Press, 1977.

_____. *Silas Marner*. New York: New American Library, 1960.

Ellman, Richard. *Ulysses on the Liffey*. New York: Oxford University Press, 1972.

Elward, Robert. *On Collecting Miniatures, Enamels, and Jewellry*. London: Arnold, 1905.

Erdman, David. *Blake: Prophet Against Empire*. Princeton: Princeton University Press, 1977.

Evans, E. Estyn. *Irish Folk Ways*. London: Routledge and Kegan Paul, 1972.

Evans Wentz, E. E. *The Fairy Faith in Celtic Countries*. 1911. Reprint. Gerrards Cross, Buckinghamshire: Colin Smythe, 1977.

Fairholt, F. W. *Gog and Magog, the Giants in Guildhall: Their Real and Legendary History, with an Account of Other Civic Giants, at Home and Abroad*. London: John Camden Hotten, 1859.

Ferry, Jean. *Une Etude sur Raymond Roussel*. Paris: Arcanes, 1953.

Fiedler, Leslie. *Freaks: Myths and Images of the Secret Self*. New York: Simon and Schuster, 1978.

Fielding, Henry. *Tom Jones*. New York: New American Library, 1963.

Fish, Stanley E. "How Ordinary Is Ordinary Language?" *New Literary History* 5 (1973): 40–54.

Fisher, Philip. "City Matters: City Minds." *Harvard English Studies* 6 (1975): 371–389.

_____. "The Construction of the Body." Photocopy.

_____. "The Recovery of the Body." *Humanities in Society* 1 (1978): 133–146.

Forsyth, J. S. *The Antiquary's Portfolio; or, Cabinet Selection of Historical and Literary Curiosities, on Subjects Principally Connected with the Manners, Customs, and Morals; Civil, Military, and Ecclesiastical Governments &c. of Great Britain, During the Middle and Later Ages*. 2 vols. London: G. Wightman, 1825.

Foucault, Michel. *Raymond Roussel*. Paris: Gallimard, 1963.

Freud, Sigmund. *Standard Works*. Translated by James Strachey. Vols. 7 and 21. London: Hogarth Press, 1953.

Fried, Michael. "Art and Objecthood." *Artforum* 5 (1967): 12–23.

Gadamer, Hans-Georg. "The Historicity of Understanding." In *Critical Sociology*, edited by Paul Connerton, pp. 117–133. Harmondsworth, Middlesex: Penguin Books, 1976.

Gifford, Don, and Robert Seidman. *Notes for Joyce*. New York: E. P. Dutton, 1974.

Glassie, Henry. *Patterns in the Material Folk Culture of the Eastern United States*. Philadelphia: University of Pennsylvania Press, 1968.

Gombrich, E. H. *Art and Illusion*. Princeton: Princeton University Press, 1972.

Gomme, George Laurence. *Folk-lore Relics of Early Village Life*. London: E. Stock, 1883.

Graburn, Nelson. *Ethnic and Tourist Arts.* Berkeley: University of California Press, 1979.

Grildrig, Solomon [pseud.]. *The Miniature: A periodical Paper*. Edited by

Thomas Rennell, H. C. Knight, G. Canning, and others. Windsor: C. Knight, 1804.

Gröber, Karl. *Children's Toys of Bygone Ages*. Translated by Philip Hereford. New York: Frederick A. Stokes, 1928.

Hall, Stanley G. *A Study of Dolls*. New York: E. L. Kellogg and Co., 1897.

Halliwell, J., ed. *The Metrical History of Tom Thumb the Little, as Issued Early in the Eighteenth Century in Three Parts*. London: Whittingham and Wilkins, 1860.

Harrison, W. H. *The Tourist in Portugal*. London: Robert Jennings and Co., 1839.

Hazlitt, William Carew. *The Coin Collector*. London: G. Redway, 1896.

Hegel, G. W. F. *The Phenomenology of Mind*. Translated by J. B. Baillie. New York: Harper and Row, 1967.

Heidegger, Martin. *An Introduction to Metaphysics*. Translated by Ralph Mannheim. New Haven: Yale University Press, 1959.

Henderson, James Dougald. *Lilliputian Newspapers*. Worcester, Mass.: A. J. St. Onge, 1936.

——. *Miniature Books*. Leipzig: Tondeur and Sauberlich, 1930.

——. *Miniature Books: Newsletter of the LXIVmos Society*, February 1, 1928.

Heppenstall, Rayner. *Raymond Roussel: A Critical Guide*. London: Calder and Boyers, 1966.

Hilliard, Nicholas. *A Treatise Concerning the Arte of Limning Together with a More Compendious Discourse Concerning Ye Art of Liming by Edward Norgate*. Edited by R. K. R. Thornton and T. G. S. Cain. Ashington, Northumberland: Mid Northumberland Arts Group and Carcanet New Press, 1981.

Hirsch, Edward. "Wisdom and Power: Yeats and the Commonwealth of Faery," *Yeats-Eliot Review*. Forthcoming.

Holland, Philip. "Robert Burton's *Anatomy of Melancholy* and Menippean Satire, Humanist and English." Diss., University of London, 1979.

Homer. *The Odyssey*. Translated by Robert Fitzgerald. Garden City, N.Y.: Doubleday, Anchor Books, 1963.

Hooke, Robert. *Micrographia; or, Some Physiological Descriptions of Minute Bodes Made by Magnifying Glasses, with Observations and Inquiries There Upon*. London: Jo. Maryn and Ja. Allestry, 1665.

Hunter, Joseph. *Antiquarian Notices of Lupset, the Heath, Sharlston and, Ackton, in the County of York*. London: J. B. Nichols and Son, 1851.

Hurston, Zora Neale. *Mules and Men*. Bloomington: Indiana University Press, 1978.

Hussey, Christopher. *The Picturesque: Studies in a Point of View*. G. P. Putnam and Sons, 1927.

Iser, Wolfgang. *The Act of Reading: A Theory of Aesthetic Response*. London: Routledge and Kegan Paul, 1978.

——. *The Implied Reader*. Baltimore: Johns Hopkins University Press, 1974.

Jackson, Emily. *Toys of Other Days*. New York: Charles Scribner's Sons, 1908.

Jacobs, Flora Gill. *A World of Doll Houses*. New York: Gramercy, 1965.

James, M. R. *Ghost-Stories of an Antiquary*. London: Edward Arnold, 1912.

James, William. *The Principles of Psychiatry*. 2 vols. New York: Dover, 1950.

Janes, Rev. Edmund S., ed. *Miniature Bible*. Philadelphia: W. N. Wiatt, 185?.

Jankélévitch, Vladimir. *L'Irréversible et la nostalgie*. Paris: Flammarion, 1974.

Jessup, Bertram. "Aesthetic Size." *Journal of Aesthetics and Art Criticism* 9 (1950): 31–38.

Jonson, Ben. "To Penshurst." In *The Complete Poetry of Ben Jonson*, edited by William B. Hunter, pp. 77–81. New York: New York University Press, 1963.

Joyce, James. *Ulysses*. New York: Random House, Vintage Books, 1961.

Kawasaki, Toshihiko. "Donne's Microcosm." In *Seventeenth Century Imagery*, edited by Earl Miner, pp. 25–43. Berkeley: University of California Press, 1971.

Kirk, Robert. *The Secret Commonwealth of Elves, Fauns, and Fairies*. 1691, 1815. Reprint. London: D. Nutt, 1893.

Klein, Melanie. *"Love, Guilt, and Reparation," and Other Works, 1921–1945*. New York: Delacorte Press, 1975.

Kowzan, Tadeusz. *Littérature et spectacle*. The Hague: Mouton, 1975.

Kristeva, Julia. "Motherhood According to Giovanni Bellini." In *Desire in Language*, edited by Leon S. Roudiez and translated by Thomas Gora, Alice Jardine, and Leon S. Roudiez, pp. 237–270. New York: Columbia University Press, 1980.

Kusamitsu, Toshio. "Great Exhibitions Before 1851." *History Workshop* 9 (1980): 70–89.

Lacan, Jacques. *Ecrits*. Paris: Editions du Seuil, 1966.

———. *Ecrits*. Translated by Alan Sheridan. New York: W. W. Norton, 1977.

———. *The Language of the Self: The Function of Language In Psychoanalysis*. Translated by Anthony Wilden. Baltimore: Johns Hopkins Press, 1968.

Lampedusa, Giuseppe di. *The Leopard*. Translated by Archibald Colquhoun. New York: Pantheon, 1960.

Lang, Andrew. Preface to *The Folk-lore Record, for Collecting and Printing Relics of Popular Antiquities*, vol. 2. London, 1879.

Latham, Minor White. *The Elizabethan Fairies: The Fairies of Folklore and the Fairies of Shakespeare*. New York: Columbia University Press, 1930.

Leach, Edmund. "Anthropological Aspects of Language: Animal Categories and Verbal Abuse." In *Reader in Comparative Religion*, edited by William Lessa and Evon Vogt, 3rd ed. pp. 206–220. New York: Harper and Row, 1972.

Leach, Maria, ed. *Standard Dictionary of Folklore, Mythology, and Legend*. 2 vols. New York: Funk and Wagnalls, 1949.

Lefebvre, Henri. *Critique de la Vie Quotidienne*. 2 vols. Paris: L'Arche, 1958.

———. *La Production de l'espace*. Paris: Editions anthropos, 1974.

Leinster, Murray. *Land of the Giants*. New York: Pyramid Publications, 1968.
Lévi-Strauss, Claude. *The Savage Mind*. Chicago: University of Chicago Press, 1973.
Lippard, Lucy. *Pop Art*. New York: Praeger, 1966.
Longinus. *On The Sublime*. Edited by D. A. Russell. Oxford: Clarendon Press, 1964.
Lotman, J. M. "Point of View in a Text." *New Literary History* 6 (1975): 339–352.
————. "Primary and Secondary Communication-Modeling Systems." In *Soviet Semiotics*, translated and edited by Daniel P. Lucid, pp. 95–98. Baltimore: Johns Hopkins University Press, 1977.
Lotze, Hermann. *Microcosmus: An Essay Concerning Man and His Relation to the World*. Translated by E. Hamilton and E. E. Constance Jones. 2 vols. New York: Scribner and Welford, 1886.
Lowenthal, Leo. *Literature, Popular Culture, and Society*. Palo Alto: Pacific Books, 1961.

MacCannell, Dean. *The Tourist: A New Theory of the Leisure Class*. New York: Schocken Books, 1976.
McClinton, Katharine. *Antiques in Miniature*. New York: Charles Scribner's Sons, 1970.
Mackay, Charles. *Extraordinary Popular Delusions and the Madness of Crowds*. London: R. Bentley, 1841. Reprint. New York: Noonday, 1970.
Macmanus, Dermot. *The Middle Kingdom*. Gerrards Cross, Buckinghamshire: Colin Smythe, 1975.
McMurtie, Douglas. *Miniature Incunabula: Some Preliminary Notes on Small Books Printed During the Fifteenth Century*. Chicago: Privately printed, 1929.
MacRitchie, David. *Fians, Fairies, and Picts*. London: K. Paul, Trench, Trubner and Co., 1893.
Magoon, E. L. "Scenery and Mind." In *The Home Book of the Picturesque*, pp. 1–48. New York: G. P. Putnam, 1852.
Maistre, Xavier de. *Voyage autour de ma chambre*. Paris: Flammarion, 1932.
Marin, Louis. *Etudes sémiologiques, ecritures, peintures*. Paris: Klincksieck, 1971.
Marquand, John P. *The Late George Apley: A Novel in the Form of a Memoir*. Boston: Little, Brown, 1937.
Marshall, Howard Wight. "Mr. Westfall's Baskets: Traditional Craftsmanship in Northcentral Missouri." In *Readings in American Folklore*, edited by Jan Harold Brunvand, pp. 168–191. New York: W. W. Norton, 1979.
Marvell, Andrew. "Upon Appleton House." In *The Poems and Letters of Andrew Marvell*, edited by H. M. Margoliouth, pp. 62–86. New York: Oxford University Press, 1971.
Marx, Karl. *Capital: A Critique of Political Economy*. Translated by Samuel Moore and Edward Aveling. New York: Modern Library, 1906.
Massingham, Harold John. *Fee, fi, fo, fum, or, The giants of England*. London: Kegan, Paul, Trench, Trubner, 1926.
Metz, Christian. *Le Signifiant Imaginaire*. Paris: 10/18, 1977.

Mingus, Charlie. *Beneath the Underdog: His World as Composed By Mingus.* Edited by Nel King. New York: Alfred A. Knopf, 1971.

A Miniature Almanack. Boston: Charles Ewer, 1819/1820, 1820/1821.

Monk, Samuel. "The Sublime: Burke's *Enquiry.*" In *Romanticism and Consciousness,* edited by Harold Bloom, pp. 24–41. New York: W. W. Norton, 1970.

Montiesor, C. *Some Hobby Horses; or, How to Collect Stamps, Coins, Seals, Crests, and Scraps.* London: W. H. Allen and Co., 1890.

Moog, Florence. "Gulliver Was a Bad Biologist." *Scientific American* 179 (1948): 52–55.

Mukařovský, Jan. "Standard Language and Poetic Language." In *A Prague School Reader on Esthetics, Literary Structure, and Style,* edited by Paul Garvin, pp. 19–35. Washington, D.C.: Washington Linguistics Club, 1955.

Murdoch, John, Jim Murrell, Patrick J. Noon, and Roy Strong. *The English Miniature.* New Haven: Yale University Press, 1981.

Napier, Charles O. G. *The Book of Nature and the Book of Man, in Which Man Is Accepted as a Type of Creation—the Microcosm—the Great Pivot on Which All Lower Forms of Life Turn.* London: J. C. Hotten, 1870.

Nicholson, Marjorie Hope. *The Microscope and English Imagination.* Smith College Studies in Modern Languages. Northampton, Mass.: Smith College, 1935.

———. *Mountain Gloom and Mountain Glory: The Development of the Aesthetics of the Infinite.* Ithaca, N.Y.: Cornell University Press, 1959.

———. *Science and Imagination.* Ithaca, N.Y.: Cornell University Press, 1956.

O'Donnell, Georgene. *Miniaturia: The World of Tiny Things.* Chicago: Lightner Publishing Co., 1943.

Olrik, Axel. "Epic Laws of Folk Narrative." In *The Study of Folklore,* edited by Alan Dundes, pp. 129–141. Englewood Cliffs, N.J.: Prentice-Hall, 1965.

O'Súilleabhain, Séan. *Storytelling in Irish Tradition.* Cork: The Mercier Press and The Cultural Relations Commission of Ireland, 1973.

Plato. *Works.* Translated by B. Jowett. 4 vols. in 1. New York: Tudor, n.d.

Ponge, Francis. *The Voice of Things.* Translated by Beth Archer. New York: McGraw-Hill, 1972.

Powell, Mel. *Miniatures for Baroque Ensemble.* Opus 8. New York: G. Schermer, 1959.

Pratt, Mary Louise. *Toward a Speech Act Theory of Literary Discourse.* Bloomington: Indiana University Press, 1977.

Praz, Mario. *The House of Life.* Translated by Angus Davidson. New York: Oxford University Press, 1964.

———. *An Illustrated History of Interior Decoration: From Pompeii to Art Nouveau.* Translated by William Weaver. New York: Thames and Hudson, 1982.

Price, Martin. *To the Palace of Wisdom.* Garden City, N.Y.: Doubleday, 1964.

Pyne, William Henry. *Microcosm; or, A Picturesque Delineation of the Arts, Agri-*

culture, and Manufactures of Great Britain in a Series of a Thousand Groups of Small Figures for the Embellishment of Landscape. 1845. Reprint. New York: B. Blom, 1971.

Rabelais, François. *Gargantua and Pantagruel.* Translated by J. M. Cohen. Harmondsworth, Middlesex: Penguin Books, 1969.

Radin, Paul. *The Trickster.* New York: Schocken Books, 1972.

Ratchford, Fannie. *The Brontës' Web of Childhood.* New York: Russell and Russell, 1941.

Riffaterre, Michael. *Semiotics of Poetry.* Bloomington: Indiana University Press, 1978.

Rigby, Douglas. *Lock, Stock, and Barrel: The Story of Collecting.* Philadelphia: J. B. Lippincott, 1944.

Ritson, Joseph. *Fairy Tales, Legends, and Romances Illustrating Shakespeare and Other Early English Writers to Which Are Prefixed Two Preliminary Dissertations: 1. On Pygmies, 2. On Fairies.* Edited by William C. Hazlitt. London: F. and W. Kerslake, 1875.

Robertson, D. W. *Preface to Chaucer.* Princeton: Princeton University Press, 1962.

Roscoe, Thomas. *The Tourist in Spain.* Vol. 3, *Biscay and the Castiles.* London: Robert Jennings and Co., 1837.

Rose, Barbara. "Blow Up—the Problem of Scale in Sculpture." *Art in America* 56 (1968): 80–91.

Roussel, Raymond. *How I Write Certain of My Books.* Translated by Trevor Winkfield. New York: Sun Press, 1977.

———. *Impressions of Africa.* Translated by Lindy Foord and Rayner Heppenstall. London: Calder and Boyers, 1966.

Salomone-Marino, Salvatore. *Customs and Habits of the Sicilian Peasants.* Edited and translated by Rosalie N. Norris. Rutherford, N.J.: Fairleigh Dickinson University Press, 1981. Originally published as *Costumi e usanze dei contadini di Sicilia,* 1897.

Schafer, Roy. *Aspects of Internalization.* New York: International Universities Press, 1968.

Scholes, Robert, and Robert Kellogg. *The Nature of Narrative.* New York: Oxford University Press, 1966.

Shuman, Amy. *Retellings: Storytelling and Writing Among Urban Adolescents.* Ph.D. diss., University of Pennsylvania, 1981.

Simmel, Georg. *The Sociology of Georg Simmel.* Translated and edited by Kurt Wolff. New York: Free Press of Glencoe, 1950.

Smithson, Robert. "The Monuments of Passaic." *Artforum* 6 (1967): 48–51.

Sokol, John. "Portraits of Modern Masters." *The Georgia Review* 32 (1979): 368–376.

Sontag, Susan. "Notes on Camp." In *"Against Interpretation" and Other Essays,* pp. 277–293. New York: Dell, 1969.

The Souvenir: By the Ladies Literary Union of Hillsdale College, Hillsdale, Michigan. August 1860, no. 1. Toledo: Pelton, Stewart, and Waggoner, 1860.

Speaight, George. *The History of the English Toy Theatre*. London: Studio Vista, 1969.

Spence, Lewis. *British Fairy Origins*. London: Watts and Co., 1946.

Spenser, Edmund. *The Poetical Works of Edmund Spenser*. Edited by J. C. Smith and E. De Selincourt. London: Oxford University Press, 1960.

Spitzer, Leo. "Milieu and Ambiance: An Essay in Historical Semantics." *Philosophy and Phenomenological Research: A Quarterly Journal* 3, no. 1 (1942): 1–42; 3, no. 2 (1942): 169–218.

Squire, Charles. *Celtic Myth and Legend*. Hollywood: Newcastle Publishing Co., 1975. Originally published in 1905 under the title *The Mythology of the British Isles*.

Stevick, Philip. "Miniaturization in Eighteenth-Century English Literature." *University of Toronto Quarterly* 38 (1969): 159–173.

Stewart, Susan. "The Epistemology of the Horror Story." *Journal of American Folklore* 95 (1982): 33–50.

————. *Nonsense: Aspects of Intertextuality in Folklore and Literature*. Baltimore: Johns Hopkins University Press, 1979.

————. "The Pickpocket: A Study in Tradition and Allusion." *MLN* 95 (1980): 1127–1154.

Stone, Wilbur Macey. *A Snuff-boxful of Bibles*. Newark: Carteret Book Club, 1926.

————. *An Unusual Collection of Miniature Books, Formed by a Lady*. New York: Flandome Press, 1928.

Storer, James, and I. Grieg. *Antiquarian and Topographical Cabinet, Containing a Series of Elegant Views of the Most Interesting Objects of Curiosity in Great Britain*. N.p., 1807–1811.

Swift, Jonathan. *Gulliver's Travels*. Edited by Robert A Greenberg. New York: W. W. Norton, 1970.

Sypher, Wylie. "Baroque Afterpiece: The Picturesque." *Gazette des Beaux-Arts* 27 (1945): 39–58.

Thomas, Gerald. *The Tall Tale and Philippe d'Alcripe*. St. John's: Department of Folklore, Memorial University of Newfoundland, 1977.

Tillim, Sidney. "Earthworks and the New Picturesque." *Artforum* 7 (1968): 42–45.

"The Toby Jug." *The Antiquarian*, November 1923.

The Tom Thumb Wedding and the Brownie's Flirtation. Boston: W. H. Baker, 1898.

Tousey, Frank. *How to Write Letters: Everybody's Friend, Samples of Every Conceivable Kind of Letters*. New York: Frank Tousey, 1890.

Townsend, John Rowe. *Written for Children*. Harmondsworth, Middlesex: Penguin Books, 1965.

Tuve, Rosemond. *Allegorical Imagery: Some Medieval Books and Their Posterity*. Princeton: Princeton University Press, 1966.

Valéry, Paul. *Aesthetics*. Translated by Ralph Mannheim. New York: Random House, 1964.

Vallois, Grace. *First Steps in Collecting Furniture, Glass, China.* New York: Medill McBride, 1950.

Van Loot, Cornelius Obenchain, Milton Kilgallen, and Murgatroyd Elphinstone [pseud. of Booth Tarkington, Kenneth Lewis Roberts, and Hugh MacNair Kahler]. *The Collector's Whatnot: A Compendium, Manual, and Syllabus of Information and Advice on All Subjects Appertaining to the Collection of Antiques, Both Ancient and Not So Ancient.* Boston: Houghton Mifflin, 1923.

Veblen, Thorstein. *The Theory of the Leisure Class.* New York: New American Library, 1953.

Vološinov, V. N. *Marxism and the Philosophy of Language.* Translated by Ladislav Matejka and I. R. Titunik. Hawthorne, N.Y.: Mouton, Seminar, 1973.

Walsh, William S. *Handy-book of Literary Curiosities.* Philadelphia: J. B. Lippincott, 1892.

Watson, Emily. *Fairies of Our Garden.* Boston: J. E. Tilton, 1862.

Watson, Patrick. *Fasanella's City: The Paintings of Ralph Fasanella, with the Story of His Life and Art.* New York: Random House, Ballantine Books, 1973.

Watt, Ian. *The Rise of the Novel.* Berkeley: University of California Press, 1974.

Wells, H. G. *Little Wars: A Game for Boys from Twelve Years of Age to 150 and for That More Intelligent Sort of Girls Who Like Boys' Games and Books; with an Appendix on Kriegspiel.* London: Frank Palmer, 1913.

Wilgus, D. K. *Anglo-American Folksong Scholarship since 1898.* New York: Rutgers University Press, 1959.

Williams, Mary. "Folklore and Placenames." *Folklore* 74 (1963): 361–376.

Williams, Raymond. *Marxism and Literature.* Oxford: Oxford University Press, 1977.

Winter, Carl. *Elizabethan Miniatures.* Harmondsworth, Middlesex: Penguin Books, 1943.

Wisdom in Miniature; or, The Youth's Pleasing Instructor. New York: Mahlon Day, 1822.

Wittgenstein, Ludwig. *The Philosophical Investigations.* Oxford: Oxford University Press, 1958.

Wood, Edward. *Giants and Dwarfs.* London: R. Bentley, 1868.

Yonge, Charlotte M. *The History of Sir Thomas Thumb.* Edinburgh: Thomas Constable, 1856.

Zigrosser, Carl. *Multum in parvo: An Essay in Poetic Imagination.* New York: George Braziller, 1965.

INDEX

Aberrations, 108, 109, 160. *See also* Freaks
Abstraction, 84, 167, 169
Accumulation, 153
Adventures of a Pincushion, The (Kilner), 55
Advertising, 32, 68, 124, 133
Alan of Lille, 127, 129
Albigensian heresies, 81, 183 n.34
"Aleph, The" (Borges), 52, 126, 179 n.38
Alice in Wonderland (Carroll), 77
Alienation, 164, 171
Allegory, 3–5, 10, 59, 174 n.1
Almanacs, 39, 42, 177 n.14
Ambience, 157
Amulet. *See* Talisman
Amusement parks, 58, 145
Analogy, 74
Anal retentiveness, 153, 154
Anatomy of Melancholy (Burton), x, 79
Andre, Carl, 76
Animation, theme of, 55–57, 172, 179–180 n.43
Anspach, Elizabeth Berkeley Craven: *The Miniature Picture*, 126–127
Anteriority, 146, 189 n.16
Antiquarian and Topographical Cabinet (Storer and Greig), 141
Antiquarianism: and nationalism, 140–144; suppression of, 141
Antiquarian Notices (Hunter), 141
Antiquarian Repertory, The (Grose), 143
Antiquary's Portfolio (Forsyth), 142
Antiques, 140, 145, 168

Antiquitates Vulgares (Bourne), 141
Aphorism, 53, 95, 98
Arbitrariness of the sign, 5, 17, 20–21, 31–32, 38. *See also* Oxymoron of the sign
Aristophanes: *The Clouds*, 71
Aristotle: *The Poetics*, 94–95
"Arrival of a Train at a Station" (Lumière), 11
Art: body as, 107; under glass, 68, 114, 144; holographic, 12; as play, 151; signs of, 32–33
Art cabinets, 61, 143, 153, 157
Artisan, the, 62, 68, 144, 149–150. *See also* Crafts; Domestic arts; Handmade goods
Atticus, 160
Aubrey, John: *Brief Lives and Miscellanies*, 141
Augusta Dorothea of Schwarzburg-Gotha, Duchess, 62–63. *See also* Dollhouses
Augustine, Saint, 14
Authenticity: and hand-labor, 39; in Lévi-Strauss, 176 n.30; of lived experience, 22; and mechanical reproduction, 91, 92; and quotation, 19; and souvenirs, 133, 136, 140, 146–147; and the subject, 171–172; and tourist art, 150
Authority: and the collection, 152; and exaggeration, xiii; and mechanical reproduction, 8, 12; and the novel, 10; and reading, 44; and writing, 26

About the Author

Susan Stewart is Professor of English at Temple
University. Her works on theory include *Nonsense:
Aspects of Intertextuality in Folklore and Literature* and
*Crimes of Writing: Problems in the Containment of
Representation*. She has also published two books of
poetry: *Yellow Stars and Ice* and *The Hive*.

Library of Congress Cataloging-in-Publication Data
Stewart, Susan.
On longing : narratives of the miniature, the
gigantic, the souvenir, the collection/Susan
Stewart. —1st paperback ed.
Originally published: Baltimore : Johns Hopkins
University Press, c1984.
Includes bibliographical references (p.   ) and index.
ISBN 0-8223-1366-9 (paper)
1. Discourse analysis, Narrative. 2. Semiotics and
literature. I. Title.
[P302.7.S68 1993]
808′.00141—dc20   92-40004 CIP